RabbitMQ in Depth

RabbitMQ in Depth

GAVIN ROY

MANNING
SHELTER ISLAND

For online information and ordering of this and other Manning books, please visit
www.manning.com. The publisher offers discounts on this book when ordered in quantity.
For more information, please contact

> Special Sales Department
> Manning Publications Co.
> 20 Baldwin Road
> PO Box 761
> Shelter Island, NY 11964
> Email: orders@manning.com

Manning Publications Co.
20 Baldwin Road
PO Box 761
Shelter Island, NY 11964

Development editor:	Karen Miller
Technical editor:	James Titcumb
Technical development editor:	Phillip Warner
Copyeditor:	Andy Carroll
Proofreader:	Alyson Brener
Technical proofreader:	Karsten Strøbæk
Typesetter:	Dennis Dalinnik
Cover designer:	Marija Tudor

ISBN: 9781617291005
Printed in the United States of America
2 3 4 5 6 7 8 9 10 – DP – 22 21 20 19 18

brief contents

v

contents

preface

When Manning Publications published *RabbitMQ in Action* back in April 2012, RabbitMQ was gaining popularity rapidly. As of today, it is one of the stalwart leaders in the world of message brokers and is ideal for a variety of application uses. Facilitating communication through distributed applications, using micro-services in a service oriented architecture, and enabling logical separation of CQRS and Event Sourcing components are just some of the common uses of RabbitMQ.

We now present a new, in-depth exploration of RabbitMQ itself, digging deep under the surface by examining things like how the Advanced Message Queuing Protocol is structured, progressive exploration into the various exchanges, and examination of various performance aspects. RabbitMQ in Depth aims to take your understanding of RabbitMQ to a new level, enabling you to further apply this knowledge in real-world applications today.

acknowledgments

This book has been some time in the making, and so first and foremost a big thank you goes out to all of our families and friends who tirelessly stood by us all, put up with us, and made those late evening coffees to keep us going through the many additional long hours of work required to write such a book – thank you!

To Alvaro Videla and Jason J.W. Williams, authors of *RabbitMQ in Action* (also published by Manning Publications, in April 2012), for laying the foundation for countless developers' insight and interest in RabbitMQ itself.

To Karen, our development editor, for her endless patience and understanding with us all over this entire period, plus the entire Manning team for the fantastic effort involved by all to finally get us to this point. It was hard work, and we ended up doing a fair few rounds, but we are grateful for the solid production effort which has emerged as a result!

Thanks, too, to technical proofreader, Karsten Strøbæk, whose contribution helped the book immensely, as did the comments of the reviewers: Phillip Warner, Jerry Kuch, Nadia Saad Noori, Bruce Snyder, Robert Kielty, Milos Milivojevic, Arathi Maddula, Ian Dallas, George Harley, Dimitri Aivaliotis, Hechen Gao, Stefan Turalski, Andrew Meredith, Artem Dayneko, David Paccoud, Barry Alexander, Biju Kunjummen, Adolfo Pérez Álvarez, Brandon Wilhite, David Pull, and Ray Lugo.

There are a great many others which have helped contribute in various ways to this book as well. We cannot mention everyone by name as this would just mean the acknowledgements roll on and on, but a big thank you goes out to everyone else who had a hand in helping make this possible!

about this book

RabbitMQ is an open source message broker written in Erlang, currently under the wing of Pivotal Software. It's based around the AMQP open protocol, with official client libraries in Java, .NET, Erlang, as well as libraries for most other popular programming languages.

This book is up-to-date with RabbitMQ 3.6.3, so with the erratic release schedule of RabbitMQ itself, by the time this book reaches you there may be newer versions released. Not to fret though, as in our experience RabbitMQ has rarely broken features with releases, only added new features and fixed issues!

The code examples used throughout the book are written with Python, but if you don't have a working setup with Python and RabbitMQ, or you'd just like to experiment without setting up the whole environment, we've included instructions on setting up a Vagrant box with everything pre-installed. Make sure you check out the appendix for instructions on how to get this up and running first.

Road Map

Chapter 1 looks at the foundation of RabbitMQ: the various features of RabbitMQ itself and the foundation of RabbitMQ, the Advanced Messaging Queuing model.

Chapter 2 explores the AMQ protocol, looking at the frame structure, and the low-level process that occurs when a message is published or retrieved from RabbitMQ.

Chapter 3 goes even further and looks at the message properties, including the headers that add important meta-data to messages, such as content-type and encoding, and how you can leverage these headers in your applications.

Chapter 4 considers performance trade-offs which must be made. With each level of guarantee, your applications risk taking a hit on performance. This chapter explores what these options are and will help you balance your environments' need for guaranteed message assurance versus lightning fast delivery, the Goldilocks Principle.

Chapter 5 explores the concept of consuming messages, looking at the fundamental difference between Basic.Get and Basic.Consume at a low level (and why the latter is usually better), as well as pre-fetching and Quality of Service, message acknowledgements, dead letter exchanges, temporary queues, and message expiry.

Chapter 6 takes an in-depth look into the four core exchange types in RabbitMQ and how they can benefit your application architecture.

Chapter 7 looks at how you can scale up RabbitMQ by managing clusters, crash recovery in a cluster, and further performance considerations when working with a clustered environment.

Chapter 8 builds on the core concepts of clustering by taking a look at federated exchanges and queues, integrating RabbitMQ clusters with Amazon Web Services, and applying policies.

Chapter 9 looks at other ways of talking to RabbitMQ: using MQTT and STOMP as alternative protocols, or using statelessd-based HTTP messaging.

Finally, Chapter 10 looks at database integration into both PostgreSQL and InfluxDB for further interesting integrations.

Code

Just about all of the code shown in the book can be found in various forms in the sample source code which accompanies this book. The sample code can be downloaded free of charge from the Manning website (https://www.manning.com/books/rabbitmq-in-depth), as well as from this Github repository: https://github.com/gmr/RabbitMQ-in-Depth.

Book forum

Purchase of *RabbitMQ in Depth* includes free access to a private web forum run by Manning Publications where you can make comments about the book, ask technical questions, and receive help from the author and from other users. To access the forum, go to https://forums.manning.com/forums/rabbitmq-in-depth. You can also learn more about Manning's forums and the rules of conduct at https://forums.manning.com/forums/about.

Manning's commitment to our readers is to provide a venue where a meaningful dialogue between individual readers and between readers and the author can take place. It is not a commitment to any specific amount of participation on the part of the author, whose contribution to the forum remains voluntary (and unpaid). We suggest you try asking the author some challenging questions lest his interest stray! The forum and the archives of previous discussions will be accessible from the publisher's website as long as the book is in print.

About the author

GAVIN M. ROY is an active open-source evangelist and advocate who has been working with internet and Enterprise technologies since the mid-90's.

About the cover

The figure on the cover of *RabbitMQ in Depth* is captioned "A man from Mikanovac, Srijem, Croatia." The illustration is taken from a reproduction of an album of Croatian traditional costumes from the mid-nineteenth century by Nikola Arsenovic, published by the Ethnographic Museum in Split, Croatia, in 2003. The illustrations were obtained from a helpful librarian at the Ethnographic Museum in Split, itself situated in the Roman core of the medieval center of the town: the ruins of Emperor Diocletian's retirement palace from around AD 304. The book includes finely colored illustrations of figures from different regions of Croatia, accompanied by descriptions of the costumes and of everyday life.

Dress codes and lifestyles have changed over the last 200 years, and the diversity by region, so rich at the time, has faded away. It's now hard to tell apart the inhabitants of different continents, let alone of different hamlets or towns separated by only a few miles. Perhaps we have traded cultural diversity for a more varied personal life—certainly for a more varied and fast-paced technological life. Manning celebrates the inventiveness and initiative of the computer business with book covers based on the rich diversity of regional life of two centuries ago, brought back to life by illustrations from old books and collections like this one.

Part 1

RabbitMQ and application architecture

In this part of the book, we'll explore the structure of the AMQ protocol, which is how your application communicates with RabbitMQ. We'll also look at the messages themselves, leveraging features such as message headers, priority, and more, to enhance message interactions. We'll explore performance trade-offs, balancing stability and transactional safety against high-performance throughput with no guarantees. Additionally, we'll investigate the different exchange types and why they work the way they do.

Foundational RabbitMQ

This chapter covers

- Unique features of RabbitMQ
- Why RabbitMQ is becoming a popular choice for the centerpiece of messaging-based architectures
- The basics of the Advanced Messaging Queuing model, RabbitMQ's foundation

Whether your application is in the cloud or in your own data center, RabbitMQ is a lightweight and extremely powerful tool for creating distributed software architectures that range from the very simple to the incredibly complex. In this chapter you'll learn how RabbitMQ, as messaging-oriented middleware, allows tremendous flexibility in how you approach and solve problems. You'll learn how some companies are using it and about key features that make RabbitMQ one of the most popular message brokers today.

1.1   *RabbitMQ's features and benefits*

RabbitMQ has many features and benefits, the most important of which are

- *Open source*—Originally developed in a partnership between LShift, LTD, and Cohesive FT as RabbitMQ Technologies, RabbitMQ is now owned by Pivotal Software Inc. and is released under the Mozilla Public License. As an open-source project written in Erlang, RabbitMQ enjoys freedom and flexibility, while leveraging the strength of Pivotal standing behind it as a product. Developers and engineers in the RabbitMQ community are able to contribute enhancements and add-ons, and Pivotal is able to offer commercial support and a stable home for ongoing product maturation.

- *Platform and vendor neutral*—As a message broker that implements the platform- and vendor-neutral Advanced Message Queuing Protocol (AMQP) specification, there are clients available for almost any programming language and on all major computer platforms.

- *Lightweight*—It is lightweight, requiring less than 40 MB of RAM to run the core RabbitMQ application along with plugins, such as the Management UI. Note that adding messages to queues can and will increase its memory usage.

- *Client libraries for most modern languages*—With client libraries targeting most modern programming languages on multiple platforms, RabbitMQ makes a compelling broker to program for. There's no vendor or language lock-in when choosing how you'll write programs that will talk to RabbitMQ. In fact, it's not uncommon to see RabbitMQ used as the centerpiece between applications written in different languages. RabbitMQ provides a useful bridge that allows for languages such as Java, Ruby, Python, PHP, JavaScript, and C# to share data across operating systems and environments.

- *Flexibility in controlling messaging trade-offs*—RabbitMQ provides flexibility in controlling the trade-offs of reliable messaging with message throughput and performance. Because it's not a "one size fits all" type of application, messages can designate whether they should be persisted to disk prior to delivery, and, if set up in a cluster, queues can be set to be highly available, spanning multiple servers to ensure that messages aren't lost in case of server failure.

- *Plugins for higher-latency environments*—Because not all network topologies and architectures are the same, RabbitMQ provides for messaging in low-latency environments and plugins for higher-latency environments, such as the internet. This allows for RabbitMQ to be clustered on the same local network and share federated messages across multiple data centers.

- *Third-party plugins*—As a center point for application integrations, RabbitMQ provides a flexible plugin system. For example, there are third-party plugins for storing messages directly into databases, using RabbitMQ directly for database writes.

- *Layers of security*—In RabbitMQ, security is provided in multiple layers. Client connections can be secured by enforcing SSL-only communication and client certificate validation. User access can be managed at the virtual-host level, providing isolation of messages and resources at a high level. In addition, access to configuration capabilities, reading from queues, and writing to exchanges is managed by regular expression (regex) pattern matching. Finally, plugins can be used for integration into external authentication systems like LDAP.

We'll explore the features on this list in later chapters, but I'd like to focus right now on the two most foundational features of RabbitMQ: the language it's programmed in (Erlang), and the model it's based on (the Advanced Message Queuing model), a specification that defines much of the RabbitMQ lexicon and its behavior.

1.1.1   RabbitMQ and Erlang

As a highly performant, stable, and clusterable message broker, it's no surprise that RabbitMQ has found a home in such mission-critical environments as the centerpiece of large-scale messaging architectures. It was written in Erlang, the telco-grade, functional programming language designed at the Ericsson Computer Science Laboratory in the mid-to-late 1980s. Erlang was designed to be a distributed, fault-tolerant, soft real-time system for applications that require 99.999% uptime. As a language and run-time system, Erlang focuses on lightweight processes that pass messages between each other, providing a high level of concurrency with no shared state.

> **REAL-TIME SYSTEM**   A real-time system is a hardware platform, software platform, or combination of both that has requirements defined for when it must return a response from an event. A soft real-time system will sacrifice less important deadlines for executing tasks in favor of more important ones.

Erlang's design, which focused on concurrent processing and message passing, made it a natural choice for a message broker like RabbitMQ: As an application, a message broker maintains concurrent connections, routes messages, and manages their states. In addition, Erlang's distributed communication architecture makes it a natural for RabbitMQ's clustering mechanism. Servers in a RabbitMQ cluster make use of Erlang's *inter-process communication* (IPC) system, offloading the functionality that many competing message brokers have to implement to add clustering capabilities (figure 1.1).

Despite the advantages RabbitMQ gains by using Erlang, the Erlang environment can be a stumbling block. It may be helpful to learn some Erlang so you're confident in managing RabbitMQ's configuration files and using Erlang to gather information about RabbitMQ's current runtime state.

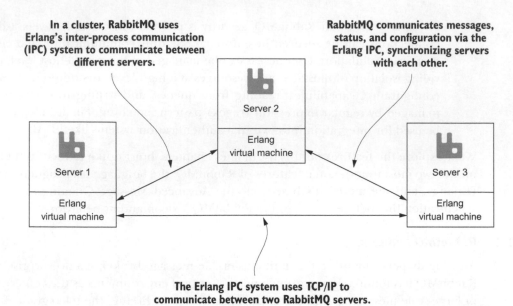

In a cluster, RabbitMQ uses Erlang's inter-process communication (IPC) system to communicate between different servers.

RabbitMQ communicates messages, status, and configuration via the Erlang IPC, synchronizing servers with each other.

Server 2
Erlang virtual machine

Server 1
Erlang virtual machine

Server 3
Erlang virtual machine

The Erlang IPC system uses TCP/IP to communicate between two RabbitMQ servers.

Figure 1.1   RabbitMQ clusters use the native Erlang inter-process communication mechanism in the VM for cross-node communication, sharing state information and allowing for messages to be published and consumed across the entire cluster.

1.1.2   RabbitMQ and AMQP

RabbitMQ was originally released in 2007, and interoperability, performance, and stability were the primary goals in mind during its development. RabbitMQ was one of the first message brokers to implement the AMQP specification. By all appearances, it set out to be the reference implementation. Split into two parts, the AMQP specification defines not only the wire protocol for talking to RabbitMQ, but also the logical model that outlines RabbitMQ's core functionality.

> **NOTE**   There are multiple versions of the AMQP specification. For the purposes of this book, we'll focus only on AMQP 0-9-1. Although newer versions of RabbitMQ support AMQP 1.0 as a plugin extension, the core RabbitMQ architecture is more closely related to AMQP 0-8 and 0-9-1. The AMQP specification is primarily comprised of two documents: a top-level document that describes both the AMQ model and the AMQ protocol, and a more detailed document that provides varying levels of information about every class, method, property, and field. More information about AMQP, including the specification documents, may be found at http://www.amqp.org.

There are multiple popular message brokers and messaging protocols, and it's important that you consider the impact that the protocol and broker will have on your application. RabbitMQ supports AMQP, but it also supports other protocols, such as MQTT,

Stomp, and XMPP. RabbitMQ's protocol neutrality and plugin extensibility make it a good choice for multiprotocol application architectures when compared to other popular message brokers.

It's RabbitMQ's roots in the AMQP specification that outline its primary architecture and communication methodologies. This is an important distinction when evaluating RabbitMQ against other message brokers. As with AMQP, RabbitMQ set out to be a vendor-neutral, platform-independent solution for the complex needs that messaging oriented architectures demand, such as flexible message routing, configurable message durability, and inter-datacenter communication, to name a few.

1.2 Who's using RabbitMQ, and how?

As an open-source software package, RabbitMQ is rapidly gaining mainstream adoption, and it powers some of the largest, most trafficked websites on the internet. Today, RabbitMQ is known to run in many different environments and at many different types of companies and organizations:

- Reddit, the popular online community, uses RabbitMQ heavily in the core of their application platform, which serves billions of web pages per month. When a user registers on the site, submits a news post, or votes on a link, a message is published into RabbitMQ for asynchronous processing by consumer applications.
- NASA chose RabbitMQ to be the message broker for their Nebula platform, a centralized server management platform for their server infrastructure, which grew into the OpenStack platform, a very popular software platform for building private and public cloud services.
- RabbitMQ sits at the core of Agoura Games' community-oriented online gaming platform, and it routes large volumes of real-time single and multiplayer game data and events.
- For the Ocean Observations Initiative, RabbitMQ routes mission-critical physical, chemical, geological, and biological data to a distributed network of research computers. The data, collected from sensors in the Southern, Pacific, and Atlantic Oceans, is integral to a National Science Foundation project that involves building a large-scale network of sensors in the ocean and seafloor.
- Rapportive, a Gmail add-on that places detailed contact information right inside the inbox, uses RabbitMQ as the glue for its data processing systems. Billions of messages pass through RabbitMQ monthly to provide data to Rapportive's web-crawling engine and analytics system and to offload long-running operations from its web servers.
- MercadoLibre, the largest e-commerce ecosystem in Latin America, uses RabbitMQ at the heart of their Enterprise Service Bus (ESB) architecture, decoupling their data from tightly coupled applications, allowing for flexible integrations with various components in their application architecture.

- Google's AdMob mobile advertising network uses RabbitMQ at the core of their RockSteady project to do real-time metrics analysis and fault-detection by funneling a fire hose of messages through RabbitMQ into Esper, the complex-event-processing system.
- India's biometric database system, Aandhaar leverages RabbitMQ to process data at various stages in its workflow, delivering data to their monitoring tools, data warehouse, and Hadoop-based data processing system. Aandhaar is designed to provide an online portable identity system for every single resident of India, covering 1.2 billion people.

As you can see, RabbitMQ isn't only used by some of the largest sites on the internet, it's also found its way into academia for large-scale scientific research, and NASA found it fitting to use RabbitMQ at the core of their network infrastructure management stack. As these examples show, RabbitMQ has been used in mission-critical applications in many different environments and industries with tremendous success.

1.3   *The advantages of loosely coupled architectures*

When I first started to implement a messaging based architecture, I was looking for a way to decouple database updates related to when a member logged in to a website. The website had grown very quickly, and due to the way we'd written it, it wasn't initially designed to scale well. When a user logged in to the website, several database servers had tables that needed to be updated with a login timestamp (figure 1.2). This timestamp needed to be updated in real time, as the most engaging activities on the site were driven in part by the timestamp value. Upon login, members were given preferential status in social games compared to those users who were actively online at any given time.

As the site continued to grow, the amount of time it took for a member to log in also grew. The reason for this was fairly straightforward: When adding a new application that used the member's last login timestamp, its database tables would carry the value to make it as fast as possible by removing cross database joins. To keep the data up to date and accurate, the new data tables would also be updated when the member logged in. It wasn't long before there were quite a few tables that were being maintained this way. The performance issue began to creep up because the database updates were being performed serially. Each query updating the member's last login timestamp would have to finish before the next began. Ten queries that were considered performant, each finishing within 50 ms, would add up to half a second in database updates alone. All of these queries would have to finish prior to sending the authorization response and redirect back to the user. In addition, any operational issues on a database server compounded the problem. If one database server started responding slowly or became unresponsive, members could no longer log in to the site.

To decouple the user-facing login application from directly writing to the database, I looked into publishing messages to message-oriented middleware or a centralized

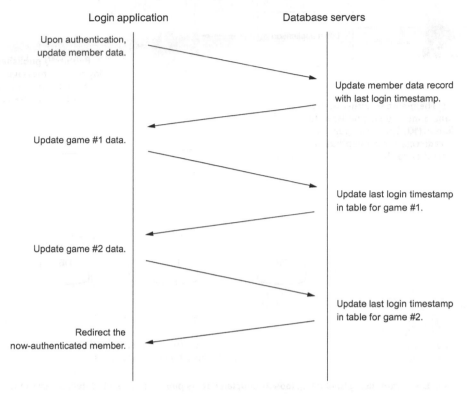

Figure 1.2   Before: once a user has logged in, each database is updated with a timestamp sequentially and dependently. The more tables you add, the longer this takes.

message broker that would then distribute the messages to any number of consumer applications that would do the database writes required. I experimented with several different message brokers, and ultimately I landed on RabbitMQ as my broker of choice.

> **DEFINITION**   Message-oriented middleware (MOM) is defined as software or hardware infrastructure that allows for the sending and receiving of messages from distributed systems. RabbitMQ fills this role handily with functionality that provides advanced routing and message distribution, even with wide area network (WAN) tolerances to support reliable, distributed systems that interconnect with other systems easily.

After decoupling the login process from the database updates that were required, I discovered a new level of freedom. Members were able to quickly log in because we were no longer updating the database as part of the authentication process. Instead, a member login message was published containing all of the information needed to update any database, and consumer applications were written that updated each database table independently (figure 1.3). This login message didn't contain authentication information for the member, but instead, only the information needed to maintain the

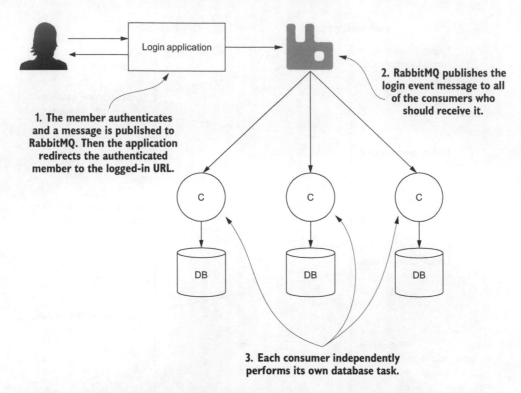

1. **The member authenticates and a message is published to RabbitMQ. Then the application redirects the authenticated member to the logged-in URL.**

2. **RabbitMQ publishes the login event message to all of the consumers who should receive it.**

3. **Each consumer independently performs its own database task.**

Figure 1.3   After: using RabbitMQ, loosely coupled data is published to each database asynchronously and independently, allowing the login application to proceed without waiting on any database writes.

member's last login status in our various databases and applications. This allowed us to horizontally scale database writes with more control. By controlling the number of consumer applications writing to a specific database server, we were able to throttle database writes for servers that had started to strain under the load created by new site growth while we worked through their own unique scaling issues.

As I detail the advantages of a messaging-based architecture, it's important to note that these advantages could also impact the performance of systems like the login architecture described. Any number of problems may impact publisher performance, from networking issues to RabbitMQ throttling message publishers. When such events happen, your application will see degraded performance. In addition to horizontally scaling consumers, it's wise to plan for horizontal scaling of message brokers to allow for better message throughput and publisher performance.

1.3.1   *Decoupling your application*

The use of messaging-oriented middleware can provide tremendous advantages for organizations looking to create flexible application architectures that are data centric. By moving to a loosely coupled design using RabbitMQ, application architectures are no longer bound to database write performance and can easily add new applications to act upon the data without touching any of the core applications. Consider figure 1.4, demonstrating the design of a tightly coupled application communicating with a database.

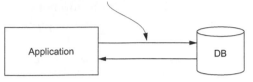

In a tightly coupled application, database writes are communicated directly with the database.

Figure 1.4   When communicating with a database, a tightly coupled application must wait for the database server to respond before it can continue processing.

1.3.2   Decoupling database writes

In a tightly coupled architecture, the application must wait for the database server to respond before it can finish a transaction. This design has the potential to create performance bottlenecks in both synchronous and asynchronous applications. Should the database server slow down due to poor tuning or hardware issues, the application will slow. Should the database stop responding or crash, the application will potentially crash as well.

By decoupling the database from the application, a loosely coupled architecture is created. In this architecture, RabbitMQ, as messaging-oriented middleware, acts as an intermediary for the data prior to some action being taken with it in the database. A consumer application picks up the data from the RabbitMQ server, performing the database action (figure 1.5).

In this model, should a database need to be taken offline for maintenance, or should the write workload become too heavy, you can throttle the consumer application or stop it. Until the consumer is able to receive the message, the data will persist

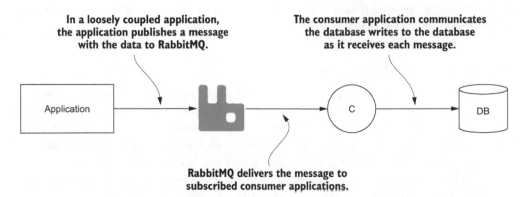

In a loosely coupled application, the application publishes a message with the data to RabbitMQ.

The consumer application communicates the database writes to the database as it receives each message.

RabbitMQ delivers the message to subscribed consumer applications.

Figure 1.5   A loosely coupled application allows the application that would have saved the data directly in the database to publish the data to RabbitMQ, allowing for the asynchronous processing of data.

in the queue. The ability to pause or throttle consumer application behavior is just one advantage of using this type of architecture.

1.3.3 *Seamlessly adding new functionality*

Loosely coupled architectures leveraging RabbitMQ allow data to be repurposed as well. The data that originally was only going to be written to a database can also be used for other purposes. RabbitMQ will handle all of the duplication of message content and can route it to multiple consumers for multiple purposes (figure 1.6).

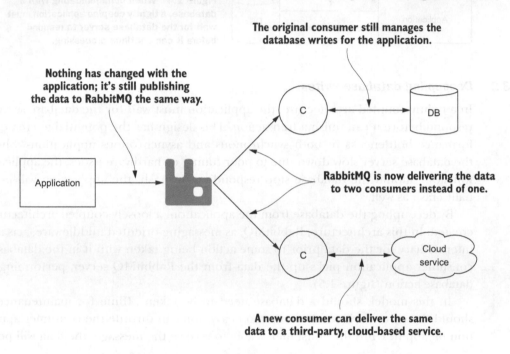

Figure 1.6   By using RabbitMQ, the publishing application doesn't need to be changed in order to deliver the same data to both a new cloud-based service and the original database.

1.3.4 *Replication of data and events*

Expanding upon this model, RabbitMQ provides built-in tools for cross–data center distribution of data, allowing for federated delivery and synchronization of applications. Federation allows RabbitMQ to push messages to remote RabbitMQ instances, accounting for WAN tolerances and network splits. Using the RabbitMQ federation plugin, it's easy to add a RabbitMQ server or cluster in a second data center. This is illustrated in figure 1.7, where the data from the original application can now be processed in two different locations over the internet.

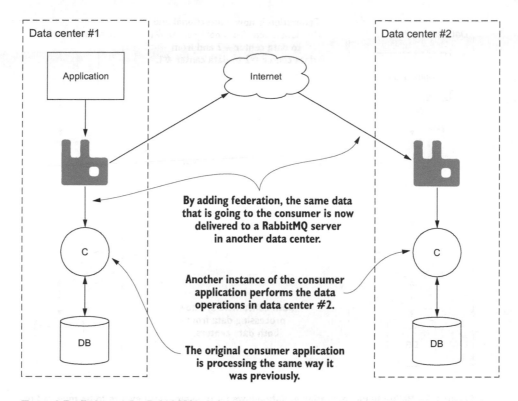

Figure 1.7   By leveraging RabbitMQ's federation plugin, messages can be duplicated to perform the same work in multiple data centers.

1.3.5   *Multi-master federation of data and events*

Expanding upon this concept by adding the same front-end application to a second data center and setting the RabbitMQ servers to bidirectionally federate data, you can have highly available applications in different physical locations. Messages from the application in either data center are sent to consumers in both data centers, allowing for redundancy in data storage and processing (figure 1.8). This approach to application architecture can allow applications to scale horizontally, also providing geographic proximity for users and a cost-effective way to distribute your application infrastructure.

> **NOTE**   As with any architecture decision, using messaging-oriented middleware introduces a degree of operational complexity. Because a message broker becomes a center point in your application design, a new single point of failure is introduced. There are strategies, which we'll cover in this book, to create highly available solutions to minimize this risk. In addition, adding a message broker creates a new application to manage. Configuration, server resources, and monitoring must be taken into account when weighing the tradeoffs of introducing a message broker to your architecture. I'll teach you how to account for these and other concerns as you proceed through the book.

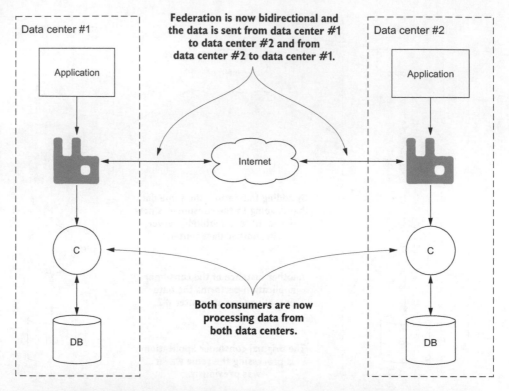

Figure 1.8   Bidirectional federation of data allows for the same data events to be received and processed in both data centers.

1.3.6   *The Advanced Message Queuing model*

Many of RabbitMQ's strengths, including its flexibility, come from the AMQP specification. Unlike protocols like HTTP and SMTP, the AMQP specification defines not only a network protocol but also server-side services and behaviors. I'll refer to this information as the Advanced Message Queuing (AMQ) model. The AMQ model logically defines three abstract components in broker software that define the routing behavior of messages:

- *Exchange*—The component of the message broker that routes messages to queues
- *Queue*—A data structure on disk or in memory that stores messages
- *Binding*—A rule that tells the exchange which queue the messages should be stored in

The flexibility of RabbitMQ comes from the dynamic nature of how messages can be routed through exchanges to queues. The bindings between exchanges and queues, and the message routing dynamics they create, are a foundational component of implementing a messaging-based architecture. Creating the right structure using these basic tools in RabbitMQ allows your applications to scale and easily change with the underlying business needs.

The first piece of information that RabbitMQ needs in order to route messages to their proper destination is an exchange to route them through.

EXCHANGES

Exchanges are one of three components defined by the AMQ model. An exchange receives messages sent into RabbitMQ and determines where to send them. Exchanges define the routing behaviors that are applied to messages, usually by examining data attributes passed along with the message or that are contained within the message's properties.

RabbitMQ has multiple exchange types, each with different routing behaviors. In addition, it offers a plugin-based architecture for custom exchanges. Figure 1.9 shows a logical view of a publisher sending a message to RabbitMQ, routing a message through an exchange.

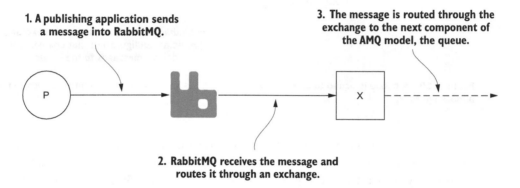

1. A publishing application sends a message into RabbitMQ.

3. The message is routed through the exchange to the next component of the AMQ model, the queue.

2. RabbitMQ receives the message and routes it through an exchange.

Figure 1.9   When a publisher sends a message into RabbitMQ, it first goes to an exchange.

QUEUES

A queue is responsible for storing received messages and may contain configuration information that defines what it's able to do with a message. A queue may hold messages in RAM only, or it may persist them to disk prior to delivering them in first-in, first-out (FIFO) order.

BINDINGS

To define a relationship between queues and exchanges, the AMQ model defines a *binding*. In RabbitMQ, bindings or *binding keys*, tell an exchange which queues to deliver messages to. For some exchange types, the binding will also instruct the exchange to filter which messages it can deliver to a queue.

When publishing a message to an exchange, applications use a *routing*-key attribute. This may be a queue name or it may be a string that semantically describes the message. When a message is evaluated by an exchange to determine the appropriate queues it should be routed to, the message's routing key is evaluated against the binding key (figure 1.10). In other words, the binding key is the glue that binds a queue to an exchange, and the routing key is the criteria that's evaluated against it.

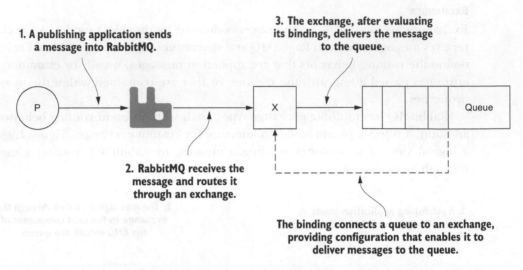

1. A publishing application sends a message into RabbitMQ.

3. The exchange, after evaluating its bindings, delivers the message to the queue.

2. RabbitMQ receives the message and routes it through an exchange.

The binding connects a queue to an exchange, providing configuration that enables it to deliver messages to the queue.

Figure 1.10   A queue is bound to an exchange, providing the information the exchange needs to route a message to it.

In the most simple of scenarios, the routing key may be the queue name, though this varies with each exchange type. In RabbitMQ, each exchange type is likely to treat routing keys in a different way, with some exchanges invoking simple equality checks and others using more complex pattern extractions from the routing key. There's even an exchange type that ignores the routing key outright in favor of other information in the message properties.

In addition to binding queues to exchanges, as defined in the AMQ model, RabbitMQ extends the AMQP specification to allow exchanges to bind to other exchanges. This feature creates a great deal of flexibility in creating different routing patterns for messages. In addition to the various routing patterns available when you use exchanges, you'll learn more about exchange-to-exchange bindings in chapter 6.

1.4   Summary

RabbitMQ, as messaging-oriented middleware, is an exciting technology that enables operational flexibility that's difficult to achieve without the loosely coupled application architecture it enables. By diving deep into RabbitMQ's AMQP foundation and behaviors, this book should prove to be a valuable reference, providing insight into how your applications can leverage its robust and powerful features. In particular, you'll soon learn how to publish messages and use the dynamic routing features in RabbitMQ to selectively sip from the fire hose of data your application can send, data that once may have been deeply buried in tightly coupled code and processes in your environment.

Whether you're an application developer or a high-level application architect, it's advantageous to have a deep level of knowledge about how your applications can benefit from RabbitMQ's diverse functionality. Thus far, you've learned the most foundational concepts that comprise the AMQ model. I'll expand on these concepts in the remainder of part 1 of this book: You'll learn about AMQP and how it defines the core of RabbitMQ's behavior.

Because this book will be hands-on, with the goal of imparting the knowledge required to use RabbitMQ in the most demanding of environments, you'll start working with code in the next chapter. By learning "how to speak Rabbit," you'll be leveraging the fundamentals of AMQP, writing code to send and receive messages with RabbitMQ. To speak Rabbit, you'll be using a Python-based library called *rabbitpy,* a library that was written specifically for the code examples in this book; I'll introduce it to you in the next chapter. Even if you're an experienced developer who has written applications that communicate with RabbitMQ, you should at least browse through the next chapter to understand what's happening at the protocol level when you're using RabbitMQ via the AMQP protocol.

How to speak Rabbit: the AMQ Protocol

This chapter covers

- Communicating with RabbitMQ via the AMQ Protocol
- Framing the AMQ Protocol at a low level
- Publishing messages into RabbitMQ
- Getting messages from RabbitMQ

The process that RabbitMQ and client libraries go through in order to get a message from your application into RabbitMQ and from RabbitMQ into consumer applications can be complex. If you're processing critical information, such as sales data, reliably delivering the canonical source of information about the sale should be a top priority. At the protocol level, the AMQP specification defines the semantics for client and broker to negotiate and speak to each other about the process for relaying your information. Oftentimes the lexicon defined in the AMQP specification bubbles its way up into RabbitMQ client libraries, with the classes and methods used by applications communicating with RabbitMQ mirroring the protocol-level classes and methods. Understanding how this communication takes place will help you learn not just the "how" of communicating with RabbitMQ but also the "why."

18

Even though the commands in client libraries tend to resemble or even directly copy the actions defined in the AMQP specification, most client libraries attempt to hide the complexity of communicating via the AMQ Protocol. This tends to be a good thing when you're looking to write an application and you don't want to worry about the intricacies of how things work. But skipping over the technical foundation of what RabbitMQ clients are doing isn't very helpful when you want to truly understand what's going on with your application. Whether you want to know why your application is slower to publish than you might expect, or you just want to know what steps a client must take in order to establish that first connection with RabbitMQ, knowing how your client is talking to RabbitMQ will make that process much easier.

To better illustrate the how and why, in this chapter you'll learn how AMQP splits communication between the client and broker into chunks of data called *frames,* and how these frames detail the actions your client application wants RabbitMQ to take and the actions RabbitMQ wants your client application to take. In addition, you'll learn how these frames are constructed at the protocol level, and how they provide the mechanism by which messages are delivered and consumed.

Building on this information, you'll write your first application in Python using a RabbitMQ client library written as a teaching aid for this book. This application will use AMQP to define an exchange and queue and then bind them together. Finally, you'll write a consumer application that will read the messages from the newly defined queue and print the contents of the message. If you're already comfortable doing these things, you should still dive into this chapter. I found that it was only after I fully understood the semantics of AMQP, the "why" instead of just the "how," that I understood RabbitMQ.

2.1 AMQP as an RPC transport

As an AMQP broker, RabbitMQ speaks a strict dialect for communication, utilizing a *remote procedure call* (RPC) pattern in nearly every aspect of communication with the core product. A remote procedure call is a type of communication between computers that allows one computer to execute a program or its methods on the other. If you've done web programming where you're talking to a remote API, you're using a common RPC pattern.

However, the RPC conversations that take place when communicating with RabbitMQ are unlike most web-based API calls. In most web API definitions, there are RPC conversations where the client issues commands and the server responds—the server doesn't issue commands back to the client. In the AMQP specification, both the server and the client can issue commands. For a client application, this means that it should be listening for communication from the server that may have little to do with what the client application is doing.

To illustrate how RPC works when a client is talking to RabbitMQ, let's consider the connection negotiation process.

2.1.1 Kicking off the conversation

When you're communicating with someone new in a foreign country, it's inevitable that one of you will kick off the conversation with a greeting, something that lets you and the other person know if you're both capable of speaking the same language. When speaking AMQP, this greeting is the *protocol header*, and it's sent by the client to the server. This greeting shouldn't be considered a request, however, as unlike the rest of the conversation that will take place, it's not a command. RabbitMQ starts the command/response sequence by replying to the greeting with a `Connection.Start` command, and the client responds to the RPC request with `Connection.StartOk` response frame (figure 2.1).

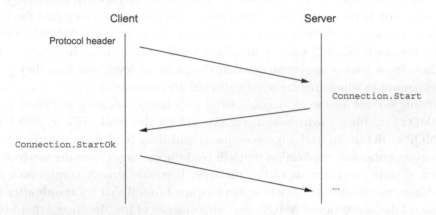

Figure 2.1   The initial communication negotiation with RabbitMQ demonstrates the RPC process in AMQP.

The full conversation for initiating a connection isn't terribly important unless you're writing a client library, but it's worth noting that to fully connect to RabbitMQ, there's a sequence of three synchronous RPC requests to start, tune, and open the connection. Once this sequence has finished, RabbitMQ will be ready for your application to make requests.

There are a whole range of different commands your application can send to RabbitMQ and that RabbitMQ can send to your client. You'll learn a small subset of these commands later in the chapter, but before that happens, you have to open a channel.

2.1.2 Tuning in to the right channel

Similar in concept to channels on a two-way radio, the AMQP specification defines channels for communicating with RabbitMQ. Two-way radios transmit information to each other using the airwaves as the connection between them. In AMQP, channels use the negotiated AMQP connection as the conduit for transmitting information to each other, and like channels on a two-way radio, they isolate their transmissions from other conversations that are happening. A single AMQP connection can have multiple channels, allowing multiple conversations between a client and server to take place. In technical terms, this is called *multiplexing*, and it can be useful for multithreaded or asynchronous applications that perform multiple tasks.

> **TIP**   In creating your client applications, it's important not to overcomplicate things with too many channels. On the wire in marshaled frames, channels are nothing more than an integer value that's assigned to the messages that are passed between a server and client; in the RabbitMQ server and client, they represent more. There are memory structures and objects set up for each channel. The more channels you have in a connection, the more memory RabbitMQ must use to manage the message flow for that connection. If you use them judiciously, you'll have a happier RabbitMQ server and a less complicated client application.

2.2   AMQP's RPC frame structure

Very similar in concept to object-oriented programming in languages such as C++, Java, and Python, AMQP uses classes and methods, referred to as *AMQP commands*, to create a common language between clients and servers. The classes in AMQP define a scope of functionality, and each class contains methods that perform different tasks. In the connection negotiation process, the RabbitMQ server sends a `Connection` `.Start` command, marshaled into a frame, to the client. As illustrated in figure 2.2, the `Connection.Start` command is composed of two components: the AMQP *class* and *method*.

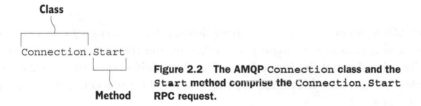

Figure 2.2   The AMQP `Connection` class and the `Start` method comprise the `Connection.Start` RPC request.

There are many commands in the AMQP specification, but if you're like me, you'll want to skip through all of that and get to the important bits of sending and receiving messages. It's important, however, to understand how the commands you'll be sending and receiving with RabbitMQ are represented on the wire to truly appreciate what's happening in your applications.

2.2.1   AMQP frame components

When commands are sent to and from RabbitMQ, all of the arguments required to execute them are encapsulated in data structures called frames that encode the data for transmission. Frames provide an efficient way for the command and its arguments to be encoded and delimited on the wire. You can think of frames as being like freight cars on a train. As a generalization, freight cars have the same basic structure and are differentiated by what they contain. The same is true with low-level AMQP frames. As figure 2.3 illustrates, a low-level AMQP frame is composed of five distinct components:

1 Frame type
2 Channel number
3 Frame size in bytes
4 Frame payload
5 End-byte marker (ASCII value 206)

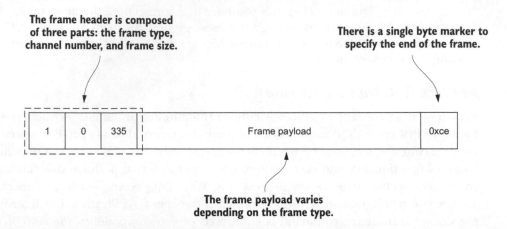

Figure 2.3   **The anatomy of a low-level AMQP frame**

A low-level AMQP frame starts off with three fields, referred to as a *frame header* when combined. The first field is a single byte indicating the frame type, and the second field specifies the channel the frame is for. The third field carries the byte size of the frame payload. The frame header, along with the end-byte marker, creates the structure for the frame.

Carried inside the frame, after the header and before the end-byte marker, is the frame payload. Much like the freight car protecting its contents on a train, the frame is designed to protect the integrity of the content it carries.

2.2.2   *Types of frames*

The AMQP specification defines five types of frames: a protocol header frame, a method frame, a content header frame, a body frame, and a heartbeat frame. Each frame type has a distinct purpose, and some are used much more frequently than others:

- The protocol header frame is only used once, when connecting to RabbitMQ.
- A method frame carries with it the RPC request or response that's being sent to or received from RabbitMQ.
- A content header frame contains the size and properties for a message.

- Body frames contain the content of messages.
- The heartbeat frame is sent to and from RabbitMQ as a check to ensure that both sides of the connection are available and working properly.

Whereas the protocol header and heartbeat frames are generally abstracted away from developers when using a client library, the method, content header, and body frames and their constructs are usually surfaced when writing applications that communicate with RabbitMQ. In the next section, you'll learn how messages that are sent into and received from RabbitMQ are marshaled into a method frame, a content header frame, and one or more body frames.

NOTE The heartbeat behavior in AMQP is used to ensure that both client and server are responding to each other, and it's a perfect example of how AMQP is a bidirectional RPC protocol. If RabbitMQ sends a heartbeat to your client application, and it doesn't respond, RabbitMQ will disconnect it. Oftentimes developers in single-threaded or asynchronous development environments will want to increase the timeout to some large value. If you find your application blocks communication in a way that makes heartbeats difficult to work with, you can turn them off by setting the heartbeat interval to 0 when creating your client connection. If, instead, you choose to use a much higher value than the default of 600 seconds, you can change RabbitMQ's maximum heartbeat interval value by changing the `heartbeat` value in the rabbitmq.config file.

2.2.3 *Marshaling messages into frames*

When publishing a message to RabbitMQ, the method, header, and body frames are used. The first frame sent is the method frame carrying the command and the parameters required to execute it, such as the exchange and routing key. Following the method frame are the content frames: a content header and body. The content header frame contains the message properties along with the body size. AMQP has a maximum frame size, and if the body of your message exceeds that size, the content will be split into multiple body frames. These frames are always sent in the same order over the wire: a method frame, content header frame, and one or more body frames (figure 2.4).

As figure 2.4 illustrates, when sending a message to RabbitMQ, a `Basic.Publish` command is sent in the method frame, and that's followed by a content header frame with the message's properties, such as the message's content type and the time when the message was sent. These properties are encapsulated in a data structure defined in the AMQP specification as `Basic.Properties`. Finally, the content of the message is marshaled into the appropriate number of body frames.

NOTE Although the default frame size is 131 KB, client libraries can negotiate a larger or smaller maximum frame size during the connection process, up to a 32-bit value for the number of bytes in a frame.

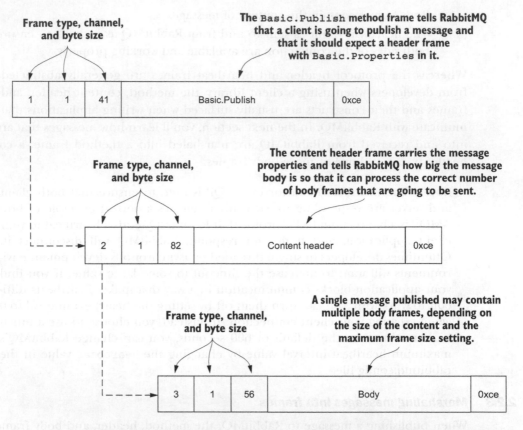

Figure 2.4   A single message published into RabbitMQ is composed of three frame types: the method frame for the `Basic.Publish` RPC call, a header frame, and one or more body frames.

In order to be more efficient and minimize the size of the data being transferred, the content in the method frame and content header frame is binary packed data and is not human-readable. Unlike the method and header frames, the message content carried inside the body frame isn't packed or encoded in any way and may be anything from plain text to binary image data.

To further illustrate the anatomy of an AMQP message, let's examine these three frame types in more detail.

2.2.4   *The anatomy of a method frame*

Method frames carry with them the class and method your RPC request is going to make as well as the arguments that are being passed along for processing. In figure 2.5, the method frame carrying a `Basic.Publish` command carries the binary packed data describing the command, and the request arguments that are passing along with it. The first two fields are numeric representations of the `Basic` class and the `Publish`

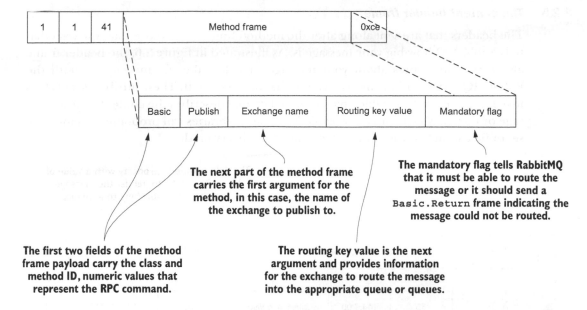

Figure 2.5 The `Basic.Publish` method frame is composed of five components: the class type and method type that identifies it as a `Basic.Publish` RPC request, the exchange name, a routing key value, and a mandatory flag.

method. These fields are followed by the string values for the exchange name and the routing key. As previously mentioned, these attributes instruct RabbitMQ on how to route a message. The `mandatory` flag tells RabbitMQ that the message must be delivered or the publishing of the message should fail.

Each data value in the method frame payload is encoded in a data-type-specific format. This format is designed to minimize byte size on the wire, ensure data integrity, and ensure that data marshaling and unmarshaling are as fast as possible. The actual format varies depending on the data type, but it's usually a single byte followed by numeric data, or a single byte followed by a byte-size field and then text data.

> **NOTE** Usually, sending a message using the `Basic.Publish` RPC request is a single-sided conversation. In fact, the AMQP specification goes as far as to say that success, as a general rule, is silent, whereas errors should be as noisy and intrusive as possible. But if you're using the `mandatory` flag when publishing your messages, your application should be listening for a `Basic.Return` command sent from RabbitMQ. If RabbitMQ isn't able to meet the requirements set by the `mandatory` flag, it will send a `Basic.Return` command to your client on the same channel. More information about `Basic.Return` is covered in chapter 4.

2.2.5   *The content header frame*

The headers that are sent along after the method frame carry more than the data that tells RabbitMQ how big your message is. As illustrated in figure 2.6, the header frame also carries attributes about your message that describe the message to both the RabbitMQ server and to any application that may receive it. These attributes, as values in a `Basic.Properties` table, may contain data that describes the content of your message or they may be completely blank. Most client libraries will prepopulate a minimal set of fields, such as the content type and the delivery mode.

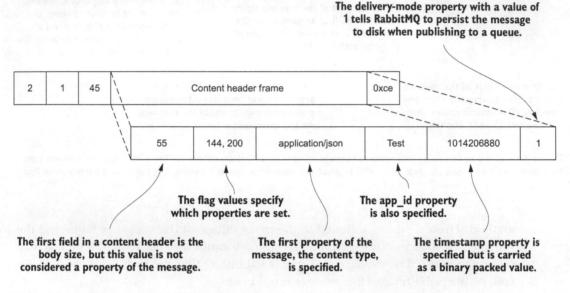

Figure 2.6   A message header carries the body size and a `Basic.Properties` table.

Properties are powerful tools in composing your message. They can be used to create a contract between publishers and consumers about the content of the message, allowing for a large amount of specificity about the message. You'll learn about `Basic` `.Properties` and the various possible uses for each field the data structure can carry in chapter 3.

2.2.6   *The body frame*

The body frame for a message is agnostic to the type of data being transferred, and it may contain either binary or text data. Whether you're sending binary data such as a JPEG image or serialized data in a JSON or XML format, the message body frame is the structure in the message that carries the actual message data (figure 2.7).

Together, the message properties and body form a powerful encapsulation format for your data. Marrying the descriptive attributes of the message with the content-agnostic body ensures you can use RabbitMQ for any type of data you deem appropriate.

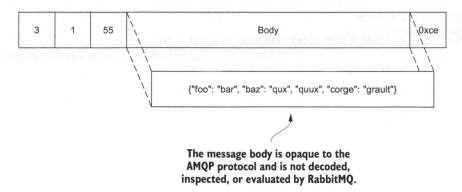

| 3 | 1 | 55 | Body | 0xce |

{"foo": "bar", "baz": "qux", "quux", "corge": "grault"}

The message body is opaque to the AMQP protocol and is not decoded, inspected, or evaluated by RabbitMQ.

Figure 2.7   A message body embedded in an AMQP frame

2.3   *Putting the protocol to use*

There are a few configuration-related steps you must take care of before you can publish messages into a queue. At a minimum, you must set up both an exchange and a queue, and then bind them together.

But before you actually perform those steps, let's look at what needs to happen at a protocol level to enable a message to be published, routed, queued, and delivered, starting with setting up an exchange for routing messages.

2.3.1   *Declaring an exchange*

Exchanges, like queues, are first-rate citizens in the AMQ model. As such, each has its own class in the AMQP specification. Exchanges are created using the Exchange .Declare command, which has arguments that define the name of the exchange, its type, and other metadata that may be used for message processing.

Once the command has been sent and RabbitMQ has created the exchange, an Exchange.DeclareOk method frame is sent in response (figure 2.8). If, for whatever reason, the command should fail, RabbitMQ will close the channel that the Exchange .Declare command was sent on by sending a Channel.Close command. This response will include a numeric reply code and text value indicating why the Exchange.Declare failed and the channel was closed.

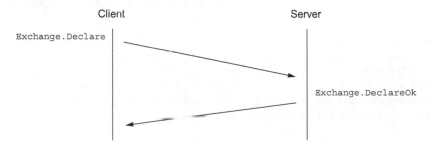

Figure 2.8   The communication sequence that occurs when declaring an exchange

2.3.2 *Declaring a queue*

Once the exchange has been created, it's time to create a queue by sending a Queue.Declare command to RabbitMQ. Like the Exchange.Declare command, there's a simple communication sequence that takes place (figure 2.9), and should the Queue .Declare command fail, the channel will be closed.

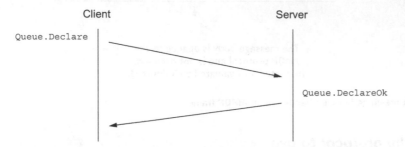

Figure 2.9   A queue-declare communication sequence consists of a Queue.Declare command and a Queue.DeclareOk response.

When declaring a queue, there's no harm in issuing the same Queue.Declare command more than once. RabbitMQ will consider subsequent queue declares to be passive and will return useful information about the queue, such as the number of pending messages in the queue and the number of consumers subscribed to it.

> ### Handling errors gracefully
>
> When you try to declare a queue with different properties than an existing queue with the same name, RabbitMQ will close the channel that the RPC request was issued on. This behavior is consistent with any other type of error that your client application may make in issuing commands to the broker. For example, if you issue a Queue .Declare command with a user that doesn't have *configuration* access on the virtual host, the channel will close with a 403 error.
>
> To correctly handle errors, your client application should be listening for a Channel .Close command from RabbitMQ so it can respond appropriately. Some client libraries may present this information as an exception for your application to handle, whereas others may use a callback passing style where you register a method that's called when a Channel.Close command is sent.
>
> If your client application isn't listening for or handling events coming from the server, you may lose messages. If you're publishing on a non-existent or closed channel, RabbitMQ may close the connection. If your application is consuming messages and doesn't know that RabbitMQ closed the channel, it may not know that RabbitMQ stopped sending your client messages and could still think that it's functioning properly and is subscribed to an empty queue.

2.3.3   Binding a queue to an exchange

Once the exchange and queue have been created, it's time to bind them together. Like with Queue.Declare, the command to bind a queue to an exchange, Queue.Bind, can only specify one queue at a time. Much like the Exchange.Declare and Queue.Declare commands, after you issue a Queue.Bind command, your application will receive a Queue.BindOk method frame if it was processed successfully (figure 2.10).

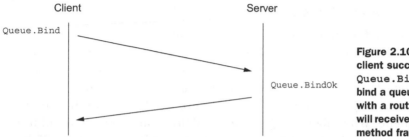

Figure 2.10   **After the client successfully issues a** Queue.Bind **command to bind a queue to an exchange with a routing key, the client will receive a** Queue.BindOk **method frame in response.**

As basic examples of RPC interactions between a RabbitMQ server and client, the Exchange.Declare, Queue.Declare, and Queue.Bind commands illustrate a common pattern that's mimicked by all synchronous commands in the AMQP specification. But there are a few asynchronous commands that break from the simple "Action" and "ActionOk" pattern. These commands deal with sending and receiving messages from RabbitMQ.

2.3.4   Publishing a message to RabbitMQ

As you previously learned, when publishing messages to RabbitMQ, multiple frames encapsulate the message data that's sent to the server. Before the actual message content ever reaches RabbitMQ, the client application sends a Basic.Publish method frame, a content header frame, and at least one body frame (figure 2.11).

When RabbitMQ receives all of the frames for a message, it will inspect the information it needs from the method frame before determining the next steps. The Basic.Publish method frame carries with it the exchange name and routing key for

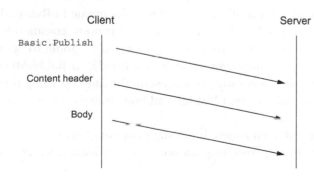

Figure 2.11   **When publishing a message to RabbitMQ, at least three frames are sent: the** Basic.Publish **method frame, a content header frame, and a body frame.**

the message. When evaluating this data, RabbitMQ will try to match the exchange name in the Basic.Publish frame against its database of configured exchanges.

> **TIP** By default, if you're publishing messages with an exchange that doesn't exist in RabbitMQ's configuration, it will silently drop the messages. To ensure your messages are delivered, either set the mandatory flag to true when publishing, or use delivery confirmations. These options are detailed in chapter 4. Be aware that using either of these methods may negatively impact the message publishing speed of your application.

When RabbitMQ finds a match to the exchange name in the Basic.Properties method frame, it evaluates the bindings in the exchange, looking to match queues with the routing key. When the criterion for a message matches any bound queues, the RabbitMQ server will enqueue the message in a FIFO order. Instead of putting the actual message into a queue data structure, a reference to the message is added to the queue. When RabbitMQ is ready to deliver the message, it will use the reference to compose the marshaled message and send it over the wire. This provides a substantial optimization for messages that are published to multiple queues. Holding only one instance of the message takes less physical memory when it's published to multiple destinations. The disposition of a message in a queue, whether consumed, expired, or sitting idle, will not impact the disposition of that message in any other queue. Once RabbitMQ no longer needs the message, because all copies of it have been delivered or removed, the single copy of the message data will be removed from memory in RabbitMQ.

By default, as long as there are no consumers listening to the queue, messages will be stored in the queue. As you add more messages, the queue will grow in size. RabbitMQ can keep these messages in memory or write them to disk, depending on the delivery-mode property specified in the message's Basic.Properties. The delivery-mode property is so important that it will be discussed in the next chapter and in even more detail in chapter 4.

2.3.5   *Consuming messages from RabbitMQ*

Once a published message has been routed and enqueued to one or more queues, there's not much left to discuss but its consumption. To consume messages from a queue in RabbitMQ, a consumer application subscribes to the queue in RabbitMQ by issuing a Basic.Consume command. Like the other synchronous commands, the server will respond with Basic.ConsumeOk to let the client know it's going to open the floodgates and release a torrent of messages, or at least a trickle. At RabbitMQ's discretion, the consumer will start receiving messages in the unsurprising form of Basic.Deliver methods and their content header and body frame counterparts (figure 2.12).

Once the Basic.Consume has been issued, it will stay active until one of a few things occurs. If a consumer wants to stop receiving messages, it can issue a Basic.Cancel

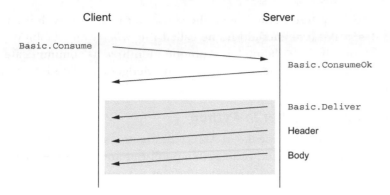

Figure 2.12   The logical frame delivery order between client and server when subscribing to a queue and receiving messages

command. It's worth noting that this command is issued asynchronously while RabbitMQ may still be sending messages, so a consumer can still receive any number of messages RabbitMQ has preallocated for it prior to receiving a `Basic.CancelOk` response frame.

When consuming messages, there are several settings that let RabbitMQ know how you want to receive them. One such setting is the `no_ack` argument for the `Basic.Consume` command. When set to true, RabbitMQ will send messages continuously until the consumer sends a `Basic.Cancel` command or the consumer is disconnected. If the `no_ack` flag is set to false, a consumer must acknowledge each message that it receives by sending a `Basic.Ack` RPC request (figure 2.13).

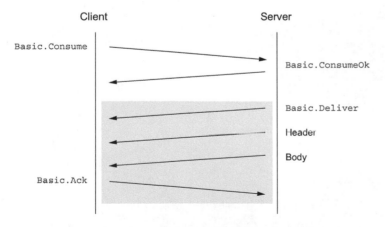

Figure 2.13   Each message successfully delivered by RabbitMQ to the client will be responded to with a `Basic.Ack`, until a `Basic.Cancel` command is sent. If `no_ack` is specified, the `Basic.Ack` step is omitted.

When the `Basic.Ack` response frame is sent, the consumer must pass with it an argument from the `Basic.Deliver` method frame called the *delivery tag*. RabbitMQ uses the delivery tag along with the channel as a unique identifier to communicate message acknowledgement, rejection, and negative acknowledgement. You'll learn more about these options in chapter 5.

2.4   *Writing a message publisher in Python*

Now that you have a healthy knowledge of AMQP fundamentals under your belt, it's time to turn theory into practice and write both a publisher and consumer. To do this we'll use the rabbitpy library. There are many libraries for communicating with RabbitMQ, but I created rabbitpy as a teaching aid for this book to keep the programming examples simple and concise while attempting to stay true to the AMQP command syntax. If you haven't done so yet, please install rabbitpy by following the VM installation instructions in the appendix.

To start this exercise, you'll make use of the IPython Notebook Server installed as part of the RabbitMQ in Depth virtual machine. If you've yet to do so, please follow the steps outlined in the appendix to set up the virtual machine on your local computer. Open your browser to http://localhost:8888 and you should see a page similar to figure 2.14.

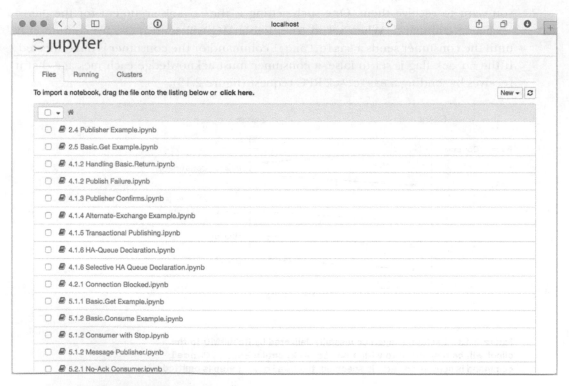

Figure 2.14   The IPython Notebook index page

The "2.4 Publisher Example" notebook in the index contains all of the code outlined in this page in order to communicate with RabbitMQ. You must import the rabbitpy library so that the Python interpreter allows you to use it:

```
In [1]:   # Import the RabbitMQ Client Library
          import rabbitpy
```

If you press the Play button or the Run Cell button in the toolbar or if you press Shift-Enter, the cell containing that code will execute. In the first cell of the notebook, the rabbitpy library will be imported.

You should also have seen the asterisk (*) change to the number 1. The active cell has automatically advanced from the first to the next one. As you read through this example code, you should execute each cell as you encounter it, advancing through the code in the IPython Notebook.

Now, with the rabbitpy library imported, you'll need to create an AMQP connection URL. The format for the URL is very similar to the format used for HTTP requests:

```
In [2]:   # Specify the URL to connect to
          url = 'amqp://guest:guest@localhost:5672/%2F'
```

This AMQP URL specifies that you'll connect over a normal AMQP connection using the username "guest" and the password "guest". It will connect you to localhost on port number 5672 with the default "/" vhost. This URL expects that you'll be connecting to RabbitMQ on your local machine with the default configuration. If you've set up RabbitMQ on a remote server or have changed the configuration of the RabbitMQ broker, you'll have to change the values accordingly.

Now that the URL has been defined, it's time to open a connection to RabbitMQ:

```
In [3]:   # Connect to RabbitMQ using the URL above
          connection = rabbitpy.Connection(url)
```

If you didn't receive an exception, you're now connected to RabbitMQ. If you did receive one, the most likely scenario is that RabbitMQ isn't running on your local machine. Please ensure that it's running and try again.

If you're successfully connected, it's time to open a channel to communicate with RabbitMQ:

```
In [4]:   # Open a new channel on the connection
          channel = connection.channel()
```

With the channel open, you can now declare an exchange by creating a new instance of the `rabbitpy.Exchange` class. Pass in the channel and the name of the exchange you'd like to create. I suggest using `chapter2-example` for now.

```
In [5]:    # Create a new exchange object, passing in the channel to use
           exchange = rabbitpy.Exchange(channel, 'chapter2-example')
```

Once it's constructed, use the exchange object's `declare` method to send the command, declaring the exchange in RabbitMQ:

```
In [6]:    # Declare the exchange on the RabbitMQ server
           exchange.declare()
```

Now that you've declared the exchange, you can set up the queue and bind it to the exchange. To do this, you first create the `Queue` object, passing in the channel and the name of the queue. In the example that follows, the name of the queue is `example`.

```
In [7]:    # Create a new queue object, passing in the channel to use
           queue = rabbitpy.Queue(channel, 'example')
```

Once the object has been created and the instance returned as the `queue` variable, you can send the `Queue.Declare` command to RabbitMQ using the `declare` method. What you should see is an output line that has a Python tuple data structure with the number of messages in the queue and the number of consumers for the queue. A tuple is an immutable set of Python objects. In this case they are integer values.

```
In [8]:    # Declare the queue on the RabbitMQ server
           queue.declare()
Out[8]:    (10, 0)
```

Now that the queue has been created, you must bind it in order for it to receive messages. To bind the queue to the exchange, send the `Queue.Bind` command by invoking the queue object's `bind` method, passing in the exchange and the routing key. In the following example, the routing key is `example-routing-key`. When the execution of this cell returns, you should see the output `True`, indicating that the binding was successful.

```
In [9]:    # Bind the queue to the exchange on the RabbitMQ server
           queue.bind(exchange, 'example-routing-key')
Out[9]:    True
```

In your application, I recommend that you use semantically appropriate period-delimited keywords to namespace your routing keys. The *Zen of Python* states that "Namespaces are one honking great idea—let's do more of those!" and this is true in RabbitMQ as well. By using period-delimited keywords, you'll be able to route messages based upon patterns and subsections of the routing key. You'll learn more about this in chapter 6.

> **TIP** Queue and exchange names, along with routing keys, can include Unicode characters.

With your exchange and queue created and bound, you can now publish test messages into RabbitMQ that will be stored in the `example` queue. To make sure you have enough messages to play with, the following example publishes 10 test messages into the queue.

```
In [10]: for message_number in range(0, 10):
             message = rabbitpy.Message(channel,
                                        'Test message #%i' % message_number,
                                        {'content_type': 'text/plain'},
                                        opinionated=True)
             message.publish(exchange, 'example-routing-key')
```

To publish test messages, a new `rabbitpy.Message` object is created in each loop iteration, passing in the channel, a message body, and a dictionary of message properties. Once the message is created, the `publish` method is invoked, creating the `Basic.Publish` method frame, the content header frame, and one body frame, and delivering them all to RabbitMQ.

> **TIP** When you write publishers for your production environment, use a data serialization format such as JSON or XML so that your consumers can easily deserialize the messages and so they're easier to read when you're troubleshooting any problems that may arise.

You should now go to the RabbitMQ web management console and see if your messages made it into the queue: Open your web browser and visit the management UI at http://localhost:15672/#/queues/%2F/example (if your broker is on a different machine, change *localhost* in the URL to the appropriate server). Once authenticated, you should see a page resembling the screenshot in figure 2.15.

If you look toward the bottom of the page, you'll see a Get Messages section. If you change the Messages field value from 1 to 10 and click Get Messages, you should see each of the 10 messages you previously published. Make sure you leave the Requeue field value set to Yes. It tells RabbitMQ to add the messages back into the queue when RabbitMQ retrieves them for display in the management UI. If you didn't, don't worry; just go back and rerun the publishing code.

Figure 2.15   The RabbitMQ web management UI showing 10 messages in the order-processing queue.

2.5   Getting messages from RabbitMQ

Now that you know how to publish messages, it's time to retrieve them. The following listing pulls together the repetitive, yet import, connection elements from the publishing code discussed in the last section, allowing you to get messages from RabbitMQ. This code is in the "2.5 Basic.Get Example" notebook. This notebook has six cells in it when using the IPython Notebook interface. You can click the Cell dropdown and then Run All instead of running each cell as in the previous example.

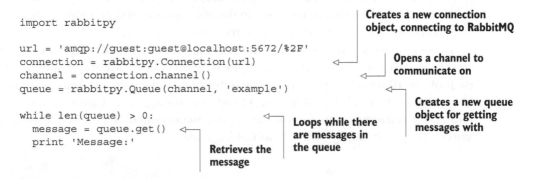

```
import rabbitpy

url = 'amqp://guest:guest@localhost:5672/%2F'
connection = rabbitpy.Connection(url)
channel = connection.channel()
queue = rabbitpy.Queue(channel, 'example')

while len(queue) > 0:
    message = queue.get()
    print 'Message:'
```

Creates a new connection object, connecting to RabbitMQ

Opens a channel to communicate on

Creates a new queue object for getting messages with

Loops while there are messages in the queue

Retrieves the message

```
print ' ID: %s' % message.properties['message_id']          ◁─┐    Gets a
print ' Time: %s' % message.properties['timestamp'].isoformat() ◁─┤  message
print ' Body: %s' % message.body    ◁─┐                               from the
message.ack()        ◁─┐                                               queue
```

Acknowledges receipt of the   **Prints the**   **Prints the timestamp**
message with RabbitMQ   **message body**   **property formatted as an**
ISO 8601 timestamp

After typing in and executing the preceding consumer code, you should see each of the 10 messages you previously published. If you were looking closely, you may have noticed that although you didn't specify the `message_id` or `timestamp` properties when publishing the messages, each message printed from the consumer has them. The rabbitpy client library will automatically populate these properties for you if you don't specify them. In addition, had you sent a Python `dict` as the message, rabbitpy would automatically serialize the data as JSON and set the content-type property as `application/json`.

2.6   *Summary*

The AMQP 0.9.1 specification defines a communication protocol that uses RPC-style commands to communicate between the RabbitMQ server and client. Now that you know how these commands are framed and how the protocol functions, you should be better equipped for writing and troubleshooting applications that interact with RabbitMQ. You've already covered a large majority of the process of communicating with RabbitMQ for publishing and consuming messages. Many applications contain little more code than what you've already implemented to work with your RabbitMQ instance.

In the next chapter you'll learn even more about using message properties, allowing your publishers and consumers to use a common contract for the messages your applications exchange.

An in-depth tour
of message properties

This chapter covers

- Message properties and their impact on message delivery
- Using message properties to create a contract with publishers and consumers

In chapter 1, I detailed how I set out to decouple member login events from database writes that were causing delays for members logging into a website. The advantages of doing so quickly became clear to our entire engineering organization, and using a loosely coupled architecture for database writes took on a life of its own. Over time, we began to leverage this architecture in new applications we were developing. No longer were we just processing member login events, we were using this architecture for account deletions, email message generation, and any application event that could be performed asynchronously. Events were being published through the message bus to consumer applications, each performing its own unique task. At first we put little thought into what the message contained and how it was formatted, but it soon became apparent that standardization was needed.

With the different message types and no standardization of message format, it became difficult to predict how a specific message type would be serialized and what data a particular message type would contain. Developers would publish messages in a format that made sense for their application and their application alone. Although they accomplished their own tasks, this mindset was shortsighted. We began to observe that messages could be reused across multiple applications, and the arbitrary formatting decisions were becoming problematic. In an effort to ease the growing pains around these and related issues, we paid more attention to describing the message being sent, both in documentation and as part of the message itself.

To provide a consistent method for self-describing our messages, we looked to AMQP's `Basic.Properties`, a data structure that's passed along with every message published via AMQP into RabbitMQ. Leveraging `Basic.Properties` opened the doors to more intelligent consumers—consumer applications that could automatically deserialize messages, validate the origin of a message and its type prior to processing, and much more. In this chapter we'll look at `Basic.Properties` in depth, covering each property and its intended use.

3.1 Using properties properly

You'll recall from chapter 2 that when you're publishing a message with RabbitMQ, your message is composed of three low-level frame types from the AMQP specification: the `Basic.Publish` method frame, the content header frame, and the body frame. These three frame types work together in sequence to get your messages where they're supposed to go and to ensure that they're intact when they get there (figure 3.1).

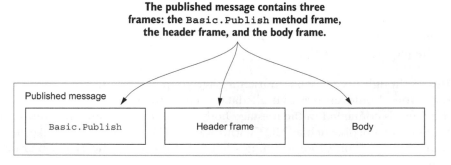

Figure 3.1   **The three components of a message published into RabbitMQ**

The message properties contained in the header frame are a predefined set of values specified by the `Basic.Properties` data structure (figure 3.2). Some properties, such as `delivery-mode`, have well-defined meanings in the AMQP specification, whereas others, such as `type`, have no exact specification.

In some cases, RabbitMQ uses well-defined properties to implement specific behaviors with regard to the message. An example of this is the previously mentioned `delivery-mode` property. The value of `delivery-mode` will tell RabbitMQ if it's allowed

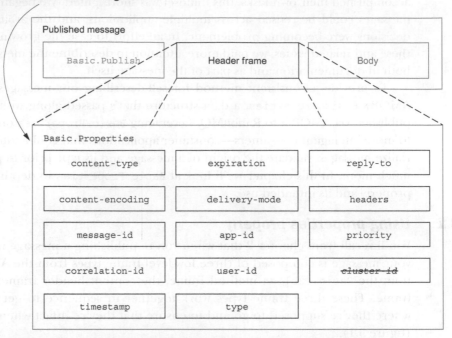

The message properties are embedded in the header frame and contain information that describes the message.

Figure 3.2 Basic.Properties, **including the deprecated** cluster-id **property from AMQP-0-8**

to keep the message in memory when the message is placed in a queue or if it must store the message to disk first.

> **TIP** Although it's advisable to use message properties to describe your message, you should ensure that all data needed by applications consuming messages is contained in the message body. Should you eventually venture to bridging protocols, such as MQTT with RabbitMQ, you'll want to make sure your messages don't lose meaning when AMQP-specific message semantics aren't available.

As we went through the message standardization process, the AMQP message properties provided a useful starting point for defining and carrying metadata about a message. That metadata, in turn, allows the reader to create strict contracts between publishers and consumers. Many of the attributes, from the content-type and message type (type) to the timestamp and application ID (app-id), have proven to be very useful not just for consistency in the engineering process but in day-to-day operational use. In short, by using message properties, you can create self-describing messages, similar to how XML is considered self-describing data markup.

In this chapter, we'll look at each of the basic properties outlined in figure 3.2:

- Using the content-type property to let consumers know how to interpret the message body
- Using content-encoding to indicate that the message body may be compressed or encoded in some special way
- Populating message-id and correlation-id to uniquely identify messages and message responses, tracking the message through your workflow
- Leveraging the timestamp property to reduce message size and create a canonical definition of when a message was created
- Expiring messages with the expiration property
- Telling RabbitMQ to write your messages to disk-backed or in-memory queues using delivery-mode
- Using app-id and user-id to help track down troublesome publishers
- Using the type property to define a contract with publishers and consumers
- Routing reply messages when implementing a pattern using the reply-to property
- Using the headers table property for free-form property definitions and RabbitMQ routing

We'll also touch on why you'll want to avoid using the priority property and on what happened to the cluster-id property and why you can't use it.

I'll discuss the properties in the order of this list, but I've also included a handy table at the end of the chapter listing each property in alphabetical order along with its data type, an indication of whether it's used by a broker or application, and instructions for its use.

NOTE When I use the term "contract" with regard to messaging, I'm referring to a specification for the format and contents of a message. In programming, the term is often used to describe the predefined specification of APIs, objects, and systems. Contract specifications often contain precise information about the data transmitted and received, such as the data type, its format, and any conditions that should be applied to it.

3.2 Creating an explicit message contract with content-type

As I quickly found, it's easy to come up with new uses for messages that are published through RabbitMQ. Our initial consumer applications were written in Python, but soon messages were being consumed by applications written in PHP, Java, and C.

When messages are not self-describing about their payload format, your applications are more likely to break due to the use of implicit contracts, which are inherently error-prone. By using self-describing messages, programmers and consumer applications don't need to guess how to deserialize the data received by messages or if deserialization is even necessary.

The Basic.Properties data structure specifies the content-type property for conveying the format of the data in the message body (figure 3.3).

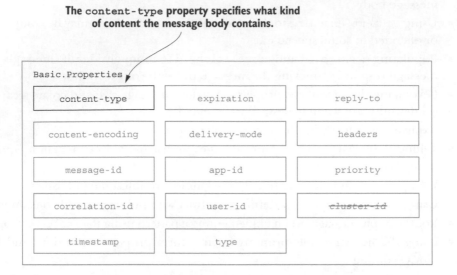

Figure 3.3 **The content-type property is the first property in Basic.Properties.**

Like in the various standardized HTTP specifications, content-type conveys the MIME type of the message body. If your application is sending a JSON-serialized data value, for example, setting the content-type property to application/json will allow for yet-to-be-developed consumer applications to inspect the message type upon receipt and correctly decode the message.

Thoughts on self-describing messages and message content

It's wise to use a standard serialization format such as JSON, Msgpack (http://msgpack.org/), or XML. These formats allow for any number of consumer applications to be written in just about any programming language. Because the data is self-describing in these formats, it's easier to write future consumer applications and it's easier to decode messages on the wire outside of your core application.

In addition, by specifying the serialization format in the content-type property, you can future-proof your consumer applications. When consumers can automatically recognize the serialization formats that they support and can selectively process messages, you don't have to worry about what happens when a new serialization format is used and routed to the same queues.

If you're using a framework for your consumer code, you may want to make it smart about how it deals with the messages it receives. By having the framework preprocess the message prior to handing it off to your consumer code, message bodies can automatically be deserialized and loaded into native data structures in your programming language. For example, in Python your framework could detect the message serialization type from the content-type header and, using this information, it could automatically deserialize the message body and place the contents into a dict, list, or other native data type. This would ultimately reduce the complexity of your code in the consumer application.

3.3 Reducing message size with gzip and content-encoding

Messages sent over AMQP aren't compressed by default. This can be problematic with overly verbose markup such as XML, or even with large messages using less markup-heavy formats like JSON or YAML. Your publishers can compress messages prior to publishing them and decompress them upon receipt, similarly to how web pages can be compressed on the server with gzip and the browser can decompress them on the fly prior to rendering.

To make this process explicit, AMQP specifies the content-encoding property (figure 3.4).

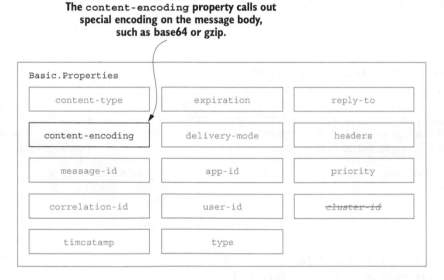

Figure 3.4 The content-encoding property indicates whether special encodings have been applied to the message body.

It's preferable not to change the contract of the message being published and consumed in production, thus minimizing any potential effects on preexisting code. But if message size is impacting overall performance and stability, using the content-encoding header will allow your consumers to prequalify messages, ensuring they can decode whatever format the message body is sent as.

> **NOTE** Don't confuse content-encoding with content-type. Like in the HTTP specification, content-encoding is used to indicate some level of encoding beyond the content-type. It's a modifier field that's often used to indicate that the content of the message body has been compressed using gzip or some other form of compression. Some AMQP clients automatically set the content-encoding value to UTF-8, but this is incorrect behavior. The AMQP specification states that content-encoding is for storing the MIME content encoding.

To draw a parallel, MIME email markup uses a content-encoding field to indicate the encoding for each of the different parts of the email. In email, the most common encoding types are Base64 and Quoted-Printable. Base64 encoding is used to ensure binary data transferred in the message doesn't violate the text-only SMTP protocol. For example, if you're creating an HTML-based email message with embedded images, the embedded images are likely to be Base64 encoded.

Unlike SMTP, however, AMQP is a binary protocol. The content in the message body is transferred as is and isn't encoded or transformed in the message marshaling and remarshaling process. Without regard to format, any content may be passed without concern of violating the protocol.

Leveraging consumer frameworks

If you're using a framework to write your consumer code, it can use the content-encoding property to automatically decode messages upon receipt. By preprocessing, deserializing, and decompressing messages prior to calling your consumer code, the logic and code in a consumer application can be simplified. Your consumer-specific code will be able to focus on the task of processing the message body.

We'll discuss consumer frameworks in more detail in chapter 5.

Combined with the content-type property, the content-encoding property empowers consumer applications to operate in an explicit contract with the publishers. This allows you to write future-proof code, hardening it against unexpected errors caused by changes in message format. For example, at some point in your application's lifetime you may find that bzip2 compression is better for your message content. If you code your consumer applications to examine the content-encoding property, they can then reject messages that they can't decode. Consumers that only know how to decompress using zlib or deflate would reject the new bzip2 compressed messages, leaving them in a queue for other consumer applications that can decompress bzip2 messages.

3.4 Referencing messages with message-id and correlation-id

In the AMQP specification, `message-id` and `correlation-id` are specified "for application use" and have no formally defined behavior (figure 3.5). This means that as far as the specification is concerned, you can use them for whatever purpose you like. Both fields allow for up to 255 bytes of UTF-8 encoded data and are stored as uncompressed values embedded in the `Basic.Properties` data structure.

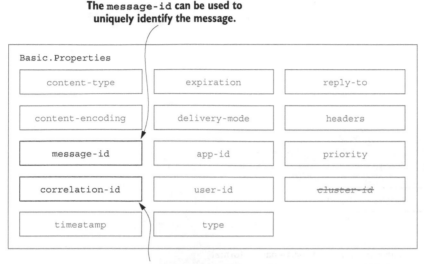

The `message-id` can be used to uniquely identify the message.

The `correlation-id` can indicate that the message is in response to another message, and, in this case, would contain the `message-id` from the previous message.

Figure 3.5 The `message-id` and `correlation-id` properties can be used to track individual messages and response messages as they flow through your systems.

3.4.1 Message-id

Some message types, such as a login event, aren't likely to need a unique message ID associated with them, but it's easy to imagine types of messages that would, such as sales orders or support requests. The `message-id` property enables the message to carry data in the header that uniquely identifies it as it flows through the various components in a loosely coupled system.

3.4.2 Correlation-id

Although there's no formal definition for the `correlation-id` in the AMQP specification, one use is to indicate that the message is a response to another message by having it carry the `message-id` of the related message. Another option is to use it to carry a transaction ID or other similar data that the message is referencing.

3.5   *Born-on dating: the timestamp property*

One of the more useful fields in `Basic.Properties` is the `timestamp` property (figure 3.6). Like `message-id` and `correlation-id`, `timestamp` is specified as "for application use." Even if your message doesn't use it, the `timestamp` property is very helpful when you're trying to diagnose any type of unexpected behavior in the flow of messages through RabbitMQ. By using the `timestamp` property to indicate when a message was created, consumers can gauge performance in message delivery.

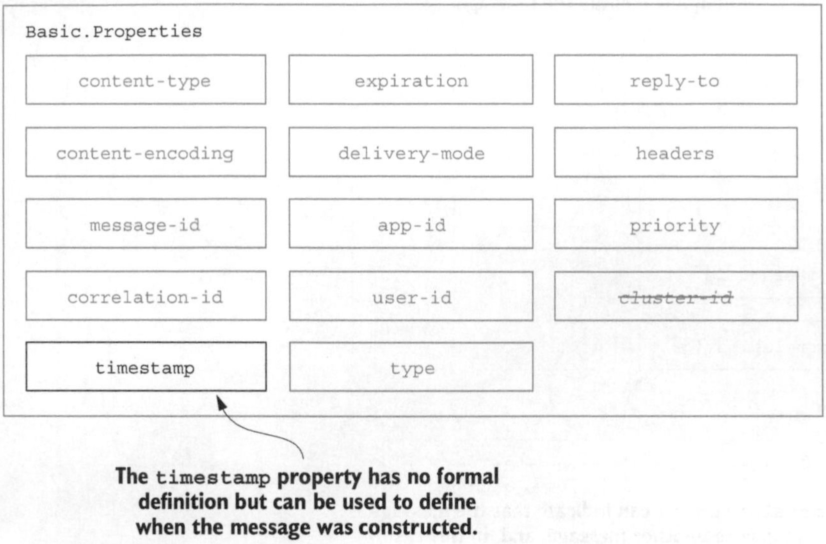

```
Basic.Properties

  content-type          expiration            reply-to

  content-encoding      delivery-mode         headers

  message-id            app-id                priority

  correlation-id        user-id               cluster-id

  timestamp             type
```

The `timestamp` **property has no formal
definition but can be used to define
when the message was constructed.**

Figure 3.6   The `timestamp` **property can carry an epoch value to specify when the
message was created.**

Is there a service level agreement (SLA) that your processes need to enforce? By evaluating the `timestamp` from the message properties, your consumer applications can decide whether they will process a message, discard it, or even publish an alert message to a monitoring application to let someone know that the age of a message is exceeding a desired value.

The timestamp is sent as a Unix epoch or integer-based timestamp indicating the number of seconds since midnight on January 1, 1970. For example, February 2, 2002, at midnight would be represented as the integer value 1329696000. As an encoded integer value, the timestamp only takes up 8 bytes of overhead in the message. Unfortunately there's no time zone context for the timestamp, so it's advisable to use UTC or another consistent time zone across all of your messages. By standardizing on the time zone up front, you'll avoid any future problems that may result from your messages traveling across time zones to geographically distributed RabbitMQ brokers.

3.6 *Automatically expiring messages*

The expiration property tells RabbitMQ when it should discard a message if it hasn't been consumed. Although the expiration property (figure 3.7) existed in both the 0-8 and 0-9-1 versions of the AMQP specification, it wasn't supported in RabbitMQ until the release of version 3.0. In addition, the specification of the expiration property is a bit odd; it's specified "for implementation use, no formal behavior," meaning RabbitMQ can implement its use however it sees fit. One final oddity is that it's specified as a short string, allowing for up to 255 characters, whereas the other property that represents a unit of time, timestamp, is an integer value.

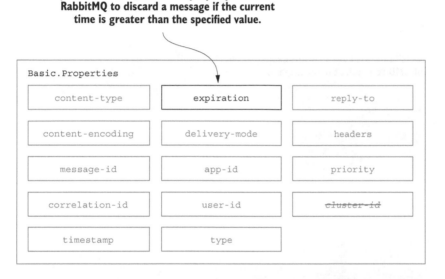

If specified, the expiration **property will instruct RabbitMQ to discard a message if the current time is greater than the specified value.**

Figure 3.7   To use the expiration **property in RabbitMQ, set the string value to a Unix epoch timestamp designating the maximum value for which the message is still valid.**

Because of the ambiguity in the specification, the expiration value is likely to have different implications when using different message brokers or even different versions of the same message broker. To auto-expire messages in RabbitMQ using the expiration property, it must contain a Unix epoch or integer-based timestamp, but stored as a string. Instead of storing an ISO-8601 formatted timestamp such as "2002-02-20T00:00:00-00", you must set the string value to the equivalent value of "1329696000".

When using the expiration property, if a message is published to the server with an expiration timestamp that has already passed, the message will not be routed to any queues, but instead will be discarded.

It's also worth noting that RabbitMQ has other functionality to expire your messages only under certain circumstances. In declaring a queue, you can pass an x-message-ttl argument along with the queue definition. This value should also be a Unix epoch timestamp, but it uses millisecond precision (value*1000) as an integer value. This value instructs the queue to automatically discard messages once the specified time has passed. The x-message-ttl queue argument and the merits of its use will be discussed in more detail in chapter 5.

3.7   *Balancing speed with safety using delivery-mode*

The delivery-mode property is a byte field that indicates to the message broker that you'd like to persist the message to disk prior to it being delivered to any awaiting consumers (figure 3.8). In RabbitMQ, persisting a message means that it will remain in the queue until it's consumed, even if the RabbitMQ server is restarted. The delivery-mode property has two possible values: 1 for a non-persisted message and 2 for a persisted message.

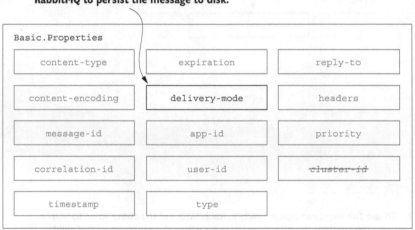

Figure 3.8   The delivery-mode property instructs RabbitMQ whether it must store the message on disk when placing it in a queue or if it may keep the message only in memory.

> **NOTE**   When you're first learning the various terms and settings in RabbitMQ, message persistence can often be confused with the durable setting in a queue. A queue's durability attribute indicates to RabbitMQ whether the definition of a queue should survive a restart of the RabbitMQ server or cluster. Only the delivery-mode of a message will indicate to RabbitMQ whether a message should be persisted or not. A queue may contain persisted and non-persisted messages. Queue durability is discussed in chapter 4.

As illustrated in figure 3.9, specifying your message as a non-persisted message will allow RabbitMQ to use memory-only queues.

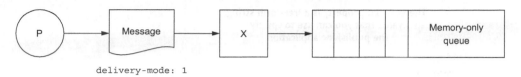

delivery-mode: 1

Figure 3.9 Publishing messages to memory-only queues

Because memory IO is inherently faster than disk IO, specifying `delivery-mode` as 1 will deliver your messages with as little latency as possible. In my web application login use case, the choice of delivery mode may be easier than in other use cases. Although it's desirable not to lose any login events if a RabbitMQ server fails, it's usually not a hard requirement. If member login event data is lost, it's not likely the business will suffer. In that case, we'd use `delivery-mode:1`. But if you're using RabbitMQ to publish financial transaction data, and your application architecture is focused on guaranteed delivery instead of message throughput, you can enable persistence by specifying `delivery-mode:2`. As illustrated in figure 3.10, when specifying a delivery mode of 2, messages are persisted to a disk-backed queue.

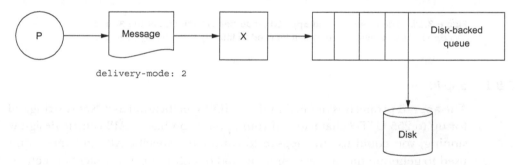

delivery-mode: 2

Figure 3.10 Publishing messages to disk-backed queues

Although this provides some guarantee that messages won't be lost in the event of a message broker crash, it comes with potential performance and scaling concerns. The `delivery-mode` property has such a significant impact on delivery and performance that it's covered in more detail in chapter 4.

3.8 *Validating message origin with app-id and user-id*

The `app-id` and `user-id` properties provide another level of information about a message and have many potential uses (figure 3.11). As with other properties that can be used to specify a behavioral contract in the message, these two properties can carry information that your consumer applications can validate prior to processing.

The `app-id` property is a free-form string
value that you can use to specify
the publishing application.

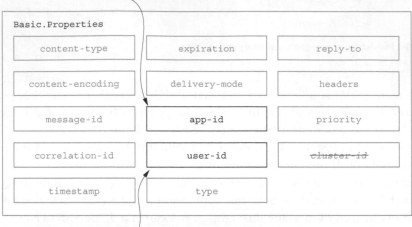

RabbitMQ validates the `user-id` property
against the authenticated RabbitMQ
user publishing the message.

**Figure 3.11   The `user-id` and `app-id` properties are the last of the `Basic`
`.Properties` values, and they can be used to identify the message source.**

3.8.1   *app-id*

The `app-id` property is defined in the AMQP specification as a "short-string," allowing
for up to 255 UTF-8 characters. If your application has an API-centric design with ver-
sioning, you could use the `app-id` to convey the specific API and version that were
used to generate the message. As a method of enforcing a contract between publisher
and consumer, examining the `app-id` prior to processing allows the application to discard the message if it's from an unknown or unsupported source.

Another possible use for `app-id` is in gathering statistical data. For example, if
you're using messages to convey login events, you could set the `app-id` property to the
platform and version of the application triggering the login event. In an environment
where you may have web-based, desktop, and mobile client applications, this would be
a great way to transparently both enforce a contract and extract data to keep track of
logins by platform, without ever inspecting the message body. This is especially handy
if you want to have single-purposed consumers allowing for a stats-gathering consumer
listening to the same messages as your login processing consumer. By providing the
`app-id` property, the stats-gathering consumer wouldn't have to deserialize or decode
the message body.

TIP   When trying to track down the source of rogue messages in your queues,
enforcing the use of `app-id` can make it easier to trace back the source of the

bad messages. This is especially useful in larger environments where many applications share the same RabbitMQ infrastructure, and a new publisher may erroneously use the same exchange and routing key as an existing publishing application.

3.8.2 user-id

In the use case of user authentication, it may seem obvious to use the user-id property to identify the user who has logged in, but in most cases this isn't advisable. RabbitMQ checks every message published with a value in the user-id property against the RabbitMQ user publishing the message, and if the two values don't match, the message is rejected. For example, if your application is authenticating with RabbitMQ as the user "www", and the user-id property is set to "linus", the message will be rejected.

Of course, if your application is something like a chat room or instant messaging service, you may very well want a user in RabbitMQ for every user of your application, and you would indeed want to use user-id to identify the actual user logging into your application.

3.9 Getting specific with the message type property

The 0-9-1 version of the AMQP specification defines the Basic.Properties type property as the "message type name," saying that it's for application use and has no formal behavior (figure 3.12). Although the routing-key value, in combination with the exchange, may often convey as much information about the message as is needed to determine the content of a message, the type property adds another tool your applications can use to determine how to process a message.

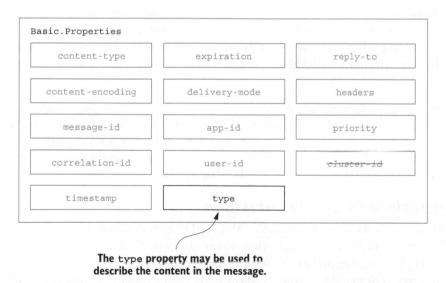

The type property may be used to
describe the content in the message.

Figure 3.12   The type property is a free-form string value that can be used to define the message type.

When self-describing serialization formats aren't fast enough

The `type` property can be very useful when creating self-describing messages, especially when the message body isn't serialized in a self-describing data format. Self-describing formats like JSON and XML are considered by some to be too verbose. They can also carry unnecessary overhead on the wire or in memory, as well as being slower to serialize and deserialize in some languages. If any of these concerns ring true to you, you can choose a serialization format like Apache Thrift (http://thrift.apache.org/) or Google's Protobuf (https://code.google.com/p/protobuf/). Unlike MessagePack (http://msgpack.org/), these binary encoded message formats aren't self-describing and require an external definition file for serialization and deserialization. This external dependency and the lack of self-description allows for smaller payloads on the wire but has tradeoffs of its own.

When trying to create self-describing AMQP messages that allow for an enforceable contract between publisher and consumer, a message payload that isn't self-describing requires the message payload to be deserialized prior to determining whether the message is OK for the consumer to process. In this case, the `type` property can be used to specify the record type or the external definition file, enabling the consumer to reject messages it can't process if it doesn't have access to the proper .thrift or .proto file required to process the message.

In my example of publishing member login events, when it came time to store the events in a data warehouse, we found it useful to carry the message type with the message. To prepare the events for storage in the data warehouse, they're first stored in a temporary location, and then a batch process reads them and stores them in the database. Because this is a very generic process, a single consumer performs the extract phase of the extract-transform-load (ETL) process using a generic queue to process all the messages. The ETL queue consumer processes multiple types of messages and uses the `type` property to decide which system, table, or cluster to store the extracted data in.

> **NOTE**   ETL processing is a standard practice where OLTP data is extracted and eventually loaded into a data warehouse for reporting purposes. If you'd like to learn more about ETL processing, Wikipedia has a very good article describing each phase, ETL performance, common challenges, and related subjects (http://en.wikipedia.org/wiki/Extract,_transform,_load).

3.10   *Using reply-to for dynamic workflows*

In a confusing and terse definition in the AMQP specification, the `reply-to` property has no formally defined behavior and is also specified for application use (figure 3.13). Unlike the previously mentioned proprieties, it has a caveat: `reply-to` may be used to designate a private response queue for replies to a message. Although the exact definition of a private response queue isn't stated in the AMQP specification,

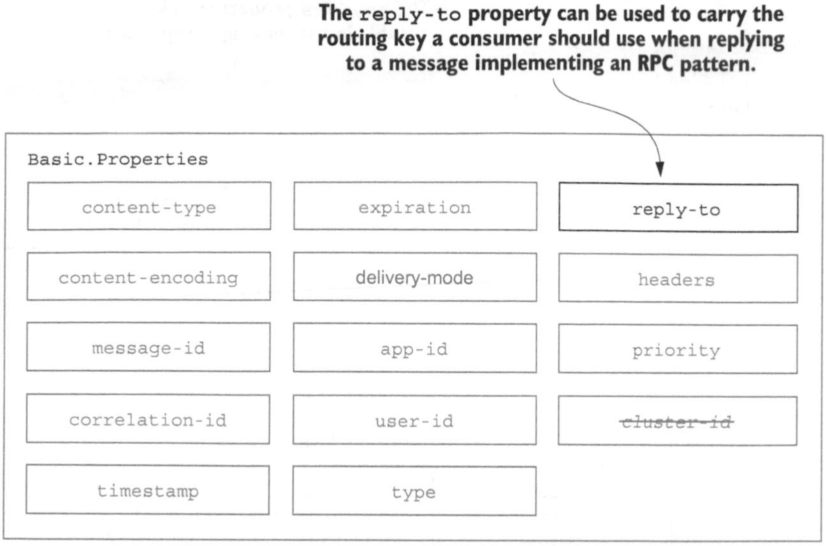

The `reply-to` property can be used to carry the
routing key a consumer should use when replying
to a message implementing an RPC pattern.

```
Basic.Properties
```

content-type	expiration	reply-to
content-encoding	delivery-mode	headers
message-id	app-id	priority
correlation-id	user-id	~~cluster-id~~
timestamp	type	

**Figure 3.13   The `reply-to` property has no formal definition but can carry a routing
key or queue name value that can be used for replies to the message.**

this property could easily carry either a specific queue name or a routing key for replies
in the same exchange through which the message was originally published.

> **WARNING**   There's a caveat in the 0-9-1 version of the AMQP specification for
> `reply-to` that states it "may hold the name of a private response queue, when
> used in request messages." There's enough ambiguity in the definition of this
> property that it should be used with caution. Although it's not likely that
> future versions of RabbitMQ will enforce routability of response messages at
> publishing time, it's better to be safe than sorry. Given RabbitMQ's behavior
> with regard to the `user-id` property and the ambiguity of the specification
> with regard to this property, it wouldn't be unreasonable for RabbitMQ to
> deny publishing of a message if response messages wouldn't be routable due
> to information in the `reply-to` property.

3.11   *Custom properties using the headers property*

The headers property is a key/value table that allows for arbitrary, user-defined keys
and values (figure 3.14). Keys can be ASCII or Unicode strings that have a maximum
length of 255 characters. Values can be any valid AMQP value type.

Unlike the other properties, the headers property allows you to add whatever data
you'd like to the headers table. It also has another unique feature: RabbitMQ can
route messages based upon the values populated in the headers table instead of rely-
ing on the routing key. Routing messages via the headers property is covered in chapter 6.

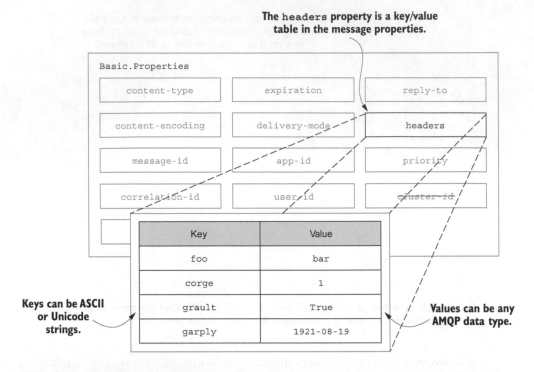

Figure 3.14 The headers property allows for arbitrary key/value pairs in the message properties.

3.12 *The priority property*

As of RabbitMQ 3.5.0, the priority field has been implemented as per the AMQP specification. It's defined as an integer with possible values of 0 through 9 to be used for message prioritization in queues. As specified, if a message with a priority of 9 is published, and subsequently a message with a priority of 0 is published, a newly connected consumer would receive the message with the priority of 0 before the message with a priority of 9. Interestingly, RabbitMQ implements the priority field as an unsigned byte, so priorities could be anywhere from 0 to 255, but the priority should be limited to 0 through 9 to maintain interoperability with the specification. See figure 3.15.

3.13 *A property you can't use: cluster-id/reserved*

There's only one more property to call to your attention, and only for the purpose of letting you know that you can't use it. You most likely noticed the cluster-id property that's crossed out in the previous figures (figure 3.16).

The cluster-id property was defined in AMQP 0-8 but was subsequently removed, and RabbitMQ never implemented any sort of behavior around it. AMQP 0-9-1 renamed it to reserved and states that it must be empty. Although RabbitMQ currently doesn't enforce the specification requiring it to be empty, you're better off avoiding it altogether.

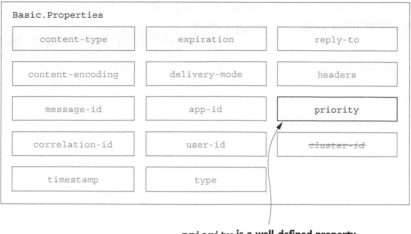

priority **is a well-defined property
that is not supported in RabbitMQ.**

Figure 3.15 The priority **property can be used to designate priority in queues for
the message.**

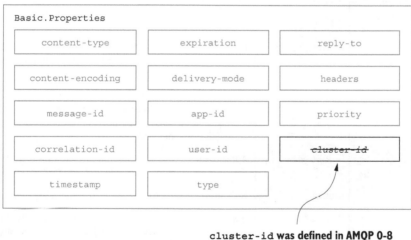

cluster-id **was defined in AMQP 0-8
and removed in AMQP 0-9-1.**

Figure 3.16 The cluster-id **property was renamed as reserved in AMQP 0-9-1 and
must not be used.**

3.14 *Summary*

By using Basic.Properties properly, your messaging architecture can create strict
behavioral contracts between publishers and consumers. In addition, you'll be able to
future-proof your messages for integration projects that you may not have considered
in your initial application and message specifications.

Table 3.1 provides a quick overview of these properties. You can come back and reference it as you're figuring out the appropriate use of properties in your applications.

Table 3.1   Properties made available by `Basic.Properties`, including their type, whether the broker or application can use them, and either the specified use or suggestions for use.

Property	Type	For use by	Suggested or specified use
app-id	short-string	Application	Useful for defining the application publishing the messages.
content-encoding	short-string	Application	Specify whether your message body is encoded in some special way, such as zlib, deflate, or Base64.
content-type	short-string	Application	Specify the type of the message body using mime-types.
correlation-id	short-string	Application	If the message is in reference to some other message or uniquely identifiable item, the correlation-id is a good way to indicate what the message is referencing.
delivery-mode	octet	RabbitMQ	A value of 1 tells RabbitMQ it can keep the message in memory; 2 indicates it should also write it to disk.
expiration	short-string	RabbitMQ	An epoch or Unix timestamp value as a text string that indicates when the message should expire.
headers	table	Both	A free-form key/value table that you can use to add additional metadata about your message; RabbitMQ can route based upon this if desired.
message-id	short-string	Application	A unique identifier such as a UUID that your application can use to identify the message.
priority	octet	RabbitMQ	A property for priority ordering in queues.
timestamp	timestamp	Application	An epoch or Unix timestamp value that can be used to indicate when the message was created.
type	short-string	Application	A text string your application can use to describe the message type or payload.
user-id	short-string	Both	A free-form string that, if used, RabbitMQ will validate against the connected user and drop messages if they don't match.

Beyond using properties for self-describing messages, these properties can carry valuable metadata about your message that will allow you to create sophisticated routing and transactional mechanisms, without having to pollute the message body with contextual information that pertains to the message. When evaluating the message for delivery, RabbitMQ will leverage specific properties, such as the `delivery-mode` and the `headers` table, to ensure that your messages are delivered how and where you specify. But these values are just the tip of the iceberg when it comes to making sure your message delivery is bulletproof.

Performance trade-offs in publishing

4

This chapter covers

- Message delivery guarantees in RabbitMQ
- Publisher vs. performance trade-offs

Message publishing is one of the core activities in a messaging-based architecture, and there are many facets to message publishing in RabbitMQ. Many of the message-publishing options available to your applications can have a large impact on your application's performance and reliability. Although any message broker is measured by its performance and throughput, reliable message delivery is of paramount concern. Imagine what would happen if there were no guarantees when you used an ATM to deposit money into your bank account. You'd deposit money with no certainty that your account balance would increase. This would inevitably be a problem for you and for your bank. Even in non-mission-critical applications, messages are published for an intended purpose, and silently dropping them could easily create problems.

Although not every system has such hard requirements around message delivery guarantees as banking applications do, it's important for software like RabbitMQ to ensure the messages it receives are delivered. The AMQP specification provides for transactions in message publishing, and for the optional persistence of messages, to provide a higher level of reliable messaging than normal message publishing provides on its own. RabbitMQ has additional functionality, such as delivery confirmations, that provide different levels of message delivery guarantees for you to choose from, including highly available (HA) queues that span multiple servers. In this chapter you'll learn about the performance and publishing guarantee trade-offs involved in using these functionalities and how to find out if RabbitMQ is silently throttling your message publisher.

4.1 Balancing delivery speed with guaranteed delivery

When it comes to RabbitMQ, the *Goldilocks Principle* applies to the different levels of guarantees in message delivery. Abstracted as a takeaway from the "Story of the Three Bears," the Goldilocks Principle describes where something is *just right*. In the case of reliable message delivery, you should apply this principle to the trade-offs encountered when using the delivery guarantee mechanisms in RabbitMQ. Some of the features may be too slow for your application, such as the ability to ensure messages survive the reboot of a RabbitMQ server. On the other hand, publishing messages without asking for additional guarantees is much faster, though it may not provide a safe enough environment for mission-critical applications (figure 4.1).

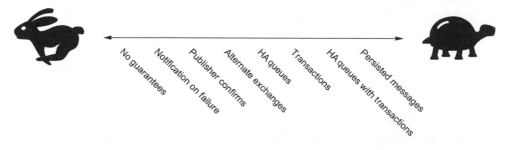

Figure 4.1 Performance will suffer when using each delivery guarantee mechanism, and even more so when they're used in combination.

In RabbitMQ, each mechanism designed to create delivery guarantees will come with some impact on performance. On their own, you may not notice a significant difference in throughput, but when they're used in combination there can be a significant impact on message throughput. Only by performing your own performance benchmarks can you determine the acceptable trade-off of performance versus guaranteed delivery.

When creating application architectures using RabbitMQ, you should keep the Goldilocks Principle in mind. The following questions can help find the right balance between high performance and message safety for a solution that's *just right*.

- How important is it that messages are guaranteed to be enqueued when published?
- Should a message be returned to a publisher if it can't be routed?

- If a message can't be routed, should it be sent somewhere else where it can later be reconciled?
- Is it okay if messages are lost when a RabbitMQ server crashes?
- Should RabbitMQ confirm that it has performed all requested routing and persistence tasks to a publisher when it processes a new message?
- Should a publisher be able to batch message deliveries and then receive confirmation from RabbitMQ that all requested routing and persistence tasks have been applied to all of the messages in the batch?
- If you're batching the publishing of messages that require confirmation of routing and persistence, is there a need for true atomic commits to the destination queues for a message?
- Are there acceptable trade-offs in reliable delivery that your publishers can use to achieve higher performance and message throughput?
- What other aspects of message publishing will impact message throughput and performance?

In this section we'll cover how these questions relate to RabbitMQ and what techniques and functionality your applications can employ to implement just the right level of reliable delivery and performance. Over the course of this chapter, you'll be presented with the options that RabbitMQ provides for finding the right balance of performance and delivery guarantees. You can pick and choose what makes the most sense for your environment and your application, as there's no one right solution. You could choose to combine mandatory routing with highly available queues, or you may choose transactional publishing along with delivery mode 2, persisting your messages to disk. If you're flexible in how you approach your application development process, I recommend trying each of the different techniques on its own and in combination with others until you find a balance that you're comfortable with—something that's just right.

4.1.1   *What to expect with no guarantees*

In a perfect world, RabbitMQ reliably delivers messages without any additional configuration or steps. Simply publish your message via `Basic.Publish` with the correct exchange and routing information, and your message will be received and sent to the proper queue. There are no network issues, server hardware is reliable and does not crash, and operating systems never have issues that will impact the runtime state of the RabbitMQ broker. Rounding out a utopian application environment, your consumer applications will never face performance constraints by interacting with services that may slow their processing. Queues never back up and messages are processed as quickly as they're published. Publishing isn't throttled in any way.

Unfortunately, in a world where Murphy's Law is a rule of thumb, the things that would never occur in a perfect world occur regularly.

In non-mission-critical applications, normal message publishing doesn't have to handle every possible point of failure; finding the right balance will get you most of the way toward reliable and predictable uptime. In a closed-loop environment where you don't have to worry about network or hardware failures and you don't have to worry about consumers not consuming quickly enough, RabbitMQ's architecture and feature set demonstrate a level of reliable messaging that's good enough for most non-mission-critical applications. For example, Graphite, the popular, highly scalable graphing system originally developed by Orbitz, has an AMQP interface for submitting your statistical data into Graphite. Individual servers running metric collection services, such as collectd, gather information about their runtime states and publish messages on a per-minute basis (figure 4.2).

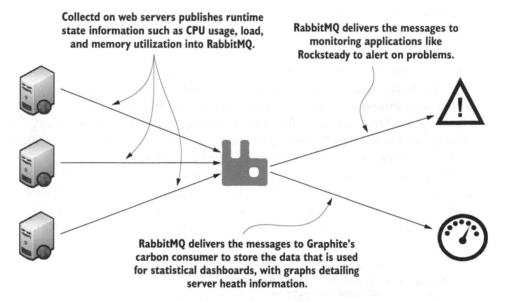

Collectd on web servers publishes runtime state information such as CPU usage, load, and memory utilization into RabbitMQ.

RabbitMQ delivers the messages to monitoring applications like Rocksteady to alert on problems.

RabbitMQ delivers the messages to Graphite's carbon consumer to store the data that is used for statistical dashboards, with graphs detailing server heath information.

Figure 4.2   Web server collectd's statistic-gathering daemons publish monitoring data to RabbitMQ for delivery to Graphite and Rocksteady consumers.

These messages carry information such as the CPU load, memory, and network utilization of the server. Graphite has a collector service called carbon that consumes these messages and stores the data in its internal data store. In most environments, this data isn't considered mission-critical, even though it may be very important in the overall operational management of the network. If data for a given minute isn't received by carbon and stored in Graphite, it wouldn't be a failure on the same level as, say, a financial transaction. Missing sample data may in fact indicate a problem with a server or process that publishes the data to Graphite, and that can be used by systems like Rocksteady to trigger events in Nagios or other similar applications to alert to the problem.

When publishing data like this, you need to be aware of the trade-offs. Delivering the monitoring data without additional publishing guarantees requires fewer configuration options, has lower processing overhead, and is simpler than making sure the messages will be delivered. In this case, *just right* is a simple setup with no additional message delivery guarantees. The collectd process is able to fire and forget the messages it sends. If it's disconnected from RabbitMQ, it will try to reconnect the next time it needs to send stats data. Likewise, the consumer applications will reconnect when they're disconnected and go back to consuming from the same queues they were consuming from before.

This works well under most circumstances, until Murphy's Law comes into play and something goes wrong. If you're looking to make sure your messages are always delivered, RabbitMQ can change gears and go from good enough to mission critical.

4.1.2 *RabbitMQ won't accept non-routable messages with mandatory set*

If you needed the server monitoring data to always be routed to RabbitMQ prior to collectd moving on, all collectd would need to do is tell RabbitMQ that the message being published is `mandatory`. The `mandatory` flag is an argument that's passed along with the `Basic.Publish` RPC command and tells RabbitMQ that if a message isn't routable, it should send the message back to the publisher via a `Basic.Return` RPC (figure 4.3). The `mandatory` flag can be thought of as turning on fault detection mode; it will only cause RabbitMQ to notify you of failures, not successes. Should the message route correctly, your publisher won't be notified.

To publish a message with the `mandatory` flag, you simply pass in the argument after passing in the exchange, routing key, message, and properties, as shown in the following example. To trigger the expected exception for the unroutable message, you can use the same exchange as in chapter 2. When the message is published, there's

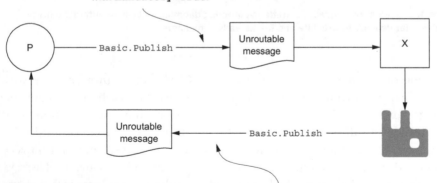

A publisher sends an unroutable message with the `Basic.Publish` RPC command with `mandatory=True`.

When the exchange can't route the message, RabbitMQ will send a `Basic.Return` back to the server with the full message as it was sent.

Figure 4.3   When an unroutable message is published with `mandatory=True`, RabbitMQ returns it via the `Basic.Return` RPC call to the client.

no bound destination and an exception should be raised when it's executed. The code is in the "4.1.2 Publish Failure" notebook.

Opens a channel to communicate on as a context manager ⟶

Connects to RabbitMQ using the connection as a context manager

Creates the message to publish, passing the channel, body, and properties ⟶

Creates the message body to deliver

Publishes the message with mandatory turned on

```python
import datetime
import rabbitpy

# Connect to the default URL of amqp://guest:guest@localhost:15672/%2F

with rabbitpy.Connection() as connection:
    with connection.channel() as channel:
        body = 'server.cpu.utilization 25.5 1350884514'
        message = rabbitpy.Message(channel,
                                   body,
                                   {'content_type': 'text/plain',
                                    'timestamp': datetime.datetime.now(),
                                    'message_type': 'graphite metric'})
        message.publish('chapter2-example',
                        'server-metrics',
                        mandatory=True)
```

When you execute this example, you should receive an exception similar to the following one. RabbitMQ can't route the message because there's no queue bound to the exchange and routing key.

```
rabbitpy.exceptions.MessageReturnedException:
        (312, 'NO_ROUTE', 'chapter2-example')
```

NOTE In the previous example, a new way of invoking the `Connection` and `Channel` objects is used: Both objects are created as a context manager. In Python, if an object is a context manager, it will automatically handle the shutdown of the object instance when you exit the scope or indentation level that you use the object in. In the case of rabbitpy, when you exit the scope, it will correctly close the channel and connection, without you having to explicitly call `Channel.close` or `Connection.close` respectively.

The `Basic.Return` call is an asynchronous call from RabbitMQ, and it may happen at any time after the message is published. For example, when collectd is publishing statistical data to RabbitMQ, it may publish multiple data points before receiving the `Basic.Return` call, should a publish fail. If the code isn't set up to listen for this call, it will fall on deaf ears, and collectd will never know that the message wasn't published correctly. This would be problematic if you wanted to ensure the delivery of messages to the proper queues.

In the rabbitpy library, `Basic.Return` calls are automatically received by the client library and will raise a `MessageReturnedException` upon receipt at the channel scope. In the following example, the same message will be sent to the same exchange using the same routing key. The code for publishing the message has been slightly refactored to wrap the channel scope in a try/except block. When the exception is raised, the code will print the message ID and return the reason extracted from the `reply-text` attribute of the Basic.Return frame. You'll still be publishing to the chapter2-example exchange, but you'll now intercept the exception being raised. This example is in the "4.1.2 Handling Basic.Return" notebook.

```
import datetime                                          Connects to RabbitMQ
import rabbitpy                                          on localhost port 5672
                                                         as guest          Opens channel to
connection = rabbitpy.Connection()                                         communicate on
try:
    with connection.channel() as channel:                              Creates message
        properties = {'content_type': 'text/plain',                    properties
                      'timestamp': datetime.datetime.now(),
                      'message_type': 'graphite metric'}
        body = 'server.cpu.utilization 25.5 1350884514'       Creates
        message = rabbitpy.Message(channel, body, properties) message body
        message.publish('chapter2-example',
                        'server-metrics',
                        mandatory=True)                       Catches the
except rabbitpy.exceptions.MessageReturnedException as error: exception as a
    print('Publish failure: %s' % error)                     variable called
                                                             error
                                     Prints exception
                                     information
```

Creates message object combining channel, body, and properties

Publishes message

When you execute this example, instead of the exception from the previous example, you should see a friendlier message, like this:

```
Message was returned by RabbitMQ: (312) NO_ROUTE for exchange chapter2-example
```

With other libraries, you may have to register a callback method that will be invoked if the Basic.Return RPC call is received from RabbitMQ when your message is published. In an asynchronous programming model where you are actually processing the Basic.Return message itself, you'll receive a Basic.Return method frame, the content header frame, and the body frame, just as if you were consuming messages. If this seems too complex, don't worry. There are other ways to simplify the process and deal with message routing failures. One is by using *Publisher Confirms* in RabbitMQ.

> **NOTE** The rabbitpy library and the examples in this section only use up to three arguments when sending a Basic.Publish command. This is in contrast to the AMQP specification, which includes an additional argument, the immediate flag. The immediate flag directs a broker to issue a Basic.Return if the message can't be immediately routed to its destination. This flag is deprecated as of RabbitMQ 2.9 and will raise an exception and close the channel if used.

4.1.3 *Publisher Confirms as a lightweight alternative to transactions*

The Publisher Confirms feature in RabbitMQ is an enhancement to the AMQP specification and is only supported by client libraries that support RabbitMQ-specific extensions. Although storing messages on disk is an important step in preventing message loss, doing so doesn't create a contract between the publisher and RabbitMQ server that assures the publisher that a message was delivered. Prior to publishing any messages, a message publisher must issue a `Confirm.Select` RPC request to RabbitMQ and wait for a `Confirm.SelectOk` response to know that delivery confirmations are enabled. At that point, for each message that a publisher sends to RabbitMQ, the server will respond with an acknowledgement response (`Basic.Ack`) or a negative acknowledgement response (`Basic.Nack`), either including an integer value specifying the offset of the message that it is confirming (figure 4.4). The confirmation number references the message by the order in which it was received after the `Confirm.Select` RPC request.

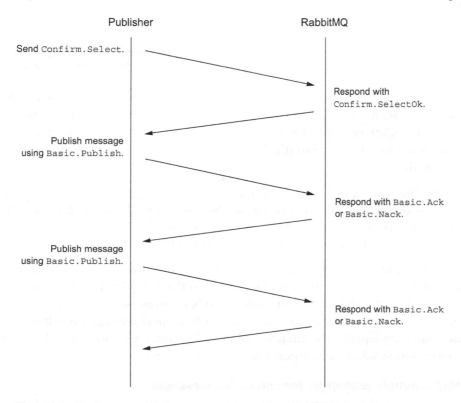

Figure 4.4 The sequence of messages sent to and from RabbitMQ for delivery confirmations

A `Basic.Ack` request is sent to a publisher when a message that it has published has been directly consumed by consumer applications on all queues it was routed to, or when the message was enqueued and persisted if requested. If a message can't be routed, the broker will send a `Basic.Nack` RPC request indicating the failure. It's then up to the publisher to decide what to do with the message.

In the following example, contained in the "4.1.3 Publisher Confirms" notebook, the publisher enables Publisher Confirms and then evaluates the response from the `Message.publish` call.

```
import rabbitpy

with rabbitpy.Connection() as connection:
    with connection.channel() as channel:
        exchange = rabbitpy.Exchange(channel, 'chapter4-example')
        exchange.declare()
        channel.enable_publisher_confirms()
        message = rabbitpy.Message(channel,
                                'This is an important message',
                                {'content_type': 'text/plain',
                                 'message_type': 'very important'})

    if message.publish('chapter4-example', 'important.message'):
        print('The message was confirmed')
```

Creates an exchange object for declaring the exchange

Connects to RabbitMQ

Opens the channel to communicate on

Declares the exchange

Enables Publisher Confirms with RabbitMQ

Creates the rabbitpy Message object to publish

Publishes the message, evaluating the response for confirmation

As you can see, it's fairly easy to use Publisher Confirms in rabbitpy. In other libraries, you'll most likely need to create a callback handler that will asynchronously respond to the `Basic.Ack` or `Basic.Nack` request. There are benefits to each style: rabbitpy's implementation is easier, but it's slower because it will block until the confirmation is received.

> **NOTE** Regardless of whether you use Publisher Confirms or not, if you publish to an exchange that doesn't exist, the channel you're publishing on will be closed by RabbitMQ. In rabbitpy, this will cause a `rabbitpy.exceptions.RemoteClosedChannelException` exception to be raised.

Publisher Confirms don't work in conjunction with transactions and is considered a lightweight and more performant alternative to the AMQP TX process (discussed in section 4.1.5). In addition, as an asynchronous response to the `Basic.Publish` RPC request, there are no guarantees made as to when the confirmations will be received. Therefore, any application that has enabled Publisher Confirms should be able to receive a confirmation at any point after sending the message.

4.1.4 *Using alternate exchanges for unroutable messages*

Alternate exchanges are another extension to the AMQ model, created by the RabbitMQ team as a way to handle unroutable messages. An alternate exchange is specified when declaring an exchange for the first time, and it specifies a preexisting exchange in RabbitMQ that the new exchange will route messages to, should the exchange not be able to route them (figure 4.5).

> **NOTE** If you set the `mandatory` flag for a message when sending it to an exchange with an alternate exchange, a `Basic.Return` won't be issued to the publisher if the intended exchange can't route the message normally. The act of sending an unroutable message to the alternate exchange satisfies the conditions for a published message when the `mandatory` flag is `true`. It's also important to realize that RabbitMQ's message routing patterns are applied to

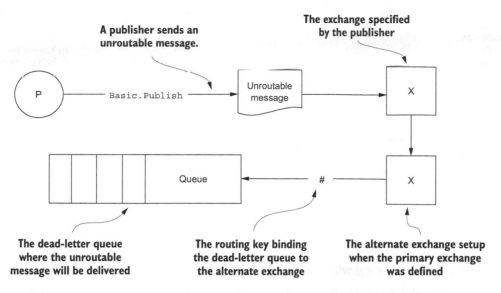

Figure 4.5 When an unroutable message is published to an exchange that has an alternate exchange defined, it will then be routed to the alternate exchange.

alternate exchanges just like any other exchange. If a queue isn't bound to receive the message with its original routing key, it won't be enqueued, and the message will be lost.

To use an alternate exchange, you must first set up the exchange that unroutable messages will be sent to. Then, when setting up the primary exchange you'll be publishing messages to, add the `alternate-exchange` argument to the `Exchange.Declare` command. This process is demonstrated in the following example, which goes one step further to create a message queue that will store any unroutable messages. This example is in the "4.1.4 Alternate-Exchange Example" notebook.

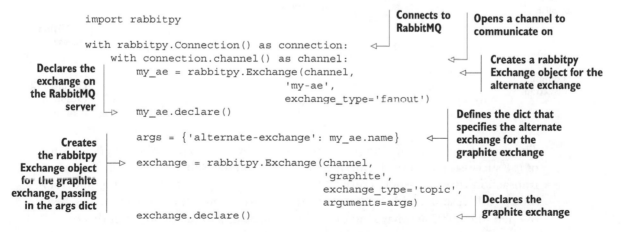

Creates a
rabbitpy
Queue
object

```
queue = rabbitpy.Queue(channel, 'unroutable-messages')
queue.declare()
if queue.bind(my_ae, '#'):
    print('Queue bound to alternate-exchange')
```

Declares the
queue on the
RabbitMQ server

Binds the queue to the
alternate exchange

When declaring the alternate exchange, a `fanout` exchange type was selected, whereas the `graphite` exchange uses a `topic` exchange. A `fanout` exchange delivers messages to all the queues it knows about; a `topic` exchange can selectively route messages based upon parts of a routing key. These two exchange types are discussed in detail in chapter 5. Once the two exchanges are declared, the `unroutable-messages` queue is bound to the alternate exchange. Any messages that are subsequently published to the `graphite` exchange and that can't be routed will end up in the `unroutable-messages` queue.

4.1.5   *Batch processing with transactions*

Before there were delivery confirmations, the only way you could be sure a message was delivered was through transactions. The AMQP transaction, or `TX`, class provides a mechanism by which messages can be published to RabbitMQ in batches and then committed to a queue or rolled back. The following example, contained in the "4.1.5 Transactional Publishing" notebook, shows that writing code that takes advantage of transactions is fairly trivial.

```
import rabbitpy

with rabbitpy.Connection() as connection:
    with connection.channel() as channel:

        tx = rabbitpy.Tx(channel)
        tx.select()

        message = rabbitpy.Message(channel,
                            'This is an important message',
                            {'content_type': 'text/plain',
                             'delivery_mode': 2,
                             'message_type': 'important'})
        message.publish('chapter4-example', 'important.message')
        try:
            if tx.commit():
                print('Transaction committed')
        except rabbitpy.exceptions.NoActiveTransactionError:
            print('Tried to commit without active transaction')
```

Connects to
RabbitMQ

Opens a channel to
communicate over

Starts the
transaction

Creates a new
instance of the
rabbitpy.Tx object

Creates the
message to
publish

Publishes
message

Commits
transaction

Catches a TX
exception if
it's raised

The transactional mechanism provides a method by which a publisher can be notified of the successful delivery of a message to a queue on the RabbitMQ broker. To begin a transaction, the publisher sends a `TX.Select` RPC request to RabbitMQ, and RabbitMQ will respond with a `TX.SelectOk` response. Once the transaction has been opened, the publisher may send one or more messages to RabbitMQ (figure 4.6).

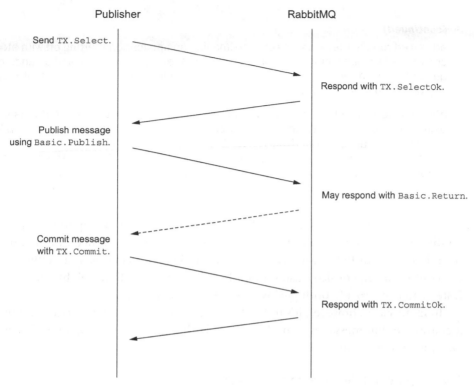

Figure 4.6   A publisher begins a transaction by sending a `TX.Select` command, publishes messages, and commits the messages with a `TX.Commit` command.

When RabbitMQ is unable to route a message due to an error, such as a non-existent exchange, it will return the message with a `Basic.Return` response prior to sending a `TX.CommitOk` response. Publishers wishing to abort a transaction should send a `TX.Rollback` RPC request and wait for a `TX.RollbackOk` response from the broker prior to continuing.

RabbitMQ and atomic transactions

Atomicity ensures that all actions in a transaction are complete as part of committing the transaction. In AMQP, this means your client won't receive the `TX.CommitOk` response frame until all actions in the transaction are complete. Unfortunately for those looking for true atomicity, RabbitMQ only implements atomic transactions when every command issued affects a single queue. If more than one queue is impacted by any of the commands in the transaction, the commit won't be atomic.

Although RabbitMQ will perform atomic transactions if all of the commands in a transaction only impact the same queue, publishers generally don't have much control over whether the message is delivered to more than one queue. With RabbitMQ's

(continued)

advanced routing methods, it's easy to imagine an application starting off with atomic commits when publishing to a single queue, but then someone may add an additional queue bound to the same routing key. Any publishing transactions with that routing key would no longer be atomic.

It's also worth pointing out that true atomic transactions with persisted messages using `delivery-mode 2` can cause performance issues for publishers. If RabbitMQ is waiting on an I/O-bound server for the write to complete prior to sending the `TX.CommitOk` frame, your client could be waiting longer than if the commands weren't wrapped in a transaction in the first place.

As implemented, transactions in RabbitMQ allow for batch-like operations in delivery confirmation, allowing publishers more control over the sequence in which they confirm delivery with RabbitMQ. If you're considering transactions as a method of delivery confirmation, consider using Publisher Confirms as a lightweight alternative—it's faster and can provide both positive and negative confirmation.

In many cases, however, it's not publishing confirmation that is required but rather a guarantee that messages won't be lost while they're sitting in a queue. This is where HA queues come into play.

4.1.6   *Surviving node failures with HA queues*

As you look to strengthen the contract between publishers and RabbitMQ to guarantee message delivery, don't overlook the important role that highly available queues (HA queues) can play in mission-critical messaging architectures. HA queues—an enhancement the RabbitMQ team created that's not part of the AMQP specification—is a feature that allows queues to have redundant copies across multiple servers.

HA queues require a clustered RabbitMQ environment and can be set up in one of two ways: using AMQP or using the web-based management interface. In chapter 8, we'll revisit HA queues and use the management interface to define policies for HA queues, but for now we'll focus on using AMQP.

In the following example, you'll set up a new queue that spans every node in a RabbitMQ cluster using arguments passed to the `Queue.Declare` AMQP command. This code is in the "4.1.6 HA-Queue Declaration" notebook.

```
import rabbitpy

connection = rabbitpy.Connection()        ◁─── Connects to RabbitMQ on localhost as guest
try:
    with connection.channel() as channel:     ◁─── Opens a channel to communicate over
        queue = rabbitpy.Queue(channel,        ◁─── Creates a new instance of the Queue object, passing in the HA policy
                               'my-ha-queue',
                               arguments={'x-ha-policy': 'all'})
```

Declares the queue

```
        if queue.declare():
            print('Queue declared')
    except rabbitpy.exceptions.RemoteClosedChannelException as error:
        print('Queue declare failed: %s' % error)
```

Catches any exception raised on error

When a message is published into a queue that's set up as an HA queue, it's sent to each server in the cluster that's responsible for the HA queue (figure 4.7). Once a message is consumed from any node in the cluster, all copies of the message will be immediately removed from the other nodes.

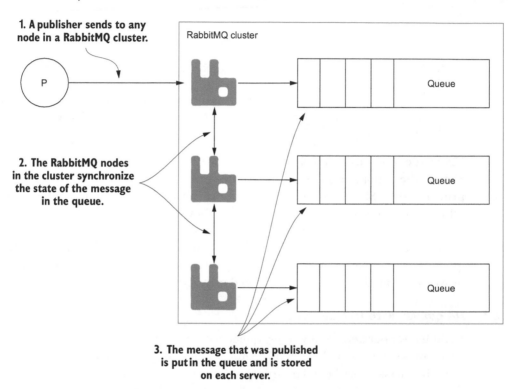

1. A publisher sends to any node in a RabbitMQ cluster.

RabbitMQ cluster

Queue

2. The RabbitMQ nodes in the cluster synchronize the state of the message in the queue.

Queue

Queue

3. The message that was published is put in the queue and is stored on each server.

Figure 4.7   A message published into an HA queue is stored on each server that's configured for it.

HA queues can span every server in a cluster, or only individual nodes. To specify individual nodes, instead of passing in an argument of x-ha-policy: all, pass in an x-ha-policy of nodes and then another argument, x-ha-nodes containing a list of the nodes the queue should be configured on. The following example is in the "4.1.6 Selective HA Queue Declaration" notebook.

```
import rabbitpy

connection = rabbitpy.Connection()
try:
    with connection.channel() as channel:
```

Connects to RabbitMQ

Opens a channel to communicate over

```
                    arguments = {'x-ha-policy': 'nodes',                  ⟵───┐  Specifies the HA
                                 'x-ha-nodes': ['rabbit@node1',                  policy the queue
                                                'rabbit@node2',                  should use
                                                'rabbit@node3']}
                    queue = rabbitpy.Queue(channel,                       ⟵───┐  Creates a new instance
                                           'my-2nd-ha-queue',                    of the Queue object,
                                           arguments=arguments)                  passing in the HA policy
   Declares    ┌──>  if queue.declare():                                         and node list
   the queue   └         print('Queue declared')
    except rabbitpy.exceptions.RemoteClosedChannelException as error:    ⟵───
        print('Queue declare failed: %s' % error)
                                                              Catches the exception if
                                                              RabbitMQ closes the channel
```

NOTE Even if you don't have node1, node2, or node3 defined, RabbitMQ will allow you to define the queue, and if you were to publish a message that's routed to my-2nd-ha-queue, it would be delivered. In the event that one or more of the nodes listed do exist, the message would live on those servers instead.

HA queues have a single primary server node, and all the other nodes are secondary. Should the primary node fail, one of the secondary nodes will take over the role of primary node. Should a secondary node be lost in an HA queue configuration, the other nodes would continue to operate as they were, sharing the state of operations that take place across all configured nodes. When a lost node is added back, or a new node is added to the cluster, it won't contain any messages that are already in the queue across the existing nodes. Instead, it will receive all new messages and only be in sync once all the previously published messages are consumed.

4.1.7   HA queues with transactions

HA queues operate like any other queue with regard to protocol semantics. If you're using transactions or delivery confirmations, RabbitMQ won't send a successful response until the message has been confirmed to be in all active nodes in the HA queue definition. This can create a delay in responding to your publishing application.

4.1.8   Persisting messages to disk via delivery-mode 2

You learned earlier how to use alternate exchanges for messages that weren't able to be routed. Now it's time to add another level of delivery guarantee for them. If the RabbitMQ broker dies for any reason prior to consuming the messages, they'll be lost forever unless you tell RabbitMQ when publishing the message that you want the messages persisted to disk while they're in its care.

As you learned in chapter 3, delivery-mode is one of the message properties specified as part of AMQP's Basic.Properties definition. If a message has delivery-mode set to 1, which is the default, RabbitMQ is instructed that it doesn't need to store the message to disk and that it may keep it in memory at all times. Thus, if RabbitMQ is restarted, the non-persisted messages won't be available when RabbitMQ is back up and running.

On the other hand, if `delivery-mode` is set to 2, RabbitMQ will ensure that the message is stored to disk. Referred to as *message persistence*, storing the message to disk ensures that if the RabbitMQ broker is restarted for any reason, the message will still be in the queue once RabbitMQ is running again.

> **NOTE** In addition to `delivery-mode` of 2, for messages to truly survive a restart of a RabbitMQ broker, your queues must be declared as *durable* when they're created. Durable queues will be covered in detail in chapter 5.

For servers that don't have sufficient I/O performance, message persistence can cause dramatic performance issues. Similar to a high-velocity web application's database server, a high-velocity RabbitMQ instance must go to disk often with persistent messages.

For most dynamic web applications, the read-to-write ratio for OLTP databases is heavily read-biased (figure 4.8). This is especially true for content sites like Wikipedia. In their case, there are millions of articles, many of which are actively being either created or updated, but the majority of users are reading the content, not writing it.

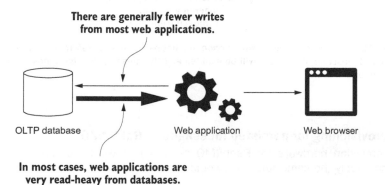

There are generally fewer writes from most web applications.

OLTP database   Web application   Web browser

In most cases, web applications are very read-heavy from databases.

Figure 4.8 Although it's not always the case, most web applications read more from a database than write to it when generating web pages.

When persisting messages in RabbitMQ, you can expect a fairly heavy write bias (figure 4.9). In a high-throughput messaging environment, RabbitMQ writes persisted messages to disk and keeps track of them by reference until they're no longer in any queue. Once all of the references for a message are gone, RabbitMQ will then remove the message from disk. When doing high-velocity writes, it's not uncommon to experience performance issues on under-provisioned hardware, because in most cases the disk write cache is much smaller than the read cache. In most operating systems, the kernel will use free RAM to buffer pages read from disk, whereas the only components caching writes to disk are the disk controller and the disks. Because of this, it's important to correctly size your hardware needs when using persisted messages. An undersized server that's tasked with a heavy write workload can bring a whole RabbitMQ server to a crawl.

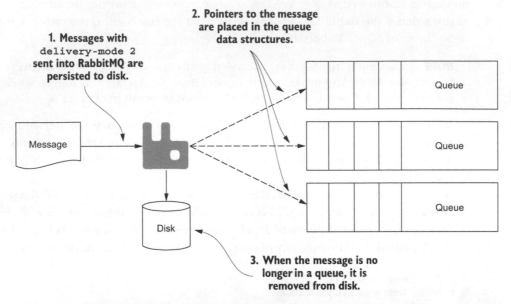

Figure 4.9   RabbitMQ stores a persisted message once and keeps track of its references across all queues it's stored in. If possible, disk reads will be avoided and the message will be removed from disk once all references are gone.

Hardware provisioning for persisted messages in RabbitMQ

To properly provision hardware for RabbitMQ servers that will be persisting messages, you can apply the same rules you would for an OLTP database.

RAM is king; beyond sizing the RAM on the server for your normal messaging workload, consider additional RAM for the operating system, to keep disk pages in the kernel disk cache. This will improve the response time of reads for messages that have already been read from disk.

The more spindles the better; although SSDs may be changing the paradigm a bit, the concept still applies. The more hard drives you have available, the better your write throughput will be. Because the system can spread the write workload across all of the disks in a RAID setup, the amount of time each physical device is blocked will be greatly reduced.

Find an appropriately sized RAID card with battery backup that has large amounts of read and write cache. This will allow the writes to be buffered by the RAID card and allow for temporary spikes in write activity that otherwise would be blocked by physical device limitations.

In I/O-bound servers, the operating system will block processes on I/O operations while the data is transferred to and from the storage device via the operating system. When the RabbitMQ server is trying to perform I/O operations, such as saving a message to disk, and the operating system kernel is blocked while waiting for the storage device to respond, there's little RabbitMQ can do but wait. If the RabbitMQ broker is waiting too often for the operating system to respond to read and write requests, message throughput will be greatly depressed (figure 4.10).

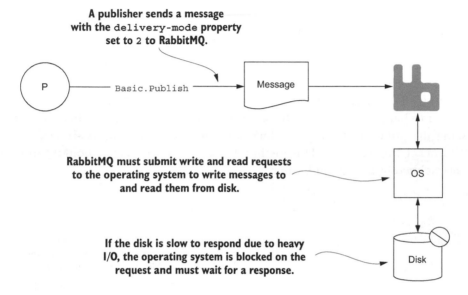

A publisher sends a message with the `delivery-mode` property set to 2 to RabbitMQ.

P — `Basic.Publish` → Message

RabbitMQ must submit write and read requests to the operating system to write messages to and read them from disk.

OS

If the disk is slow to respond due to heavy I/O, the operating system is blocked on the request and must wait for a response.

Disk

Figure 4.10 When a message is received with the `delivery-mode` property set to 2, RabbitMQ must write the message to disk.

Although message persistence is one of the most important ways to guarantee that your messages will ultimately be delivered, it's also one of the most costly. Poor disk performance can greatly degrade your RabbitMQ message publishing velocity. In extreme scenarios, I/O delays caused by improperly provisioned hardware can cause messages to be lost. Simply stated, if RabbitMQ can't respond to publishers or consumers because the operating system is blocking on I/O, your messages can't be published or delivered.

4.2   *When RabbitMQ pushes back*

In the AMQP specification, assumptions were made about publishers that weren't favorable for server implementations. Prior to version 2.0 of RabbitMQ, if your publishing application started to overwhelm RabbitMQ by publishing messages too quickly, it would send the `Channel.Flow` RPC method (figure 4.11) to instruct your publisher to block and not send any more messages until another `Channel.Flow` command was received.

"I say, would you please stop sending me messages?"

Figure 4.11   When RabbitMQ asked for `Channel.Flow`, there were no guarantees publishers were listening.

This proved to be a fairly ineffective method of slowing abusive or "impolite" publishers who weren't required to respect the `Channel.Flow` command. If a publisher continued to publish messages, RabbitMQ could eventually be overwhelmed, causing performance and throughput issues, possibly even causing the broker to crash. Before RabbitMQ 3.2, the RabbitMQ team deprecated the use of `Channel.Flow`, replacing it with a mechanism called TCP Backpressure to address the issue. Instead of politely asking the publisher to stop, RabbitMQ would stop accepting low-level data on the TCP socket (figure 4.12). This method works well to protect RabbitMQ from being overwhelmed by a single publisher.

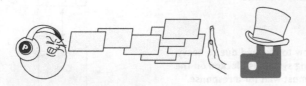

Figure 4.12   RabbitMQ applies TCP Backpressure to stop impolite publishers from oversaturating it.

Internally, RabbitMQ uses the notion of credits to manage when it's going to push back against a publisher. When a new connection is made, the connection is allotted a predetermined amount of credits it can use. Then, as each RPC command is received by RabbitMQ, a credit is decremented. Once the RPC request has been internally processed, the connection is given the credit back. A connection's credit balance is evaluated by RabbitMQ to determine if it should read from a connection's socket. If a connection is out of credits, it's simply skipped until it has enough credits.

As of RabbitMQ 3.2, the RabbitMQ team extended the AMQP specification, adding notifications that are sent when the credit thresholds are reached for a connection, notifying a client that its connection has been blocked. `Connection.Blocked` and `Connection.Unblocked` are asynchronous methods that can be sent at any time to notify the client when RabbitMQ has blocked the publishing client and when that block has been removed. Most major client libraries implement this functionality; you should check with the specific client library you're using to see how your application should determine the connection state. In the next section you'll see how to perform this check with rabbitpy and how the management API can be leveraged for versions of RabbitMQ prior to 3.2 to check if a connection's channels are blocked.

NOTE Ultimately, TCP Backpressure and connection blocking aren't issues you should run into every day, and they could be an indication that the server hardware you have RabbitMQ on is not properly sized. If you find that this is becoming an issue, it's time to evaluate your scaling strategy and perhaps implement some of the concepts covered in chapter 8.

4.2.1 Checking the connection status with rabbitpy

Whether you're using a version of RabbitMQ that supports the `Connection.Blocked` notification or not, the rabbitpy library wraps up this functionality into one easy-to-use API. When connected to a version of RabbitMQ that supports `Connection.Blocked` notifications, rabbitpy will receive the notification and will set an internal flag stating that the connection is blocked.

When you use the following example from the "4.2.1 Connection Blocked" notebook, the output should report that the connection isn't blocked.

```
import rabbitpy                                          Connects to        Checks to see
                                                         RabbitMQ           if the client is
connection = rabbitpy.Connection()          <--                            blocked
print('Connection is Blocked? %s' % connection.blocked)  <--
```

4.2.2 Using the management API for connection status

If you're using a version of RabbitMQ prior to 3.2, your application can poll for the status of its connection using the web-based management API. Doing this is fairly straightforward, but if it's used too frequently, it can cause unwanted load on the RabbitMQ server. Depending on the size of your cluster and the number of queues you have, this API request can take multiple seconds to return.

The API provides RESTful URL endpoints for querying the status of a connection, channel, queue, or just about any other externally exposed object in RabbitMQ. In the management API, the blocked status applies to a channel in a connection, not to the connection itself. There are multiple fields available when querying the status of a channel: `name`, `node`, `connection_details`, `consumer_count`, and `client_flow_blocked`, to name a few. The `client_flow_blocked` flag indicates whether RabbitMQ is applying TCP Backpressure to the connection.

To get the status of a channel, you must first construct the appropriate name for it. A channel's name is based upon the connection name and its channel ID. To construct the connection name you need the following:

- The local host IP address and outgoing TCP port
- The remote host IP address and TCP port

The format is `"LOCAL_ADDR: PORT -> REMOTE_ADDDR: PORT"`. Expanding on that, the format for the name of a channel is `"LOCAL_ADDR: PORT -> REMOTE_ADDDR. PORT (CHANNEL_ID)"`.

The API endpoint for querying RabbitMQ's management API for channel status is http://host:port/api/channels/[CHANNEL_NAME]. When queried, the management

API will return the result as a JSON-serialized object. The following is an abbreviated example of what the API returns for a channel status query:

```
{
    "connection_details": {…},
    "publishes": […],
    "message_stats": {…},
    "consumer_details": [],
    "transactional": false,
    "confirm": false,
    "consumer_count": 0,
    "messages_unacknowledged": 0,
    "messages_unconfirmed": 0,
    "messages_uncommitted": 0,
    "acks_uncommitted": 0,
    "prefetch_count": 0,
    "client_flow_blocked": false,
    "node": "rabbit@localhost",
    "name": "127.0.0.1:45250 -> 127.0.0.1:5672 (1)",
    "number": 1,
    "user": "guest",
    "vhost": "guest"
}
```

In addition to the `channel_flow_blocked` field, the management API returns rate and state information about the channel.

4.3 Summary

One of the major steps in creating your application architecture is defining the role and behavior of publishers. Questions you should be asking yourself include the following:

- Should publishers request that messages are persisted to disk?
- What guarantees do the various components of my application need that a message published will be a message received?
- What will happen in my environment if my application is blocked by TCP Backpressure or when the connection is blocked while publishing messages to RabbitMQ?
- How important are my messages? Can I sacrifice delivery guarantees for higher message throughput?

By asking yourself these questions, you'll be well on the way to creating an application architecture that's just right. RabbitMQ provides a large amount of flexibility—perhaps too much in some instances. But by taking advantage of its customization capabilities, you're empowered to make trade-offs between performance and high reliability and to decide what the right level of metadata is for your messages. Which properties you use and what mechanisms you use for reliable delivery are better decided by you than anyone else, and RabbitMQ will be a solid foundation for whatever you choose.

Don't get messages; consume them

This chapter covers

- Consuming messages
- Tuning consumer throughput
- When consumers and queues are exclusive
- Specifying a quality of service for your consumers

Having gone deep into the world of message publishers in the last chapter, it's now time to talk about consuming the messages your publishers are sending. Consumer applications can be dedicated applications with the sole purpose of receiving messages and acting on them, or receiving messages may be a very small part of a much bigger application. For example, if you're implementing an RPC pattern with RabbitMQ, the application publishing an RPC request is also consuming the RPC reply (figure 5.1).

With so many patterns available for implementing messaging in your applications, it's only appropriate that RabbitMQ has various settings for finding the right balance between performance and reliable messaging. Deciding how your applications will consume messages is the first step in finding this balance, and it starts off

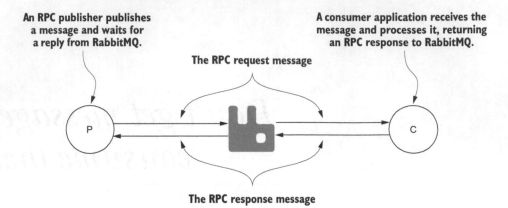

An RPC publisher publishes
a message and waits for
a reply from RabbitMQ.

A consumer application receives the
message and processes it, returning
an RPC response to RabbitMQ.

The RPC request message

The RPC response message

**Figure 5.1   An RPC publisher that publishes a message to RabbitMQ and waits as a consumer
for the RPC reply from the RPC consumer**

with one easy choice: Do you *get* messages, or do you *consume* messages? In this chapter
you'll learn

- Why you should avoid getting messages in favor of consuming them
- How to balance message delivery guarantees with delivery performance
- How to use RabbitMQ's per-queue settings to automatically delete queues, limit
  the age of messages, and more

5.1   Basic.Get vs. Basic.Consume

RabbitMQ implements two different AMQP RPC commands for retrieving messages
from a queue: Basic.Get and Basic.Consume. As the title of this chapter implies,
Basic.Get is not the ideal way to retrieve messages from the server. In the simplest
terms, Basic.Get is a polling model, whereas Basic.Consume is a push model.

5.1.1   Basic.Get

When your application uses a Basic.Get request to retrieve messages, it must send a new
request each time it wants to receive a message, even if there are multiple messages in the
queue. If the queue you're retrieving a message from has a message pending when issuing a Basic.Get, RabbitMQ responds with a Basic.GetOk RPC response (figure 5.2).

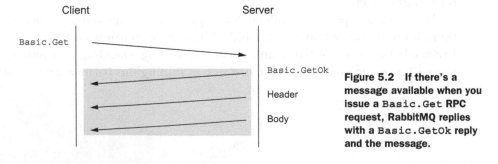

**Figure 5.2   If there's a
message available when you
issue a Basic.Get RPC
request, RabbitMQ replies
with a Basic.GetOk reply
and the message.**

If there are no messages pending in the queue, it will reply with `Basic.GetEmpty`, indicating that there are no messages in the queue (figure 5.3).

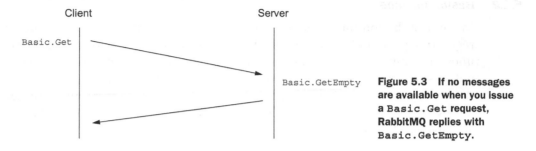

Figure 5.3 **If no messages are available when you issue a `Basic.Get` request, RabbitMQ replies with `Basic.GetEmpty`.**

When using `Basic.Get`, your application should evaluate the RPC response from RabbitMQ to determine if a message has been received. For most long-running processes that are receiving messages from RabbitMQ, this isn't an efficient way to receive and process messages.

Consider the code in the "5.1.1 Basic.Get Example" notebook. After it connects to RabbitMQ and opens the channel, it infinitely loops while requesting messages from RabbitMQ.

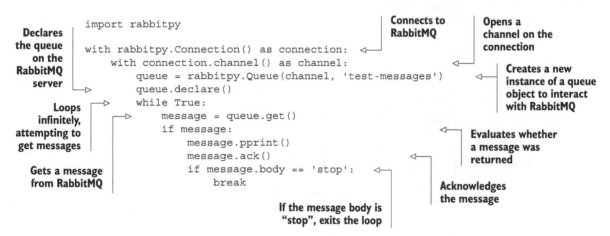

Although this is the simplest way of interacting with RabbitMQ to retrieve your messages, in most cases the performance will be underwhelming at best. In simple message velocity tests, using `Basic.Consume` is at least twice as fast as using `Basic.Get`. The most obvious reason for the speed difference is that with `Basic.Get`, each message delivered carries with it the overhead of the synchronous communication with RabbitMQ, consisting of the client application sending a request frame and RabbitMQ sending the reply. A potentially less obvious reason to avoid `Basic.Get`, yet one with more impact on throughput, is that due to the ad hoc nature of `Basic.Get`, RabbitMQ can't optimize the delivery process in any way because it never knows when an application is going to ask for a message.

5.1.2 *Basic.Consume*

In contrast, by consuming messages with the `Basic.Consume` RPC command, you're registering your application with RabbitMQ and telling it to send messages asynchronously to your consumer as they become available. This is commonly referred to as a publish-subscribe pattern, or pub-sub. Instead of the synchronous conversation with RabbitMQ that occurs when using `Basic.Get`, consuming messages with `Basic.Consume` means your application automatically receives messages from RabbitMQ as they become available until the client issues a `Basic.Cancel` (figure 5.4).

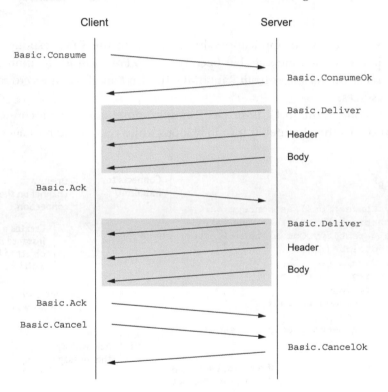

Figure 5.4   When a client issues a `Basic.Consume`, RabbitMQ sends messages to it as they become available until the client issues a `Basic.Cancel`.

Consuming messages from RabbitMQ also requires one less step in your code when you receive a message. As illustrated in the following example, when your application receives a message from RabbitMQ as a consumer, it doesn't need to evaluate the message to determine whether the value is a message or an empty response (`Basic.GetEmpty`). But like with `Basic.Get`, your application still needs to acknowledge the message to let

RabbitMQ know the message has been processed. This code is contained in the "5.1.2 Basic.Consume Example" notebook.

```
import rabbitpy

for message in rabbitpy.consume('amqp://guest:guest@localhost:5672/%2f',
                        'test-messages'):
    message.pprint()
    message.ack()
```

Iterates through the messages in the test-messages queue

Acknowledges receipt of the message

> **NOTE** You might have noticed that the code in the preceding example is shorter than that in previous examples. This is because rabbitpy has shorthand methods that encapsulate much of the logic required to connect to RabbitMQ and use channels.

CONSUMER-TAG

When your application issues `Basic.Consume`, a unique string is created that identifies the application on the open channel with RabbitMQ. This string, called a consumer tag, is sent to your application with each message from RabbitMQ.

The consumer tag can be used to cancel any future receipt of messages from RabbitMQ by issuing a `Basic.Cancel` RPC command. This is especially useful if your application consumes from multiple queues at the same time, because each message received contains the consumer tag it's being delivered for in its method frame. Should your application need to perform different actions for messages received from different queues, it can use the consumer tag used in the `Basic.Consume` request to identify how it should process a message. However, in most cases, the consumer tag is handled under the covers by the client library, and you don't need to worry about it.

In the "5.1.2 Consumer with Stop" notebook, the following consumer code will listen for messages until it receives a message with the message body that only contains the word "stop".

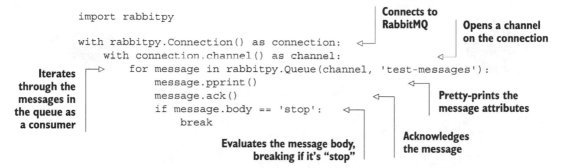

```
import rabbitpy

with rabbitpy.Connection() as connection:
    with connection.channel() as channel:
        for message in rabbitpy.Queue(channel, 'test-messages'):
            message.pprint()
            message.ack()
            if message.body == 'stop':
                break
```

Connects to RabbitMQ

Opens a channel on the connection

Iterates through the messages in the queue as a consumer

Pretty-prints the message attributes

Evaluates the message body, breaking if it's "stop"

Acknowledges the message

Once you have the consumer running, you can publish messages to it using the code in the "5.1.2 Message Publisher" notebook in a new browser tab:

```
import rabbitpy                                              Loops 10          Publishes the
                                                            times             same message
for iteration in range(10):                                                   to RabbitMQ
    rabbitpy.publish('amqp://guest:guest@localhost:5672/%2f',
                     '', 'test-messages', 'go')
    rabbitpy.publish('amqp://guest:guest@localhost:5672/%2f',
                     '', 'test-messages', 'stop')            Publishes the
                                                             stop message
                                                             to RabbitMQ
```

When you run the publisher, the running code in the "5.1 Consumer with Stop Example" notebook will stop once it receives the stop message by exiting the `Queue.consume_messages` iterator. A few things are happing under the covers in the rabbitpy library when you exit the iterator. First, the library sends a `Basic.Cancel` command to RabbitMQ. Once the `Basic.CancelOk` RPC response is received, if RabbitMQ has sent any messages to your client that weren't processed, rabbitpy will send a negative acknowledgment command (`Basic.Nack`) and instruct RabbitMQ to requeue the messages.

Choosing between the synchronous `Basic.Get` and the asynchronous `Basic.Consume` is the first of several choices you'll need to make when writing your consumer application. Like the trade-offs involved when publishing messages, the choices you make for your application can directly impact message delivery guarantees and performance.

5.2   *Performance-tuning consumers*

As when publishing messages, there are trade-offs in consuming messages that balance throughput with message delivery guarantees. As figure 5.5 points out, there are several options that can be used to speed message delivery from RabbitMQ to your application. Also as when publishing messages, RabbitMQ offers fewer guarantees for message delivery with the faster delivery throughput options.

In this section you'll learn how you can tune RabbitMQ's message delivery throughput to consumers by toggling the requirements for message acknowledgments, how to adjust RabbitMQ's message preallocation thresholds, and how to assess the impact transactions have when used with a consumer.

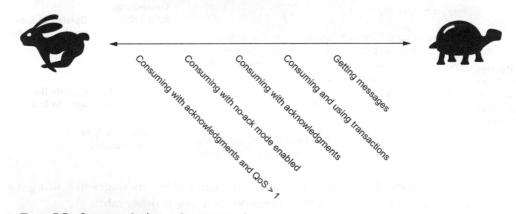

Figure 5.5   Consumer-tuning performance scale

5.2.1 Using no-ack mode for faster throughput

When consuming messages, your application registers itself with RabbitMQ and asks for messages to be delivered as they become available. Your application sends a `Basic` `.Consume` RPC request, and with it, there's a `no-ack` flag. When enabled, this flag tells RabbitMQ that your consumer won't acknowledge the receipt of messages and that RabbitMQ should just send them as quickly as it is able.

The following example in the "5.2.1 No-Ack Consumer" notebook demonstrates how to consume messages without having to acknowledge them. By passing `True` as an argument to the `Queue.consumer` method, rabbitpy sends a `Basic.Consume` RPC request with `no_ack=True`.

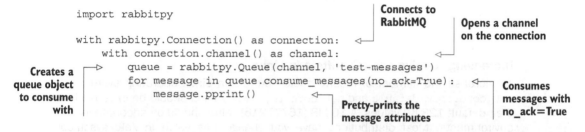

```
import rabbitpy

with rabbitpy.Connection() as connection:
    with connection.channel() as channel:
        queue = rabbitpy.Queue(channel, 'test-messages')
        for message in queue.consume_messages(no_ack=True):
            message.pprint()
```

Connects to RabbitMQ
Opens a channel on the connection
Creates a queue object to consume with
Consumes messages with no_ack=True
Pretty-prints the message attributes

Consuming messages with `no_ack=True` is the fastest way to have RabbitMQ deliver messages to your consumer, but it's also the least reliable way to send messages. To understand why this is, it's important to consider each step a message must go through prior to being received by your consumer application (figure 5.6).

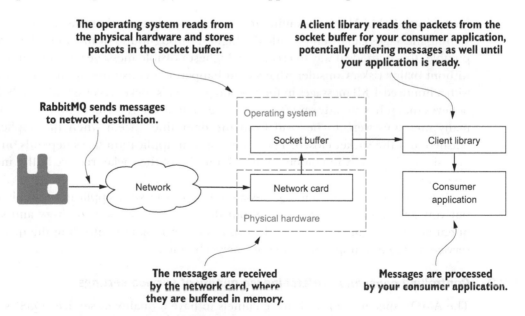

The operating system reads from the physical hardware and stores packets in the socket buffer.

A client library reads the packets from the socket buffer for your consumer application, potentially buffering messages as well until your application is ready.

RabbitMQ sends messages to network destination.

The messages are received by the network card, where they are buffered in memory.

Messages are processed by your consumer application.

Figure 5.6 There are multiple data buffers that receive the message data prior to your consumer application.

When RabbitMQ sends a message over an open connection, it's communicating to the client via a TCP socket connection. If this connection is open and writable, RabbitMQ assumes that everything is in proper working order and that the message was delivered. Should there be a network issue when RabbitMQ tries to write to the socket to deliver the message, the operating system will raise a socket error letting RabbitMQ know there was a problem. If no errors are raised, RabbitMQ assumes the message has been delivered. A message acknowledgment, sent via a `Basic.Ack` RPC response, is one way for a client to let RabbitMQ know that it has successfully received and, in most cases, processed the message. But if you turn off message acknowledgments, RabbitMQ will send another message without waiting, if one is available. In fact, RabbitMQ will continue to send messages, if they're available, to your consumer until the socket buffers are filled.

Increasing receive socket buffers in Linux

To increase the number of receive socket buffers in Linux operating systems, the `net.core.rmem_default` and `net.core.rmem_max` values should be increased from their default 128 KB values. A 16 MB (16777216) value should be adequate for most environments. Most distributions have you change this value in /etc/sysctl.conf, though you could set the value manually by issuing the following commands:

```
echo 16777216 > /proc/sys/net/core/rmem_default
echo 16777216 > /proc/sys/net/core/rmem_max
```

It's because RabbitMQ isn't waiting for an acknowledgment that this method of consuming messages can often provide the highest throughput. For messages that are disposable, this is an ideal way to create the highest possible message velocity, but it's not without major risks. Consider what would happen if a consumer application crashed with a hundred 1 KB messages in the operating system's socket receive buffer. RabbitMQ believes that it has already sent these messages, and it will receive no indication of how many messages were to be read from the operating system when the application crashed and the socket closed. The exposure your application faces depends on message size and quantity in combination with the size of the socket receive buffer in your operating system.

If this method of consuming messages doesn't suit your application architecture but you want faster message throughput than a single message delivery and subsequent acknowledgment can provide, you'll want to look at controlling the quality of service prefetch settings on your consumer's channel.

5.2.2   *Controlling consumer prefetching via quality of service settings*

The AMQP specification calls for channels to have a quality of service (QoS) setting where a consumer can ask for a prespecified number of messages to be received prior to the consumer acknowledging receipt of the messages. The QoS setting allows RabbitMQ to more efficiently send messages by specifying how many messages to pre-allocate for the consumer.

Unlike a consumer with acknowledgments disabled (no_ack=True), if your consumer application crashes before it can acknowledge the messages, all the prefetched messages will be returned to the queue when the socket closes.

At the protocol level, sending a Basic.QoS RPC request on a channel specifies the quality of service. As part of this RPC request, you can specify whether the QoS setting is for the channel it's sent on or all channels open on the connection. The Basic.QoS RPC request can be sent at any time, but as illustrated in the following code from the "5.2.2 Specifying QoS" notebook, it's usually performed prior to a consumer issuing the Basic.Consume RPC request.

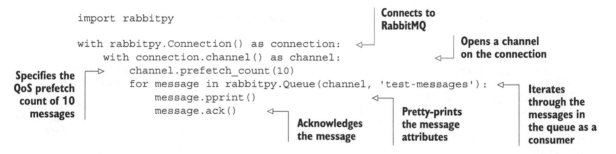

```
import rabbitpy

with rabbitpy.Connection() as connection:
    with connection.channel() as channel:
        channel.prefetch_count(10)
        for message in rabbitpy.Queue(channel, 'test-messages'):
            message.pprint()
            message.ack()
```

Connects to RabbitMQ

Opens a channel on the connection

Specifies the QoS prefetch count of 10 messages

Acknowledges the message

Pretty-prints the message attributes

Iterates through the messages in the queue as a consumer

> **NOTE** Although the AMQP specification calls for both a prefetch count and a prefetch size for the Basic.QoS method, the prefetch size is ignored if the no-ack option is set.

CALIBRATING YOUR PREFETCH VALUES TO AN OPTIMAL LEVEL

It's also important to realize that over-allocating the prefetch count can have a negative impact on message throughput. Multiple consumers on the same queue will receive messages in a round-robin fashion from RabbitMQ, but it's important to benchmark prefetch count performance in high-velocity consumer applications. The benefit of particular settings can vary based on the message composition, consumer behavior, and other factors such as operating system and language.

In figure 5.7, a simple message was benchmarked with a single consumer, showing that in these circumstances, a prefetch count value of 2,500 was the best setting for peak message velocity.

ACKNOWLEDGING MULTIPLE MESSAGES AT ONCE

One of the nice things about using the QoS setting is that you don't need to acknowledge each message received with a Basic.Ack RPC response. Instead, the Basic.Ack RPC response has an attribute named multiple, and when it's set to True it lets RabbitMQ know that your application would like to acknowledge all previous unacknowledged

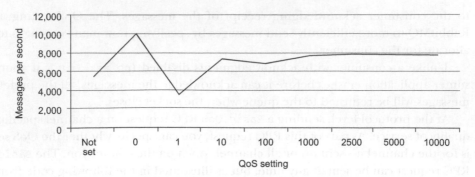

Figure 5.7   Simple benchmark results for consuming with no QoS set and different prefetch count values

messages. This is demonstrated in the following example from the "5.2.2 Multi-Ack Consumer" notebook.

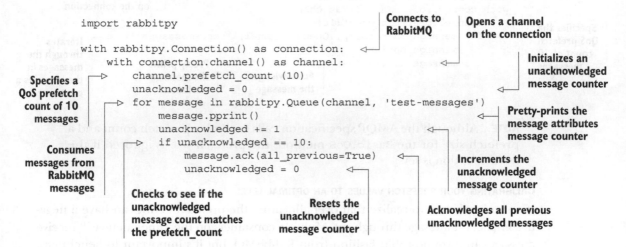

Acknowledging multiple messages at the same time allows you to minimize the network communications required to process your messages, improving message throughput (figure 5.8). It is worth noting that this type of acknowledgment carries with it some level of risk. Should you successfully process some messages and your application dies prior to acknowledging them, all the unacknowledged messages will return to the queue to be processed by another consumer process.

As with publishing messages, the Goldilocks principle applies to consuming messages—you need to find the sweet spot between acceptable risk and peak performance. In addition to QoS, you should consider transactions as a way to improve message delivery guarantees for your application. The source code for these benchmarks is available on the book's website at http://www.manning.com/roy.

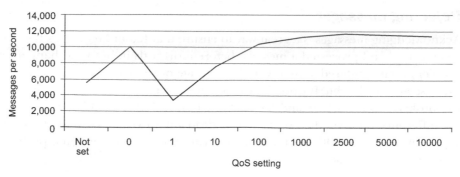

Figure 5.8 Acknowledging multiple messages at the same time improves throughput.

5.2.3 *Using transactions with consumers*

Like when publishing messages into RabbitMQ, transactions allows your consumer applications to commit and roll back batches of operations. Transactions (AMQP TX class) can have a negative impact on message throughput with one exception. If you aren't using QoS settings, you may actually see a slight performance improvement when using transactions to batch your message acknowledgments (figure 5.9).

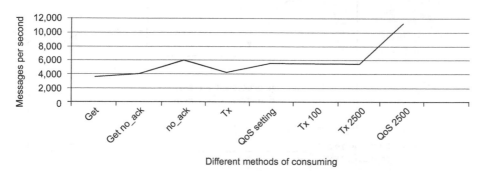

Figure 5.9 Message velocities when using transactions compared to non-transactional message velocities

As with specific QoS settings, you should benchmark your consumer application performance as part of your evaluation in determining whether transactions should play a role in your consumer application. Whether you're using them to batch message acknowledgments or to ensure that you can roll back RPC responses when consuming messages, knowing the true performance impact of transactions will help you find the proper balance between message delivery guarantees and message throughput.

NOTE   Transactions don't work for consumers with acknowledgments disabled.

5.3   *Rejecting messages*

Acknowledging messages is a great way to ensure that RabbitMQ knows the consumer has received and processed a message before it discards it, but what happens when a problem is encountered, either with the message or while processing the message? In these scenarios, RabbitMQ provides two mechanisms for kicking a message back to the broker: `Basic.Reject` and `Basic.Nack` (figure 5.10). In this section we'll cover the difference between the two, as well as dead-letter exchanges, a RabbitMQ-specific extension to the AMQP specification that can help identify systemic problems with batches of rejected messages.

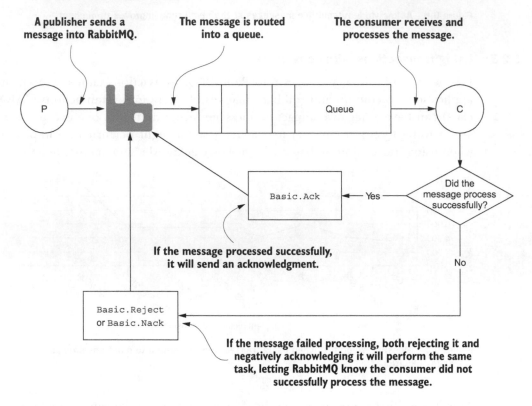

Figure 5.10   **A consumer can acknowledge, reject, or negatively acknowledge a message.**
`Basic.Nack` **allows for multiple messages to be rejected at once, whereas** `Basic.Reject`
allows just one message to be rejected at a time.

5.3.1   *Basic.Reject*

`Basic.Reject` is an AMQP-specified RPC response to a delivered message that informs the broker that the message couldn't be processed. Like `Basic.Ack`, it carries with it the delivery tag created by RabbitMQ to uniquely identify the message on the channel on which your consumer is communicating with RabbitMQ. When a consumer rejects a message, you can instruct RabbitMQ to either discard the message or to requeue the message with the requeue flag. When the requeue flag is enabled, RabbitMQ will put the message back into the queue to be processed again.

I often use this feature in writing consumer applications that communicate with other services, such as databases or remote APIs. Instead of writing logic in my consumer for retrying on failure due to a remote exception, such as a disconnected database cursor or failure to contact a remote API, I simply catch the exception and reject the message with requeue set to True. This allows me to simplify my code paths in a consumer, and when used in conjunction with a stats program such as Graphite, I can see trends in exception behavior by watching the requeue velocity.

The following example, from the "5.3.1 Message Rejection" notebook, demonstrates how when a message is requeued, the redelivered flag is set in the message, informing the message's next consumer that it had been previously delivered. I've used this functionality to implement a "two-strikes and you're out" policy. A malformed message may cause havoc in a consumer, but if you're uncertain whether the problem is due to the message or something else in the consumer, inspecting the redelivered flag is a good way to determine if you should reject the message to be requeued or discarded when an error is encountered.

```
import rabbitpy                                                    Iterates over messages
                                                                  as a consumer

for message in rabbitpy.consume('amqp://guest:guest@localhost:5672/%2f',
                                'test-messages'):
    message.pprint()
    print('Redelivered: %s' % message.redelivered)
    message.reject(True)
```

Pretty-prints the message attributes → `message.pprint()`

`message.reject(True)` ← **Rejects the message and requeues the message to be consumed again**

Prints out the redelivered attribute of the message ← `print('Redelivered: %s' % message.redelivered)`

Like Basic.Ack, using Basic.Reject releases the hold on a message after it has been delivered without no-ack enabled. Although you can confirm the receipt or processing of multiple messages at once with Basic.Ack, you can't reject multiple messages at the same time using Basic.Reject—that's where Basic.Nack comes in.

5.3.2   Basic.Nack

Basic.Reject allows for a single message to be rejected, but if you are using a workflow that leverages Basic.Ack's multiple mode, you may want to leverage the same type of functionality when rejecting messages. Unfortunately, the AMQP specification doesn't provide for this behavior. The RabbitMQ team saw this as a shortcoming in the specification and implemented a new RPC response method called Basic.Nack. Short for "negative acknowledgment," the similarity of the Basic.Nack and Basic.Reject response methods may be understandably confusing upon first inspection. To summarize, the Basic.Nack method implements the same behavior as the Basic.Reject

response method but it adds the missing multiple argument to complement the Basic
.Ack multiple behavior.

> **WARNING**   As with any proprietary RabbitMQ extension to the AMQP proto-
> col, Basic.Nack isn't guaranteed to exist in other AMQP brokers such as
> QPID or ActiveMQ. In addition, generic AMQP clients that don't have the
> RabbitMQ-specific protocol extensions won't support it.

5.3.3   *Dead letter exchanges*

RabbitMQ's dead-letter exchange (DLX) feature is an extension to the AMQP specification and is an optional behavior that can be tied to rejecting a delivered message.
This feature is helpful when trying to diagnose why there are problems consuming
certain messages.

For example, one type of consumer application I've written takes XML-based messages and turns them into PDF files using a standard markup language called XSL:FO.
By combining the XSL:FO document and the XML from the message, I was able to
use Apache's FOP application to generate a PDF file and subsequently file it electron-
ically. The process worked pretty well, but every now and then it would fail. By using a
dead-letter exchange on the queue, I was able to inspect the failing XML documents
and manually run them against the XSL:FO document to troubleshoot the failures.
Without the dead-letter exchange, I would have had to add code to my consumer that
wrote out the XML document to some place where I could then manually process it
via the command line. Instead, I was able to interactively run my consumer by pointing it at a different queue, and I was able to figure out that the problem was related to
how Unicode characters were being treated when the message publisher was generating the document.

Although it may sound like a special type of exchange in RabbitMQ, a dead-letter
exchange is a normal exchange. Nothing special is required or performed when creating it. The only thing that makes an exchange a dead-letter exchange is the declared
use of the exchange for rejected messages when creating a queue. Upon rejecting a
message that isn't requeued, RabbitMQ will route the message to the exchanged specified in the queue's x-dead-letter-exchange argument (figure 5.11).

> **NOTE**   Dead-letter exchanges aren't the same as the alternate exchanges dis-
> cussed in chapter 4. An expired or rejected message is delivered via a dead-
> letter exchange, whereas an alternate exchange routes messages that otherwise
> couldn't be routed by RabbitMQ.

Specifying a dead-letter exchange when declaring a queue is fairly trivial. Simply pass
in the exchange name as the dead_letter_exchange argument when creating the
rabbitpy Queue object or as the x-dead-letter-exchange argument when issuing the
Queue.Declare RPC request. Custom arguments allow you to specify arbitrary key/
value pairs that are stored with the queue definition. You'll learn more about them in

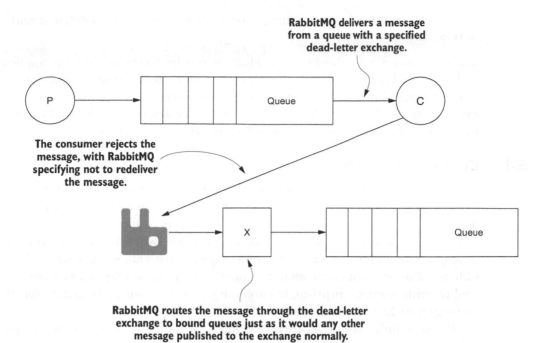

RabbitMQ delivers a message from a queue with a specified dead-letter exchange.

P → Queue → C

The consumer rejects the message, with RabbitMQ specifying not to redeliver the message.

X → Queue

RabbitMQ routes the message through the dead-letter exchange to bound queues just as it would any other message published to the exchange normally.

Figure 5.11   A rejected message can be routed as a dead-letter message through another exchange.

section 5.4.6. The following example is in the "5.3.3 Specifying a Dead Letter Exchange" notebook.

```
import rabbitpy

with rabbitpy.Connection() as connection:
    with connection.channel() as channel:
        rabbitpy.Exchange(channel, 'rejected-messages').declare()
        queue = rabbitpy.Queue(channel, 'dlx-example',
                               dead_letter_exchange='rejected-messages')
        queue.declare()
```

Connects to RabbitMQ

Opens a channel on the connection

Declares the dead-letter exchange

Declares the "example" queue with the "rejected-messages" dead-letter exchange

Creates the rabbitpy Queue object

In addition to the exchange, the dead-lettering functionality allows you to override the routing key with a prespecified value. This allows you to use the same exchange for your dead-lettered messages as your non-dead-lettered messages but to ensure that the dead-lettered messages aren't delivered to the same queue. Setting the prespecified routing key requires an additional argument, x-dead-letter-routing-key, to be specified when declaring the queue.

NOTE Per the AMQP standard, all queue settings in RabbitMQ are immutable, meaning they can't be changed after a queue has been declared. In order to change the dead-letter exchange for a queue, you'd have to delete it and redeclare it.

There are many ways dead-letter exchanges can be leveraged in your application architecture. From providing a safe place to store malformed messages to more directly integrating workflow concepts such as processing rejected credit card authorizations, the dead-letter exchange feature is very powerful, yet it's often overlooked due to its secondary placement as a custom argument for a queue.

5.4   Controlling queues

There are many different use cases for consumer applications. For some applications, it's acceptable for multiple consumers to listen to the same queue, and for others a queue should only have a single consumer. A chat application may create a queue per room or user, where the queues are considered temporary, whereas a credit card processing application may create one durable queue that's always present. With such a wide set of use cases, it's difficult to provide for every option that may be desired when dealing with queues. Surprisingly RabbitMQ provides enough flexibility for almost any use case when creating queues.

When defining a queue, there are multiple settings that determine a queue's behavior. Queues can do the following, and more:

- Auto-delete themselves
- Allow only one consumer to consume from them
- Automatically expire messages
- Keep a limited number of messages
- Push old messages off the stack

It's important to realize that per the AMQP specification, a queue's settings are immutable. Once you've declared a queue, you can't change any of the settings you used to create it. To change queue settings, you must delete the queue and re-create it.

To explore the various settings available for creating a queue, let's first explore options for temporary queues, starting with queues that delete themselves.

5.4.1   Temporary queues

AUTOMATICALLY DELETING QUEUES

Like a briefcase from *Mission Impossible*, RabbitMQ provides for queues that will delete themselves once they've been used and are no longer needed. Like a dead drop from a spy movie, queues that automatically delete themselves can be created and populated with messages. Once a consumer connects, retrieves the messages, and disconnects, the queue will be removed.

Creating an auto-delete queue is as easy as setting the `auto_delete` flag to `True` in the `Queue.Declare` RPC request, as in this example from the "5.4.1 Auto-Delete Queue" IPython notebook.

```
import rabbitpy

with rabbitpy.Connection() as connection:        ◁── Connects to RabbitMQ          Opens a channel
    with connection.channel() as channel:            ◁──                            on the connection
        queue = rabbitpy.Queue(channel, 'ad-example',
                                auto_delete=True)
        queue.declare()        ◁──                                        Declares the "ad-example"
                                                                          queue with auto_delete
                                                                          set to True
```

Creates the rabbitpy Queue object — (points to `queue = rabbitpy.Queue(...)`)

It's important to note that any number of consumers can consume from an automatically deleting queue; the queue will only delete itself when there are no more consumers listening to it. It's a fun use case to think of automatically deleting queues as a form of spy craft, but that's not the only use of automatically deleting queues.

One use case is a chat style application where each queue represents a user's inbound chat buffer. If a user's connection is severed, it's not unreasonable for such an application to expect that the queue and any unread messages should be deleted.

Another example use is with RPC-style applications. For an application that sends RPC requests to consumers and expects the responses to be delivered by RabbitMQ, creating a queue that deletes itself when the application terminates or disconnects allows RabbitMQ to automatically clean up after the application. In this use case, it's important that the RPC reply queue be only consumable by the application that's publishing the original RPC request.

ALLOWING ONLY A SINGLE CONSUMER

Without the exclusive setting enabled on a queue, RabbitMQ allows for very promiscuous consumer behavior. It sets no restrictions on the number of consumers that can connect to a queue and consume from it. In fact, it encourages multiple consumers by implementing a round-robin delivery behavior to all consumers who are able to receive messages from the queue.

There are certain scenarios, such as the RPC reply queue in an RPC workflow, where you'll want to ensure that only a single consumer is able to consume the messages in a queue. Enabling the exclusive use of a queue involves passing an argument during queue creation, and, like the auto_delete argument, enabling exclusive queues automatically removes the queue once the consumer has disconnected. This is demonstrated in the following example from the "5.4.1 Exclusive Queue" notebook.

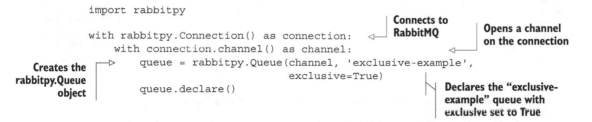

```
import rabbitpy

with rabbitpy.Connection() as connection:        ◁── Connects to RabbitMQ          Opens a channel
    with connection.channel() as channel:            ◁──                            on the connection
        queue = rabbitpy.Queue(channel, 'exclusive-example',
                                exclusive=True)
        queue.declare()                                                   Declares the "exclusive-
                                                                          example" queue with
                                                                          exclusive set to True
```

Creates the rabbitpy.Queue object — (points to `queue = rabbitpy.Queue(...)`)

A queue that's declared as exclusive may only be consumed by the same connection and channel that it was declared on, unlike queues that are declared with auto_delete set to `True`, which can have any number of consumers from any number of connections. An exclusive queue will also automatically be deleted when the channel that the queue was created on is closed, which is similar to how a queue that has `auto-delete` set will be removed once there are no more consumers subscribed to it. Unlike an `auto_delete` queue, you can consume and cancel the consumer for an `exclusive` queue as many times as you like, until the channel is closed. It's also important to note that the auto-deletion of an `exclusive` queue occurs without regard to whether a `Basic.Consume` request has been issued, unlike an `auto-delete` queue.

AUTOMATICALLY EXPIRING QUEUES

While we're on the subject of queues that are automatically deleted, RabbitMQ allows for an optional argument when declaring a queue that will tell RabbitMQ to delete the queue if it has gone unused for some length of time. Like exclusive queues that delete themselves, automatically expiring queues are easy to imagine for RPC reply queues.

Suppose you have a time-sensitive operation and you don't want to wait around indefinitely for an RPC reply. You could create an RPC reply queue that has an expiration value, and when that queue expires the queue is deleted. Using a passive queue declare, you can poll for the presence of the queue and act when you either see there are messages pending or when the queue no longer exists.

Creating an automatically expiring queue is as simple as declaring a queue with an x-expires argument with the queue's time to live (TTL) specified in milliseconds, as is demonstrated in this example from the "5.4.1 Expiring Queue" notebook.

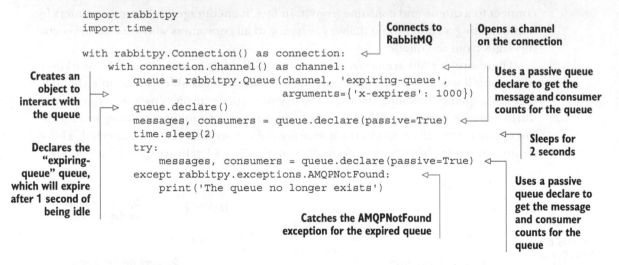

There are some strict rules around automatically expiring queues:

- The queue will only expire if it has no consumers. If you have a queue with connected consumers, it will only be automatically removed once they issue a `Basic` `.Cancel` or disconnect.

- The queue will only expire if there has been no `Basic.Get` request for the TTL duration. Once a single `Basic.Get` request has been made of a queue with an expiration value, the expiration setting is nullified and the queue won't be automatically deleted.
- As with any other queue, the settings and arguments declared with an `x-expires` argument can't be redeclared or changed. If you were able to redeclare the queue, extending the expiration by the value of the `x-expires` argument, you'd be violating a hard-set rule in the AMQP specification that a client must not attempt to redeclare a queue with different settings.
- RabbitMQ makes no guarantees about how promptly it will remove the queue post expiration.

5.4.2 Permanent queues

QUEUE DURABILITY

When declaring a queue that should persist across server restarts, the `durable` flag should be set to `True`. Often queue durability is confused with message persistence. As we discussed in the previous chapter, messages are stored on disk when a message is published with the `delivery-mode` property set to `2`. The `durable` flag, in contrast, instructs RabbitMQ that you want the queue to be configured until a `Queue.Delete` request is called.

Whereas RPC-style applications generally want queues that come and go with consumers, durable queues are very handy for application workflows where multiple consumers connect to the same queue, and the routing and message flow don't change dynamically. The "5.4.2 Durable Queue" notebook demonstrates how a durable queue is declared.

```
import rabbitpy                                        Connects to        Opens a channel
                                                       RabbitMQ           on the connection
with rabbitpy.Connection() as connection:
    with connection.channel() as channel:
        queue = rabbitpy.Queue(channel, 'durable-queue',
                               durable=True)
        if queue.declare():                                               Creates an object
            print('Queue declared')         Declares the                 to interact with
                                             durable queue                the queue
```

AUTO-EXPIRATION OF MESSAGES IN A QUEUE

With non-mission-critical messages, sometimes it's better to have them automatically go away if they hang around too long without being consumed. Whether you're accounting for stale data that should be removed after its usefulness has expired or you want to make sure that you can recover easily should a consumer application die with a high-velocity queue, per-message TTL settings allow for server-side constraints on the maximum age of a message. Queues declared with both a dead-letter exchange and a TTL value will result in the dead-lettering of messages in the queue at time of expiration.

In contrast to the expiration property of a message, which can vary from message to message, the `x-message-ttl` queue setting enforces a maximum age for all messages in the queue. This is demonstrated in the following example from the "5.4.2 Queue with Message TTL" notebook.

```
import rabbitpy                                          Connects to
                                                         RabbitMQ
with rabbitpy.Connection() as connection:    ◄──┘                    Opens a channel
    with connection.channel() as channel:                   ◄──┘     on the connection
        queue = rabbitpy.Queue(channel, 'expiring-msg-queue',
                                        arguments={'x-message-ttl': 1000})
        queue.declare()                                 ◄──┐
                                                         Declares
                                                         the queue
```

Creates an object to interact with the queue

Using per-message TTLs with queues provides inherent value for messages that may have different value to different consumers. For some consumers, a message may hold transactional value that has monetary value, and it must be applied to a customer's account. Creating a queue that automatically expires messages would prevent a real-time dashboard listening on a queue from receiving stale information.

MAXIMUM LENGTH QUEUES

As of RabbitMQ 3.1.0, queues may be declared with a maximum size. If you set the `x-max-length` argument on a queue, once it reaches the maximum size, RabbitMQ will drop messages from the front of the queue as new messages are added. In a chat room with a scroll-back buffer, a queue declared with an `x-max-length` will ensure that a client asking for the n most recent messages always has them available.

Like the per message expiration setting and the dead-letter settings, the maximum length setting is set as a queue argument and can't be changed after declaration. Messages that are removed from the front of the queue can be dead-lettered if the queue is declared with a dead-letter exchange. The following example shows a queue with a predefined maximum length. You'll find it in the "5.4.2 Queue with a Maximum Length" notebook.

```
import rabbitpy                                          Connects to
                                                         RabbitMQ
with rabbitpy.Connection() as connection:    ◄──┘                    Opens a channel
    with connection.channel() as channel:                   ◄──┘     on the connection
        queue = rabbitpy.Queue(channel, 'max-length-queue',
                                        arguments={'x-max-length': 1000})
        queue.declare()                                 ◄──┐
                                                         Declares the queue with a maximum
                                                         length of 1000 messages
```

Creates an object to interact with the queue

5.4.3 *Arbitrary queue settings*

As the RabbitMQ team implements new features that extend the AMQP specification with regard to queues, queue arguments are used to carry the setting for each feature set. Queue arguments are used for highly available queues, dead-letter exchanges, message expiration, queue expiration, and queues with a maximum length.

The AMQP specification defines queue arguments as a table where the syntax and semantics of the values are to be determined by the server. RabbitMQ has reserved arguments, listed in table 5.1, and it ignores any other arguments passed in. Arguments can be any valid AMQP data type and can be used for whatever purpose you like. Personally, I have found arguments to be a very useful way to set per-queue monitoring settings and thresholds.

Table 5.1 Reserved queue arguments

Argument name	Purpose
x-dead-letter-exchange	An exchange to which non-requeued rejected messages are routed
x-dead-letter-routing-key	An optional routing key for dead-lettered messages
x-expires	Queue is removed after the specified number of milliseconds
x-ha-policy	When creating HA queues, specifies the mode for enforcing HA across nodes
x-ha-nodes	The nodes that an HA queue is distributed across (see section 4.1.6)
x-max-length	The maximum message count for a queue
x-message-ttl	Message expiration in milliseconds, enforced at the queue level
x-max-priority	Enables priority sorting of a queue with a maximum priority value of 255 (RabbitMQ versions 3.5.0 and greater)

5.5 *Summary*

Performance-tuning your RabbitMQ consumer applications requires benchmarking and consideration of the trade-offs between fast throughput and guaranteed delivery (much like tuning for publishing messages). When setting out to write consumer applications, consider the following questions in order to find the sweet spot for your application:

- Do you need to ensure that all messages are received, or can they be discarded?
- Can you receive messages and then acknowledge or reject them as a batch operation?
- If not, can you use transactions to improve performance by automatically batching your individual operations?
- Do you really need transactional commit and rollback functionality in your consumers?

- Does your consumer need exclusive access to the messages in the queues it's consuming from?
- What should happen when your consumer encounters an error? Should the message be discarded? Requeued? Dead-lettered?

These questions provide the starting points for creating a solid messaging architecture that helps enforce the contract between your publishing and consuming applications.

Now that you have the basics of publishing and consuming under your belt, we'll examine how you can put them into practice with several different messaging patterns and use cases in the next chapter.

Message patterns via exchange routing

This chapter covers

- The four basic types of exchanges available through RabbitMQ, plus a plugin exchange
- Which type of exchange is appropriate for your application architecture
- How the use of exchange-to-exchange routing can add numerous routing options for your messages

Perhaps RabbitMQ's greatest strength is the flexibility it offers for routing messages to different queues based upon routing information provided by the publisher. Whether it's sending messages to a single queue, multiple queues, exchanges, or another external source provided by an exchange plugin, RabbitMQ's routing engine is both extremely fast and highly flexible. Although your initial application may not need complex routing logic, starting with the right type of exchange can have a dramatic impact on your application architecture.

In this chapter, we'll take a look at four basic types of exchanges and the types of architectures that can benefit from them:

- Direct exchange
- Fanout exchange

- Topic exchange
- Headers exchange

We'll start with some simple message routing using the *direct exchange*. From there, we'll use a *fanout exchange* to send images to both a facial-recognition consumer and an image-hashing consumer. A *topic exchange* will allow us to selectively route messages based upon wildcard matching in the routing key, and a *headers exchange* presents an alternative approach to message routing using the message itself. I'll dispel the myth that certain exchanges aren't as performant as others, and then I'll show you how exchange-to-exchange binding can open up an *Inception*-like reality, but for message routing, not dreams. Finally, we'll cover the *consistent-hashing exchange*, a plugin exchange type that should help if your consumer throughput needs to grow beyond the capabilities of multiple consumers sharing a single queue.

6.1   Simple message routing using the direct exchange

The direct exchange is useful when you're going to deliver a message with a specific target, or a set of targets. Any queue that's bound to an exchange with the same routing key that's being used to publish a message will receive the message. RabbitMQ uses string equality when checking the binding and doesn't allow any type of pattern matching when using a direct exchange (figure 6.1).

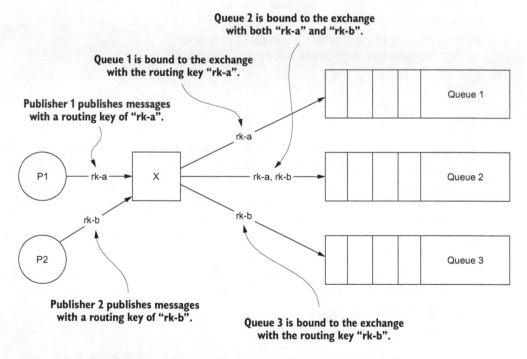

Figure 6.1   Using a direct exchange, messages published by publisher 1 will be routed to queue 1 and queue 2, whereas messages published by publisher 2 will be routed to queues 2 and 3.

As illustrated in figure 6.1, multiple queues can be bound to a direct exchange using the same routing key. Every queue bound with the same routing key will receive all of the messages published with that routing key.

The direct exchange type is built into RabbitMQ and doesn't require any additional plugins. Creating a direct exchange is as simple as declaring an exchange type as "direct," as demonstrated in this snippet in the "6.1 Direct Exchange" notebook.

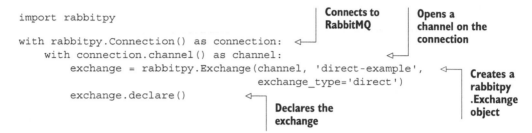

Because of its simplicity, the direct exchange is a good choice for routing reply messages used in RPC messaging patterns. Writing decoupled applications using RPC is an excellent way to create highly scalable applications with different components that are provisioned across multiple servers.

This architecture is the basis for our first example. You'll write an RPC worker that consumes images to perform facial recognition and then publishes them back to the publishing application. In computationally complex processes such as image or video processing, leveraging remote RPC workers is a great way to scale an application. If this application were running in the cloud, for example, the application publishing the request could live on small-scale virtual machines, and the image processing worker could make use of larger hardware—or, if the workload supported it, on GPU-based processing.

To get started building the example application, you'll write the worker, a single purpose image-processing consumer.

6.1.1 *Creating the application architecture*

Suppose you wanted to implement a web-based API service that processes photos uploaded by mobile phones. The pattern illustrated in figure 6.1 can be implemented as a lightweight, highly scalable, asynchronous front-end web application by leveraging a technology like the Tornado web framework (http://tornadoweb.org) or Node.js (http://nodejs.org). When the front-end application starts up, it will create a queue in RabbitMQ using a name that's unique to that process for RPC responses.

As illustrated in figure 6.2, the request process begins when a mobile client application uploads the image and your application receives the content. The application then creates a message with a unique ID that identifies the remote request. When publishing the image to the exchange, the response queue name will be set in the reply-to field in the message's properties and the request ID will be placed in

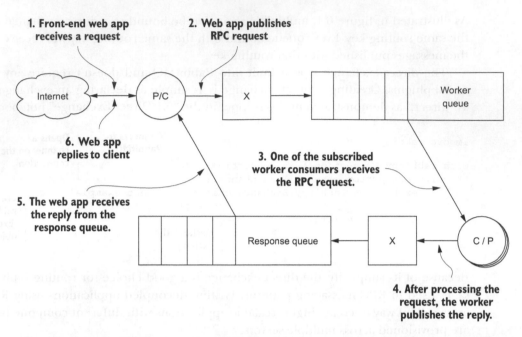

Figure 6.2 A simple RPC pattern where a publisher sends a request using a direct exchange and a worker consumes the message, publishing the result to be consumed by the original publisher

the correlation-id field. The body of the message will contain only the opaque binary data of the image.

We discussed some low-level frame structures in chapter 2. Let's review the frames required to create such an RPC request (figure 6.3).

In figure 6.3, the reply-to and correlation-id field values are carried in the Content-Headers property payload. The image that's being sent as the message body is split up into three chunks, sent in AMQP body frames. RabbitMQ's maximum frame size of 131,072 bytes means that any message body that exceeds that size must be chunked at the AMQP protocol level. Because there are 7 bytes of overhead that must be taken into account, each body frame may only carry 131,065 bytes of the opaque binary image data.

Once the message is published and routed, a consumer subscribed to the work queue consumes it, as you learned in chapter 5. This consumer can do the heavy lifting and perform the blocking, computationally expensive, or I/O intensive operations that the front-end web application wouldn't be able to perform without blocking other clients. Instead, by offloading the computationally or I/O intensive tasks to a consumer, an asynchronous front end is free to process other client requests while it's waiting for a response from the RPC worker. Once a worker has completed its processing of the image, the result of the RPC request is sent back to the web front end,

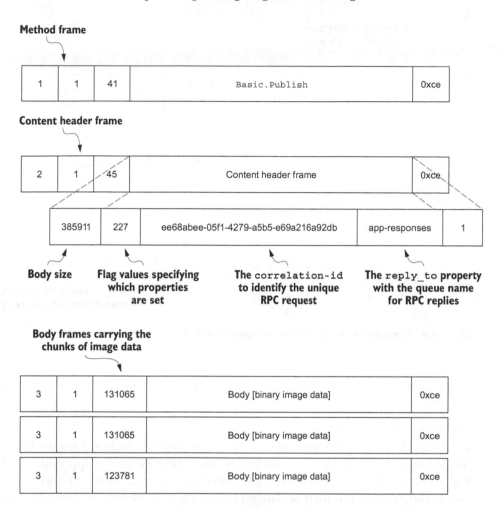

Figure 6.3   The low-level frame structure for an RPC message carrying a 385,911 byte image

enabling it to send a reply to the remote mobile client, completing the client's original request.

We won't write the full web application in the following listings, but we will write a simple consumer that will attempt to detect faces in images that are published to it and then return the same image to the publisher with boxes drawn around the detected faces. To demonstrate how the publishing side operates, we'll write a publisher that will dispatch work requests for every image located in a prespecified directory. As you can see in figure 6.4, the abbreviated workflow you'll be implementing is most of the application; it's just missing the web application.

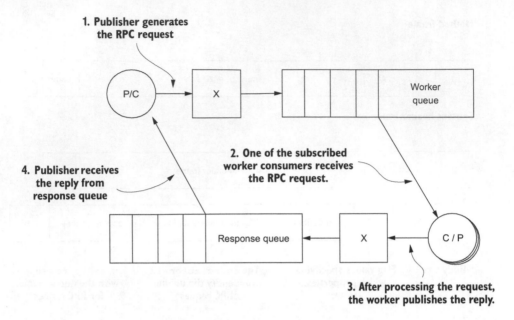

1. Publisher generates the RPC request

P/C

X

Worker queue

4. Publisher receives the reply from response queue

2. One of the subscribed worker consumers receives the RPC request.

Response queue

X

C / P

3. After processing the request, the worker publishes the reply.

Figure 6.4   The abbreviated application flow implemented in this section

With the structure outlined, we now need to do a bit of preparation before we get to the code.

DECLARING THE EXCHANGES

Before writing the consumer and publisher, you need to declare a few exchanges. In the following code, the URL to connect to isn't specified, so the application will connect to RabbitMQ using the default URL of amqp://guest:guest@localhost:5672/%2F. Once connected, it will then declare an exchange to route RPC requests through and an exchange to route RPC replies through. The following code to declare the direct RPC exchange is in the "6.1 RPC Exchange Declaration" notebook.

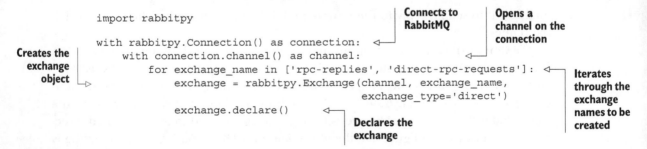

```
import rabbitpy

with rabbitpy.Connection() as connection:        ← Connects to RabbitMQ
    with connection.channel() as channel:        ← Opens a channel on the connection
        for exchange_name in ['rpc-replies', 'direct-rpc-requests']:   ← Iterates through the exchange names to be created
            exchange = rabbitpy.Exchange(channel, exchange_name,
                                     exchange_type='direct')
        exchange.declare()        ← Declares the exchange
```

Creates the exchange object

Unlike previous examples for declaring an exchange, this code declares multiple exchanges instead of just one. To limit the amount of code required to perform this task, a Python `list` or array of exchange names is iterated upon. For each iteration of the loop, a rabbitpy `Exchange` object is created, and then the exchange is declared with RabbitMQ.

Once you've declared the RPC exchanges for the RPC workflow, go ahead and move on to creating the RPC worker.

6.1.2 *Creating the RPC worker*

We'll create the RPC worker as a consumer application that will receive messages containing image files and perform image recognition on them using the excellent OpenCV (http://opencv.org), drawing a box around each face in the photo. Once an image has been processed, the new image will be published back through RabbitMQ, using the routing information provided in the original message's properties (figure 6.5).

Figure 6.5   A photo processed by the RPC facial recognition worker

The RPC consumer is a more complex example than those we've looked at so far, so it deserves a bit more than a single code listing. To keep us from getting sidetracked by the details of facial recognition, all of the code that performs the facial recognition is imported as a module named `detect` in the `ch6` Python package. In addition, the `ch6.utils` module provides functionality to manage the image file on disk, for the consumer's use. The consumer code is in the "6.1.2 RPC Worker" notebook.

IMPORTING THE PROPER LIBRARIES
To start building the facial recognition consumer, you must first import the Python packages or modules required by the application. These include the modules from the previously mentioned `ch6` package, `rabbitpy`, `os`, and `time`.

```
import os
import rabbitpy
import time
from ch6 import detect
from ch6 import utils
```

The os package is used to remove the image file from disk and get the current process ID, whereas the time package supplies timing information while providing processing information to the system console.

CONNECTING, DECLARING, AND BINDING A QUEUE

With the imports out of the way, you can use rabbitpy to connect to RabbitMQ and open a channel:

```
connection = rabbitpy.Connection()
channel = connection.channel()
```

As with previous consumer examples, a rabbitpy.Queue object is required to declare, bind, and consume from the RabbitMQ queue that will receive the messages. Unlike previous examples, this queue is temporary and exclusive to a single instance of the consumer application. To let RabbitMQ know that the queue should go away as soon as the consumer application does, the auto_delete flag is set to True and the durable flag is set to False. To let RabbitMQ know that no other consumer should be able to access the messages in the queue, the exclusive flag is set to True. If another consumer should attempt to consume from the queue, RabbitMQ will prevent the consumer from doing so, and it will send it an AMQP Channel.Close frame.

To create a meaningful name for the queue, an easily identifiable string name is created, including the operating system's process ID for the Python consumer application.

```
queue_name = 'rpc-worker-%s' % os.getpid()
queue = rabbitpy.Queue(channel, queue_name,
                       auto_delete=True,
                       durable=False,
                       exclusive=True)
```

> **NOTE** If you omit a queue name when creating the queue, RabbitMQ will automatically create a queue name for you. You should recognize these queues in the RabbitMQ management interface as they follow a pattern similar to amq.gen-oCv2kwJ2H0KYxIunVI-xpQ.

Once the Queue object has been created, the AMQP Queue.Declare RPC request is issued to RabbitMQ. That's followed by the AMQP Queue.Bind RPC request to bind the queue to the proper exchange, using the detect-faces routing key, so you only get messages sent as facial recognition RPC requests from the publisher you'll write in the next section.

```
if queue.declare():
    print('Worker queue declared')
if queue.bind('direct-rpc-requests', 'detect-faces'):
    print('Worker queue bound')
```

CONSUMING THE RPC REQUESTS

With the queue created and bound, the application is ready to consume messages. To consume messages from RabbitMQ, the consumer will use the `rabbitpy.Queue .consume_messages` iterator method that also acts as a Python context manager. A Python context manager is a language construct that's invoked by the `with` statement. For an object to provide context manager support, it defines magic methods (`__enter__` and `__exit__`) that execute when a code block is entered or exited using the `with` statement.

Using a content manager allows rabbitpy to deal with sending the `Basic.Consume` and the `Basic.Cancel` AMQP RPC requests so you can focus on your own code:

```
for message in queue.consume_messages():
```

As you iterate through each message that RabbitMQ delivers, you'll have a look at the message's `timestamp` property in order to display how long the message was sitting in the queue before the consumer received it. The publishing code will automatically set this value on every message, providing a source of information outside of RabbitMQ that details when the message was first created and published.

Because rabbitpy will automatically transform the `timestamp` property into a Python `datetime` object, the consumer needs to transform the value back into a UNIX epoch to calculate the number of seconds since the message was published:

```
duration = (time.time() -
            int(message.properties['timestamp'].strftime('%s')))
print('Received RPC request published %.2f seconds ago' %
      duration)
```

PROCESSING AN IMAGE MESSAGE

Next, to perform the facial recognition, the message body containing the image file must be written to disk. Because these files are only needed for a short time, the image will be written out as a temporary file. The `content-type` of the message is also passed in, so the proper file extension can be used when naming the file.

```
temp_file = utils.write_temp_file(message.body,
                                  message.properties['content_type'])
```

With the file written to the filesystem, the consumer can now perform the facial recognition using the `ch6.detect.faces` method. The method returns the path to a new file on disk that contains the original image with the detected faces in box overlays:

```
result_file = detect.faces(temp_file)
```

SENDING THE RESULT BACK

Now that the hard work is done, it's time to publish the result of the RPC request back to the original publisher. To do so, you must first construct the properties of the response message, which will contain the correlation-id of the original message, so the publisher knows which image to correlate with the response. In addition, the headers property is used to set the timestamp for when the message was first published. This will allow the publisher to gauge total time from request to response, which could be used for monitoring purposes.

```
properties = {'app_id': 'Chapter 6 Listing 2 Consumer',
              'content_type': message.properties['content_type'],
              'correlation_id':
                  message.properties['correlation_id'],
              'headers': {
                  'first_publish':
                      message.properties['timestamp']}}
```

With the response properties defined, the result file with the image is read from disk, and both the original temp file and the result file are removed from the filesystem:

```
body = utils.read_image(result_file)
os.unlink(temp_file)
os.unlink(result_file)
```

Finally, it's time to create and publish the response message and then acknowledge the original RPC request message so that RabbitMQ can remove it from the queue:

```
response = rabbitpy.Message(channel, body, properties)
response.publish('rpc-replies', message.properties['reply_to'])
message.ack()
```

RUNNING THE CONSUMER APPLICATION

With the consumer code done, it's time to run the consumer application. Like with previous examples, you can select Cell > Run All to bypass having to run each cell independently. Note that the last cell of this application in the IPython notebook will keep running until you stop it. You'll know it's running when the Kernel Busy indicator is displayed (figure 6.6). You can leave this browser tab open and go back to the IPython dashboard for the next section.

6.1.3 *Writing a simple RPC publisher*

You now have a running RPC consumer application that will receive messages, perform facial recognition on them, and return the result. It's time to write an application that can publish messages to it. In this sample use case, our goal is to move blocking and slow processes to external consumers so that a high-performance,

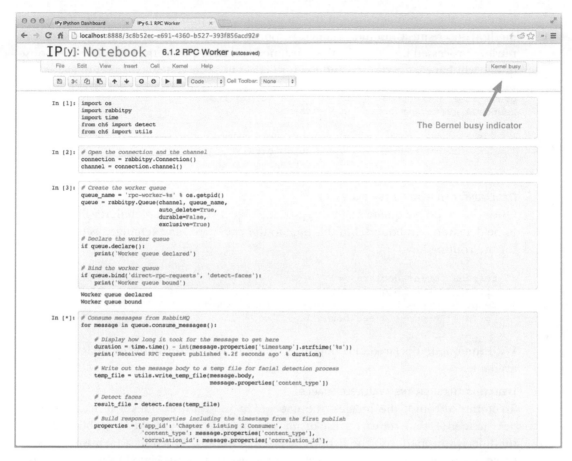

Figure 6.6 The IPython notebook running the RPC worker

asynchronous web application can receive requests and process them without blocking other requests while the processing is taking place.

Because it's outside the scope of this book to write a full asynchronous web application, the publisher code will simply publish the RPC request message and display the RPC response message once it has been received. Also, the images used for this example are already in the Vagrant virtual machine and are all in the public domain.

SPECIFYING THE IMPORTED LIBRARIES

To get started, you must first import the requisite Python packages and modules to perform the task at hand. In the case of the publisher, all of the same packages and modules are used, with the exception of the ch6.detect module.

```
import os
import rabbitpy
import time
from ch6 import utils
```

Similar to the consumer's use of the os package, the publisher uses the `os.getpid()` method to create a uniquely named response queue from which the publisher will retrieve processed images. Like the consumer's request queue, the publisher's response queue will have `auto_delete` and `exclusive` set to True and `durable` set to False.

```
queue_name = 'response-queue-%s' % os.getpid()
response_queue = rabbitpy.Queue(channel,
                                queue_name,
                                auto_delete=True,
                                durable=False,
                                exclusive=True)
```

DECLARING AND BINDING THE EXCHANGE

Once the response queue's `rabbitpy.Queue` object has been created, it will also need to be declared and bound, but this time to the `rpc-replies` exchange, using its name for the routing key:

```
if response_queue.declare():
    print('Response queue declared')
if response_queue.bind('rpc-replies', queue_name):
    print('Response queue bound')
```

With the queue declared and bound, it's time to iterate through the images that are available.

ITERATING THROUGH THE AVAILABLE IMAGES

To iterate through the images, the `ch6.utils` module provides a function named `get_images()` that returns a list of images on disk that should be published. The method is wrapped with the Python `enumerate` iterator function, which will return a tuple of the current index of the value in the list and its associated value. A tuple is a common data structure. In Python, it's an immutable sequence of objects.

```
for img_id, filename in enumerate(utils.get_images()):
```

Inside this control block, you'll construct the message and publish to RabbitMQ. But before the publisher creates the message, let's have it print out information that tells you about the image being published for processing:

```
print('Sending request for image #%s: %s' % (img_id, filename))
```

CONSTRUCTING THE REQUEST MESSAGE

Creating the message is a fairly straightforward one-liner. The `rabbitpy.Message` object is constructed, with the first argument passed in being the channel, and then it uses the `ch6.utils.read_image()` method to read the raw image data from disk and passes it in as the message body argument.

Finally, the message properties are created. The `content-type` for the message is set using the `ch6.utils.mime_time()` method, which returns the mime type for the image. The `correlation-id` property is set using the `img_id` value provided by the enumerate iterator function. In an asynchronous web application, this might be a connection ID for the client or a socket file descriptor number. Finally the message's `reply_to` property is set to the publisher's response queue name. The rabbitpy library automatically sets the `timestamp` property if it's omitted by setting the `opinionated` flag to `True`.

```
message = rabbitpy.Message(channel,
                    utils.read_image(filename),
                    {'content_type':
                        utils.mime_type(filename),
                     'correlation_id': str(img_id),
                     'reply_to': queue_name},
                    opinionated=True)
```

With the message object created, it's time to publish it to the `direct-rpc-requests` exchange using the `detect-faces` routing key:

```
message.publish('direct-rpc-requests', 'detect-faces')
```

As soon as this is run, the message is sent and should quickly be received by the RPC consumer application.

WAITING FOR A REPLY

In an asynchronous web application, the application would handle another client request while waiting for a response from the RPC consumer. For the purposes of this example, we'll create a blocking application instead of an asynchronous server. Instead of consuming the response queue and performing other work asynchronously, our publisher will use the `Basic.Get` AMQP RPC method to check whether a message is in the queue and receive it, as follows:

```
message = None
while not message:
    time.sleep(0.5)
    message = response_queue.get()
```

ACKNOWLEDGING THE MESSAGE

Once a message is received, the publisher should acknowledge so RabbitMQ can remove it from the queue:

```
message.ack()
```

PROCESSING THE RESPONSE

If you're like me, you'll want to know how long the facial recognition and message routing took, so add a line that prints out the total duration from original publishing until the response is received. In complex applications, the message properties can be used to carry metadata like this, that's used for everything from debugging information to data that's used for monitoring, trending, and analytics.

```
duration = (time.time() -
        time.mktime(message.properties['headers']['first_publish']))
print('Facial detection RPC call for image %s duration %.2f sec' %
      (message.properties['correlation_id'], duration))
```

This code that prints out the duration uses the `first_publish` timestamp value set in the message properties header table that was set by the consumer. That way you know the full round-trip time from initial RPC request publishing to the receipt of the RPC reply.

Finally, you can display the image in the IPython notebook using the `ch6.utils .display_image()` function:

```
utils.display_image(message.body,
                    message.properties['content_type'])
```

CLOSING UP

With the main publisher code block complete, the following lines close the channel and connection and should no longer be indented by four spaces:

```
channel.close()
connection.close()
```

TESTING THE WHOLE APPLICATION

It's time to test. Open up "6.1.3 RPC Publisher" in the IPython notebook and click the Run Code play button to fire off the messages and see the results (figure 6.7).

As you may have noticed, the facial recognition code isn't perfect, but it performs pretty well for a low-powered virtual machine. To improve the quality of the facial recognition, additional algorithms can be employed to look for a quorum of results from each algorithm. Such work is way too slow for a real-time web app, but not for an army of RPC consumer applications on specialty hardware. Fortunately, RabbitMQ provides multiple ways to route the same message to different queues. In the next section, we'll tap the messages sent by the RPC publisher without impacting the already established workflow. To achieve this, we'll use a fanout exchange instead of a direct exchange for RPC requests.

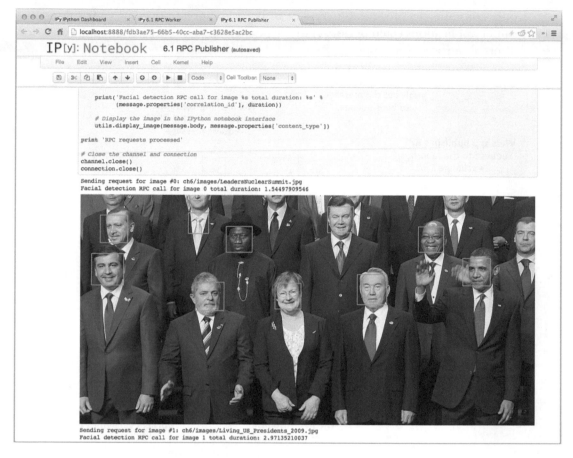

Figure 6.7   The RPC publisher receiving results from the consumer

6.2   *Broadcasting messages via the fanout exchange*

Where a direct exchange allows for queues to receive targeted messages, a fanout exchange doesn't discriminate. All messages published through a fanout exchange are delivered to all queues in the fanout exchange. This provides significant performance advantages because RabbitMQ doesn't need to evaluate the routing keys when delivering messages, but the lack of selectivity means all applications consuming from queues bound to a fanout exchange should be able to consume messages delivered through it.

Suppose that, in addition to detecting faces, you wanted to create tools so your mobile application could identify spammers in real time. Using a fanout exchange that the web application publishes to when it performs a facial recognition RPC request, you could bind the RPC consumer queues and any other consumer applications you'd like to act on the messages. The facial recognition consumer would be the only consumer to provide RPC replies to the web application, but your other consumer applications could perform other types of analysis on the images published, for internal purposes only (figure 6.8).

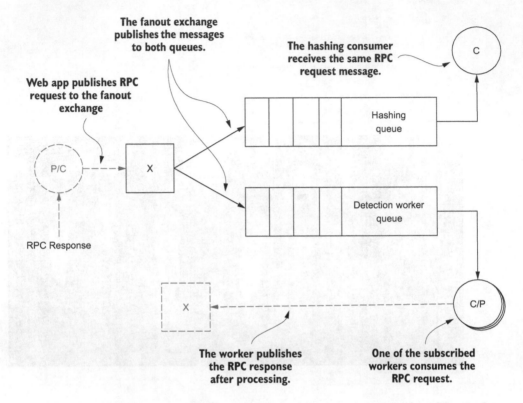

Figure 6.8   Adding another consumer that receives the same message as the RPC consumer by using a fanout exchange

In my experience, spammers often use the same images when registering for a service or submitting content to the service. One way to mitigate spam attacks is to fingerprint images and keep a database of image fingerprints identified as spam, taking action when a new image is uploaded with the same fingerprint. In the following code examples, we'll use an RPC request message that triggers the facial recognition consumer to fingerprint images.

6.2.1   *Modifying the facial detection consumer*

In the examples that follow, we'll build upon the examples in section 6.1, making some small modifications and adding a new image-hashing consumer that will create a hash of an image when the RPC request is made.

To get started, you first need to create the fanout exchange. The following snippet is from the "6.2.1 Fanout Exchange Declaration" notebook.

```
import rabbitpy                                    Connects to
                                                   RabbitMQ          Opens a
with rabbitpy.Connection() as connection:  ◄─┘                       channel on the
    with connection.channel() as channel:                       ◄─┘ connection
        exchange = rabbitpy.Exchange(channel,
                        'fanout-rpc-requests',                    ◄─┐ Creates
                        exchange_type='fanout')                      the fanout
        exchange.declare()              ◄─┐                          exchange
                                          │  Declares the            object
                                             exchange
```

In addition, the original consumer code from section 6.1 needs a slight modification in how the queue is bound. Instead of binding to the `direct-rpc-requests` exchange with a routing key, the consumer will need to bind to `fanout-rpc-requests` without a routing key. The change is already made in the "6.2.1 RPC Worker" notebook, and it changes this line:

```
if queue.bind('direct-rpc-requests', 'detect-faces'):
```

to use the new fanout exchange:

```
if queue.bind('fanout-rpc-requests'):
```

The only modification you need to make to the publisher code is to change the exchange that's being published to. Again, the code is already modified in the IPython notebook as "6.2.1 RPC Publisher," and changes this line:

```
message.publish('direct-rpc-requests', 'detect-faces')
```

to use the new exchange as follows:

```
message.publish('fanout-rpc-requests')
```

Before you publish and consume the messages, let's write the image-hashing or fingerprinting consumer.

6.2.2 Creating a simple image-hashing consumer

For the sake of simplicity, the consumer will use a simple binary hashing algorithm, MD5. There are much more sophisticated algorithms that do a much better job of creating image hashes, allowing for variations in cropping, resolution, and bit depth, but the point of this example is to illustrate RabbitMQ exchanges, not cool image-recognition algorithms.

IMPORTING THE BASE LIBRARIES AND CONNECTING TO RABBITMQ

To get started, the consumer in the "6.2.2 Hashing Consumer" notebook shares much of the same code as the RPC consumer. Most notably, though, instead of importing ch6.detect, this consumer imports Python's hashlib package:

```
import os
import hashlib
import rabbitpy
```

Similar to the RPC publisher and worker previously discussed, the image-hashing consumer will need to connect to RabbitMQ and create a channel:

```
connection = rabbitpy.Connection()
channel = connection.channel()
```

CREATING AND BINDING A QUEUE TO WORK OFF OF

Once the channel is open, you can create a queue that's automatically removed when the consumer goes away and that's exclusive to this consumer:

```
queue_name = 'hashing-worker-%s' % os.getpid()
queue = rabbitpy.Queue(channel, queue_name,
                       auto_delete=True,
                       durable=False,
                       exclusive=True)

if queue.declare():
    print('Worker queue declared')
if queue.bind('fanout-rpc-requests'):
    print('Worker queue bound')
```

HASHING THE IMAGES

The consumer is very straightforward. It will iterate through each message received and create a hashlib.md5 object, passing in the binary message data. It will then print a line with the hash. The output line could just as easily be a database insert or an RPC request to compare the hash against the database of existing hashes. Finally, the message is acknowledged and the consumer will wait for the next message to be delivered.

```
for message in queue.consume_messages():
    hash_obj = hashlib.md5(message.body)
    print('Image with correlation-id of %s has a hash of %s' %
          (message.properties['correlation_id'],
           hash_obj.hexdigest()))
message.ack()
```

> **NOTE** For storing a materialized set of hashes, Redis (http://redis.io) is an excellent choice of database. It provides quick, in-memory data structures for hash lookups and can provide very quick responses to inquiries with this type of data.

TESTING THE NEW WORKFLOW

With the new consumer written and the other applications modified, it's time to test things out. Open the "6.2.2 Hashing Consumer," "6.2.1 RPC Worker," and "6.2.1 RPC Publisher" notebooks in their own tabs in your web browser. Start by running all the cells in the "6.2.2 Hashing Consumer" notebook, then all the cells in the "6.2.1 RPC Worker" notebook, and finally send the images to kick off the process by running all the cells in the "6.2.1 RPC Publisher" notebook. You should see the same responses to the RPC publisher and consumer applications as when you ran the examples in the previous section. In addition, you should now have output similar to figure 6.9 in your "6.2.2 Hashing Consumer" application output.

```
In [*]:  # Consume messages from RabbitMQ
         for message in queue.consume_messages():

             # Create the hashing object
             hash_obj = hashlib.md5(message.body)

             # Print out the info, this might go into a database or log file
             print('Image with correlation-id of %s has a hash of %s' %
                   (message.properties['correlation_id'],
                    hash_obj.hexdigest()))

             # Acknowledge the delivery of the RPC request message
             message.ack()

Image with correlation-id of 0 has a hash of ba3acb1d632c42c4a7b7ea0eaf32b50a
Image with correlation-id of 1 has a hash of 3b2bb8455f68943745c3a362a567cba5
```

Figure 6.9   Example output of the hashing consumer in an IPython notebook

Fanout exchanges provide a great way to allow every consumer access to the fire hose of data. This can be a double-edged sword, however, because consumers can't be selective about the messages they receive. For example, let's say you wanted a single exchange that allowed different types of RPC requests to be routed through it but that performs common tasks, such as auditing each RPC request without regard to type. In such a scenario, a topic exchange would allow your RPC worker consumers to bind to routing keys specific to their task and for request audit consumers to bind with wild-card matching to all messages or a subset of them.

6.3   *Selectively routing messages with the topic exchange*

Like direct exchanges, topic exchanges will route messages to any queue bound with a matching routing key. But by using a period-delimited format, queues may bind to routing keys using wildcard-based pattern matching. By using the asterisk (*) and pound (#) characters, you can match specific parts of the routing key or even multiple parts at the same time. An asterisk will match all characters up to a period in the routing key, and the pound character will match all characters that follow, including any subsequent periods.

Figure 6.10 shows a topic exchange routing key with three parts that you can use for new profile images that have been uploaded. The first part indicates the message

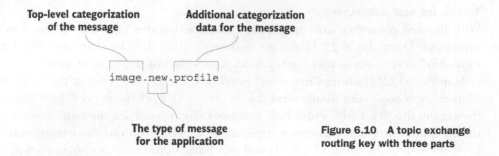

Figure 6.10   A topic exchange routing key with three parts

should be routed to consumers that know how to act on image-related messages. The second part indicates that the message contains a new image, and the third contains additional data that can be used to route the message to queues for consumers that are specific to profile-related functionality.

If we were to build out upon the image-upload process, creating a messaging-based architecture for managing all of the image-related tasks on the website, the following routing keys could describe a few of the messages that would be published.

- `image.new.profile`—For messages containing a new profile image
- `image.new.gallery`—For messages containing a new photo gallery image
- `image.delete.profile`—For messages with metadata for deleting a profile image
- `image.delete.gallery`—For messages with metadata for deleting a gallery image
- `image.resize`—For messages requesting the resizing of an image

In the preceding example routing keys, the semantic importance of the routing key should clearly stand out, describing the intent or content of the message. By using semantically named keys for messages routed through the topic exchange, a single message can be routed by subsections of the routing key, delivering the message to task-specific queues. In figure 6.11, the topic exchange determines which consumer application queues will receive a message based on how they were bound to the exchange.

A topic exchange is excellent for routing a message to queues so that single-purpose consumers can perform different actions with it. In figure 6.11, the queue for the facial-detection RPC worker is bound to `image.new.profile`, behaving as if it were bound to a direct exchange, receiving only new profile image requests. The queue for the image-hashing consumer is bound to `image.new.#`, and will receive new images regardless of origin. A consumer that maintains a materialized user directory could consume from a queue bound to `#.profile` and receive all messages ending in `.profile` to perform its materialization tasks. Image-deletion messages would be published to a queue bound to `image.delete.*`, allowing a single consumer to remove all images uploaded to the site. Finally, an auditing consumer bound to `image.#` would receive every image-related message so it could log information to help with troubleshooting or behavioral analysis.

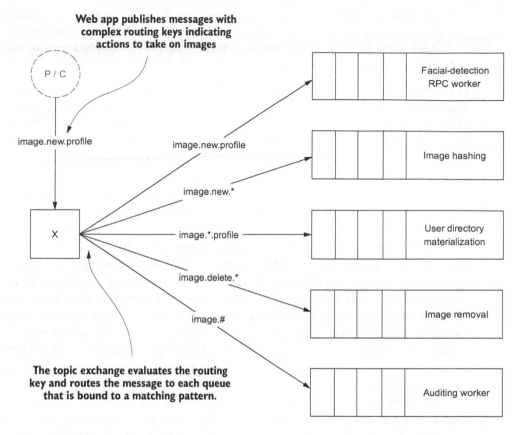

Figure 6.11   Messages are selectively routed to different queues based on the composition of their routing keys.

Single-purpose consumers leveraging architecture like this can be both easier to maintain and to scale, compared to a monolithic application performing the same actions on messages delivered to a single queue. A monolithic application increases operational and code complexity. Consider how a modular approach to writing consumer code simplifies what would otherwise be complex actions, such as moving hardware, increasing processing throughput by adding new consumers, or even just adding or removing application functionality. With a single-purpose, modular approach using a topic exchange, appropriate new functionality can be composed of a new consumer and queue without impacting the workflow and processing of other consumer applications.

NOTE   It can be useful to create routing keys that are semantically relevant to the message, describing either its intent or content. Instead of thinking about the message and its routing key as an application-specific detail, a generic, event-based approach to messaging encourages message reusability. Reduced code complexity and reduced message throughput are key benefits when developers are able to reuse existing messages in their applications. Along with virtual hosts and exchanges, routing keys should be able to provide enough semantic data about messages for any number of applications to use them without any awkward namespace-related issues.

The use of a topic exchange instead of a direct exchange is demonstrated in the "6.3 Topic Exchange Declaration," "6.3 RPC Publisher," and "6.3 RPC Worker" notebooks. The only major difference in these notebooks, as compared to the notebooks from section 6.1, is the exchange type that's declared and the routing key that's used. Running these examples should demonstrate that there's little difference between using the topic and direct exchanges when you're matching on the full routing key. But by using the topic exchange, you'll be able to perform partial pattern matching on the routing key for any other purpose in the future without having to change your messaging architecture.

Using a topic exchange with namespaced routing keys is a good choice for future-proofing your applications. Even if the pattern matching in routing is overkill for your needs at the start, a topic exchange (used with the right queue bindings) can emulate the behavior of both direct and fanout exchanges. To emulate the direct exchange behavior, bind queues with the full routing key instead of using pattern matching. Fanout exchange behavior is even easier to emulate, as queues bound with # as the routing key will receive all messages published to a topic exchange. With such flexibility, it's easy to see why the topic exchange can be a powerful tool in your messaging-based architecture.

RabbitMQ has another built-in exchange type that allows similar flexibility in routing but also allows messages to be self-describing as part of the routing process, doing away with the need for structured routing keys. The headers exchange uses a completely different routing paradigm than the direct and topic exchanges, offering an alternative view of message routing.

6.4   Selective routing with the headers exchange

The fourth built-in exchange type is the headers exchange. It allows for arbitrary routing in RabbitMQ by using the `headers` table in the message properties. Queues that are bound to the headers exchange use the `Queue.Bind` arguments parameter to pass in an array of key/value pairs to route on and an `x-match` argument. The `x-match` argument is a string value that's set to `any` or `all`. If the value is `any`, messages will be routed if any of the `headers` table values match any of the binding values. If the value of `x-match` is `all`, all values passed in as `Queue.Bind` arguments must be matched. This doesn't preclude the message from having additional key/value pairs in the `headers` table.

To demonstrate how the headers exchange is used, we'll modify the RPC worker and publisher examples from section 6.1, moving the routing key to `headers` table values. Unlike using a topic exchange, the message itself will contain the values that compose the routing criteria.

Before we modify the RPC publisher and worker to use the headers exchange, let's first declare the headers exchange. The following example creates a headers exchange named `headers-rpc-requests`; it's in the "6.4 Headers Exchange Declaration" notebook.

```
import rabbitpy

with rabbitpy.Connection() as connection:           ←──  Connects to RabbitMQ
    with connection.channel() as channel:           ←──  Opens a
        exchange = rabbitpy.Exchange(channel,             channel on the
                            'headers-rpc-requests',       connection
                            exchange_type=' headers')  ←──  Creates the
                                                            exchange
        exchange.declare()          ←──  Declares the          object
                                          exchange
```

With the exchange declared, let's examine the changes to the RPC publisher code contained in the "6.4 RPC Publisher" notebook. There are two primary changes. The first is in constructing the message that will be published. In this example, the message's `headers` property is being populated:

```
message = rabbitpy.Message(channel,
                    utils.read_image(filename),
                    {'content_type': utils.mime_type(filename),
                     'correlation_id': str(img_id),
                     'headers': {'source': 'profile',
                                 'object': 'image'
                                 'action': 'new'},
                     'reply_to': queue_name})
```

You can see that three values are being set: A value is assigned to the source, object, and action entries in the `headers` property. These are the values that will be routed on when the messages are published. Because we'll be routing on these values, there's no need for a routing key, so the `message.publish()` call is changed to only name the headers exchange the message will be routed through:

```
message.publish('headers-rpc-requests')
```

Before you run the code in this notebook, let's examine the changes to the RPC worker in the "6.4 RPC Worker" notebook and run the code there to start the consumer. The primary change is with the `Queue.Bind` call. Instead of binding to a routing key, the `Queue.Bind` call specifies the type of match required to route images to the queue and each attribute that will be matched on:

```
if queue.bind('headers-rpc-requests',
            arguments={'x-match': 'all',
                       'source': 'profile',
                       'object': 'image',
                       'action': 'new'}):
```

The value of the x-match argument is specified as all, indicating that the values of source, object, and action in the message headers must all match the values specified in the binding arguments. If you now run the "6.4 RPC Worker" notebook and then the "6.4 RPC Publisher" notebook, you should see the same results you saw with both the direct and topic exchange examples.

Is the extra metadata in the message properties worth the flexibility that the headers exchange offers? Although the headers exchange does create additional flexibility with the any and all matching capabilities, it comes with additional computational overhead in routing. When using the headers exchange, all of the values in the headers property have to be sorted by key name prior to evaluating the values when routing the message. Conventional wisdom is that the headers exchange is significantly slower than the other exchange types due to the additional computational complexity. But in benchmarking for this chapter, I found that there was no significant difference between any of the built-in exchanges with regard to performance when using the same quantity of values in the headers property.

NOTE If you're interested in the internal behavior RabbitMQ employs for sorting the headers table, check the rabbit_misc module in the rabbit-server Git repository for the sort_field_table function. The code is available on GitHub: https://github.com/rabbitmq/rabbitmq-server/blob/master/src/rabbit_misc.erl.

6.5   *Exchange performance benchmarking*

It's worth noting that the use of the headers property directly impacts the performance of message publishing regardless of the exchange type it's being published into (figure 6.12).

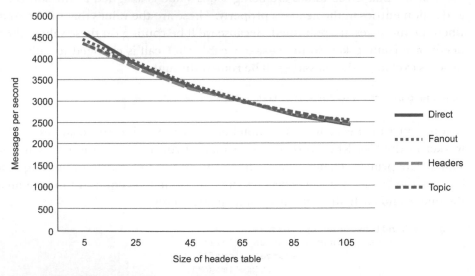

Figure 6.12   Overall publishing velocity by exchange type and header table size

As you can see, performance across the four built-in exchange types is relatively consistent. This benchmark shows that when comparing the same message with the same message headers, you won't see a dramatic difference in message publishing velocity, regardless of the exchange type.

What about a more ideal test case for the topic and the headers exchanges? Figure 6.13 compares the publishing velocity for the same message body with an empty `headers` table for the topic exchange and the routing key values in the `headers` property for the headers exchange. In this scenario, it's clear that the topic exchange is more performant than the headers exchange when doing an apples-to-apples comparison of only publishing the baseline requirements to route the message.

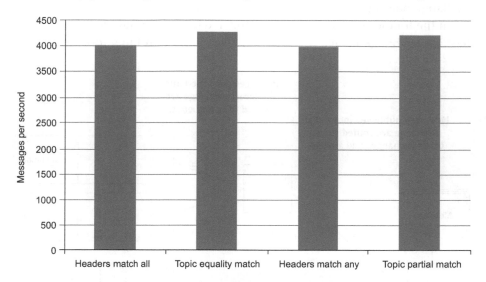

Figure 6.13   Publishing velocity of the headers and topic exchanges

If you use the `headers` property, it appears your overall message-publishing velocity won't be dramatically impacted by choosing the headers exchange, unless you end up with a fairly large table of values in the `headers` property. But this performance penalty applies to all of the built-in exchange types.

Now that you have a good idea of the capabilities of the built-in exchange types and how they perform in comparison to each other, it's time to learn how you can leverage multiple types of exchanges for a single message published to RabbitMQ.

6.6   *Going meta: exchange-to-exchange routing*

If you don't think you've been presented with enough message-routing flexibility and find that your application needs a little of one exchange type and a little of another for the exact same message, you're in luck. The RabbitMQ team added a very flexible mechanism in RabbitMQ that's not in the AMQP specification, allowing you to route messages through any combination of exchanges. The mechanism for exchange-to-exchange binding is very similar to queue binding, but instead of binding a queue to an exchange, you bind an exchange to another exchange using the Exchange.Bind RPC method.

When using exchange-to-exchange binding, the routing logic that's applied to a bound exchange is the same as it would be if the bound object were a queue. Any exchange can be bound to another exchange, including all of the built-in exchange types. This functionality allows you to chain exchanges in all sorts of imaginative ways. Do you want to route messages using namespaced keys through a topic exchange and then distribute them based upon the properties header table? If so, an exchange-to-exchange binding is the tool for you (figure 6.14).

In the following example from the "6.6 Exchange Binding" notebook, a consistent-hashing exchange named distributed-events is bound to a topic exchange named

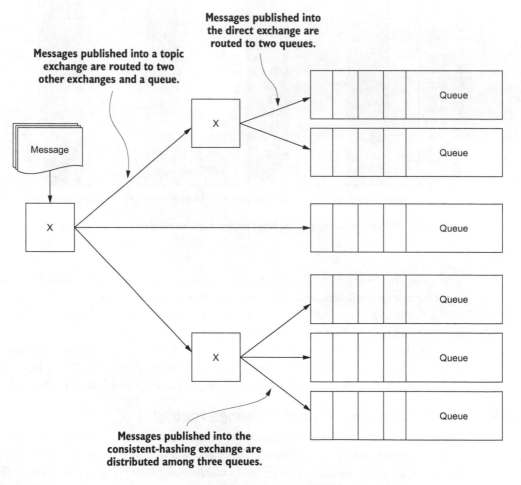

Figure 6.14   A small example of the flexibility that exchange-to-exchange binding offers

events to distribute messages routed with the any routing key among the queues bound to the consistent-hashing exchange.

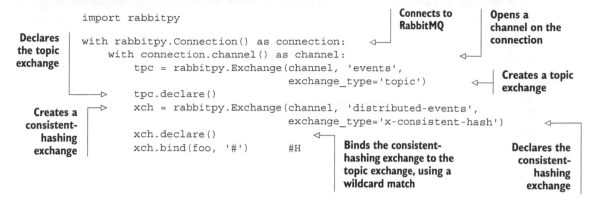

Declares the topic exchange

Connects to RabbitMQ

Opens a channel on the connection

Creates a topic exchange

Creates a consistent-hashing exchange

Binds the consistent-hashing exchange to the topic exchange, using a wildcard match

Declares the consistent-hashing exchange

```
import rabbitpy

with rabbitpy.Connection() as connection:
    with connection.channel() as channel:
        tpc = rabbitpy.Exchange(channel, 'events',
                                exchange_type='topic')
        tpc.declare()
        xch = rabbitpy.Exchange(channel, 'distributed-events',
                                exchange_type='x-consistent-hash')
        xch.declare()
        xch.bind(foo, '#')         #H
```

As a tool, exchange-to-exchange bindings create a huge amount of flexibility in the messaging patterns available to you. But with that flexibility comes extra complexity and overhead. Before you go crazy with super-complex exchange-to-exchange binding patterns, remember that simple architectures are easier to maintain and diagnose when things go wrong. If you're considering using exchange-to-exchange bindings, you should make sure that you have a use case for the functionality that warrants the extra complexity and overhead.

6.7 *Routing messages with the consistent-hashing exchange*

The consistent-hashing exchange, a plugin that's distributed with RabbitMQ, distributes data among the queues that are bound to it. It can be used to load-balance the queues that receive messages published into it. You can use it to distribute messages to queues on different physical servers in a cluster or to queues with single consumers, providing the potential for faster throughput than if RabbitMQ were distributing messages to multiple consumers in a single queue. When using databases or other systems that can directly integrate with RabbitMQ as a consumer, the consistent-hashing exchange can provide a way to shard out data without having to write middleware.

> **NOTE** If you're considering using the consistent-hashing exchange to improve consumer throughput, you should benchmark the difference between multiple consumers on a single queue and single consumers on multiple queues before deciding which is right for your environment.

The consistent-hashing exchange uses a consistent-hashing algorithm to pick which queue will receive which message, with all queues being potential destinations. Instead of queues being bound with a routing key or header values, they're bound with an integer-based weight that's used as part of the algorithm for determining message delivery. Consistent-hashing algorithms are commonly used in clients for network-based caching systems like memcached and in distributed database systems like Riak and Cassandra, and in PostgreSQL (when using the PL/Proxy sharding methodology). For data sets or in the case of messages with a high level of entropy in the string values for routing, the consistent-hashing exchange provides a fairly uniform method of distributing data. With two queues bound to a consistent-hashing exchange, each with an equal weight, the distribution of messages will be approximately split in half (figure 6.15).

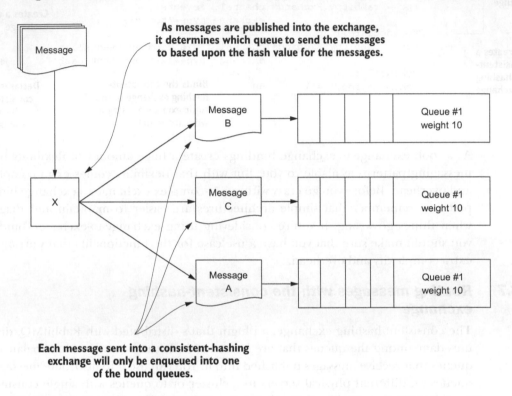

Figure 6.15 Messages published into the consistent-hashing exchange are distributed among the bound queues.

When selecting a destination for a message, there's no explicit effort made to ensure an even distribution of the messages. The consistent-hashing exchange doesn't round-robin the messages, but rather deterministically routes messages based upon a hash value of the routing key or a message properties header-type value. But a queue with a higher weight than any other queue should receive a higher percentage of the messages published into the exchange. Of course, the distribution of messages across multiple queues assumes that you're publishing messages with different routing keys or header table values. The differences in those values provide the entropy required to distribute the messages. Five messages sent with the same routing key would all end up in the same queue.

In our image-processing RPC system, it's likely that images will need to be stored in some fashion to be served to other HTTP clients. At some point in dealing with the scaling demands of image storage, it's common to need to use a distributed storage solution. In the following examples, we'll employ the consistent-hashing exchange to distribute messages across four queues that could be used to store the images on four different storage servers.

By default, the routing key is the value that's hashed for distributing the messages. For an image, one possible routing key value is a hash of the image itself, similar to the hash that's generated in the "6.2.2 Hashing Consumer" notebook. If you intend to distribute messages via hashes of the routing key values, nothing special is required when declaring the exchange. This is demonstrated in the "6.7 A Consistent-Hashing Exchange that Routes on a Routing Key" notebook.

```
import rabbitpy                                          Connects to
                                                          RabbitMQ              Opens a
with rabbitpy.Connection() as connection:         <——                          channel on the
    with connection.channel() as channel:                           <——        connection
        exchange = rabbitpy.Exchange(channel, 'image-storage',
                                      exchange_type='x-consistent-hash')
        exchange.declare()                        <——
                                                       Declares the
                                                       exchange
```

Creates the consistent-hash exchange object →

Alternatively, you could hash on a value in the headers property table. To route this way, you must pass a `hash-header` value in when declaring the exchange. The `hash-header` value contains the single key in the `headers` table that will contain the value to hash the message with. This is demonstrated in the following code snippet from the "6.7 A Consistent-Hashing Exchange that Routes on a Header" notebook.

```
import rabbitpy                                          Connects to
                                                          RabbitMQ              Opens a
with rabbitpy.Connection() as connection:         <——                          channel on the
    with connection.channel() as channel:                           <——        connection
        exchange = rabbitpy.Exchange(channel, 'image-storage',
                                      exchange_type='x-consistent-hash',
                                      arguments={'hash-header':
                                                  'image-hash'})
        exchange.declare()                        <——
                                                       Declares
                                                       exchange
```

Creates the consistent-hash exchange object that hashes on the headers table value for key →

When binding a queue to the consistent-hash exchange, you enter the weight of the queue for the hashing algorithm as a string value. For example, if you'd like to declare a queue with a weight of 10, you'd pass in the string value of 10 as the binding key in the `Queue.Bind` AMQP RPC request. Using the image storage example, suppose that your servers for storing the images each have different storage capacities. You could use the weight value to prefer larger servers over smaller ones. You could even specify the weights as the capacity size in gigabytes or terabytes to try to balance the distribution as closely as possible. The following example, from the "6.7 Creating Multiple Bound Queues" notebook, will create four queues named q0, q1, q2, and q3 and bind all of them equally against an exchange named image-storage.

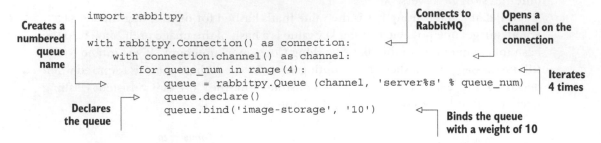

It's important to note that, because of the way the consistent-hashing algorithm works, should you change the number of queues that are bound to the exchange, the distribution of messages will most likely change. If a message with a specific routing key or header table value always goes into q0, and you add a new queue named q4, it may end up in any of the five queues, and messages with the same routing key will consistently go to that queue until the number of queues changes again.

To further illustrate how the distribution of data with a consistent-hashing exchange works, the following code, from the "6.7 Simulated Image Publisher" notebook, publishes 100,000 messages to the image-storage exchange. The routing keys are MD5 hashes of the current time and message number concatenated, because providing 100,000 images would be a bit excessive for this example. The results of the distribution are shown in the bar graph in figure 6.16.

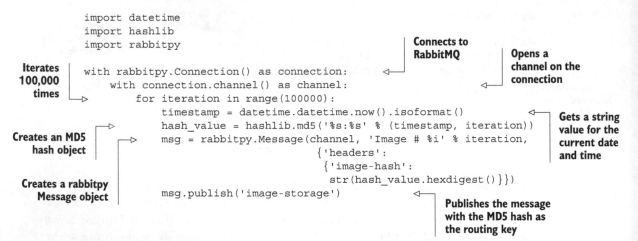

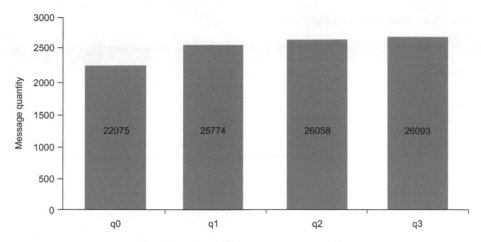

Figure 6.16 The distribution of 100,000 messages with fairly random hashes

As you can see, the distribution is close but not exact. This is because the decision of where to place the queue is determined by the value used in routing, and it can't truly load-balance messages in a round-robin way without very specific routing key values being crafted to ensure this behavior. If you're looking to load-balance your messages among multiple queues but don't want to use the consistent hashing approach, take a look at John Brisbin's random exchange (https://github.com/jbrisbin/random-exchange). Instead of looking at the routing key to distribute the message among the queues, it uses random number generation. Given RabbitMQ's plugin flexibility, it wouldn't be surprising if a true round-robin exchange were to surface in the future. If this is something that interests you, perhaps it's something you'll be able to write.

If you're looking to leverage a consistent-hashing exchange to increase throughput, you should look before you leap, as it's not typically required to increase performance or message throughput. But if you need to perform tasks like distributing subsets of messages across data centers or RabbitMQ clusters, the consistent-hashing exchange can be a valuable tool.

6.8 Summary

By now you should have a good understanding of the various routing mechanisms built into RabbitMQ. If you need to come back for reference, table 6.1 contains a quick summary of the exchanges and their descriptions. Each exchange type offers distinct functionality that can be leveraged in your applications to ensure that messages are routed to the proper consumers as quickly as possible.

Remember that messages can often be reused in ways that aren't initially evident when creating your architecture, so I recommend incorporating as much flexibility as possible when creating your messaging architecture. By using topic exchanges with namespaced semantic routing keys, you can easily tap into the flow of messages, a task

Table 6.1   Summary of exchange types

Name	Plugin	Description
Direct	No	Routes to bound queues based upon the value of a routing key. Performs equality matches only.
Fanout	No	Routes to all bound queues regardless of the routing key presented with a message.
Topic	No	Routes to all bound queues using routing key pattern matching and string equality.
Headers	No	Routes messages to bound queues based upon the values in the message properties `headers` table.
Consistent-hashing	Yes	Behaves like a fanout exchange but routes to bound queues, distributing messages based on the hashed value of a routing key or message properties header value.

that may be more difficult than if you use a direct exchange as your main routing mechanism. Topic exchanges should be able to provide almost the same level of flexibility that the headers exchange allows for, without the protocol lock-in of having to have AMQP message properties for routing.

At their core, exchanges are simply routing mechanisms for the messages that flow through RabbitMQ. A wide variety of exchange plugins exist, from exchanges that store messages in databases, like the Riak exchange (https://github.com/jbrisbin/riak-exchange), to exchanges with a memory, like the Message History exchange (https://github.com/videlalvaro/rabbitmq-recent-history-exchange).

In the next chapter you'll learn how to join two or more RabbitMQ servers into a cohesive messaging cluster, providing a way to scale out your messaging throughput and add stronger message guarantees using highly available queues.

Part 2

Managing RabbitMQ
in the data center
or the cloud

Introducing RabbitMQ in the early stages of an application's development lifecycle is a real boost to the application's architecture. But code isn't thrown "over the fence" to production infrastructure teams anymore; as developers, it's our responsibility to have a good understanding of the setup in our infrastructure.

This part of the book deals with using RabbitMQ in clusters: setting up clusters, exploring how they behave, and managing them. We'll also look at message distribution and replication across the web: dealing with federated exchanges and queues allowing the physical separation of two or more clusters, and replicating through these clusters.

Scaling RabbitMQ with clusters

7

This chapter covers

- Cluster management
- How queue location can impact performance
- The steps involved in setting up a cluster
- What to do when nodes crash

As a message broker, RabbitMQ is perfect for standalone applications. But suppose your application needs additional delivery guarantees that only highly available queues will satisfy. Or maybe you want to use RabbitMQ as a central messaging hub for many applications. RabbitMQ's built-in clustering capabilities provide a robust, cohesive environment that can span multiple servers.

I'll start by describing the features and behaviors of RabbitMQ clusters, and then you'll set up a two-node RabbitMQ cluster in the Vagrant virtual machine (VM) environment. In addition, you'll learn how queue placement is important for a performant cluster and how to set up HA queues. You'll also learn how RabbitMQ's clustering works at a low level and what server resources are most important to ensure cluster performance and stability. Closing out the chapter, you'll learn how to recover from crashes and node failures.

7.1   *About clusters*

A RabbitMQ cluster creates a seamless view of RabbitMQ across two or more servers. In a RabbitMQ cluster, runtime state containing exchanges, queues, bindings, users, virtual hosts, and policies are available to every node. Because of this shared runtime state, every node in a cluster can bind, publish, or delete an exchange that was created when connected to the first node (figure 7.1).

RabbitMQ's cohesive clusters create a compelling way to scale RabbitMQ. In addition, clusters provide a mechanism that allows you to create a structured architecture for your publishers and consumers. In larger cluster environments, it's not uncommon to have nodes dedicated to specific tasks or queues. For example, you might have cluster nodes that act strictly as publishing front ends and others that are strictly used for queues and consumers. If you're looking to create fault tolerance in your RabbitMQ environment, clusters provide an excellent way to create HA queues. HA queues span multiple cluster nodes and share a synchronized queue state, including message data. Should any node with an HA queue fail, the other nodes in the cluster will still contain the messages and queue state. When the failed node rejoins the cluster, the newly rejoined node will fully synchronize once any messages that were added while the node was down are consumed.

Despite the advantages of using RabbitMQ's built-in clustering, it's important to recognize the limitations and downsides of RabbitMQ clustering. First, clusters are designed for low-latency environments. You should never create RabbitMQ clusters across a WAN or internet connection. State synchronization and cross-node message delivery demand low-latency communication that can only be achieved on a LAN. You can run RabbitMQ in cloud environments such as Amazon EC2, but not across availability zones. To synchronize RabbitMQ messages in high-latency environments, you'll want to look at the Shovel and Federation tools outlined in the next chapter.

Another important issue to consider with RabbitMQ clusters is cluster size. The work and overhead of maintaining the shared state of a cluster is directly proportionate to

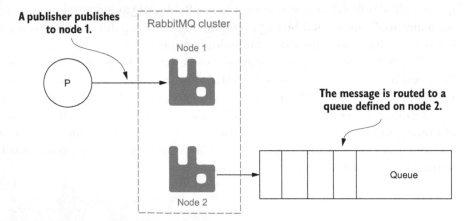

Figure 7.1   Cross-node publishing of messages in a cluster

the number of nodes in the cluster. For example, using the management API to gather statistical data in a large cluster can take considerably longer than in a single node. Such actions can only be as fast as the slowest node to respond. Conventional wisdom in the RabbitMQ community calls for an upper bound of 32 to 64 nodes in a cluster. Remember, as you add a node to a cluster, you're adding complexity to the synchronization of the cluster. Each node in a cluster must know about every other node in the cluster. This non-linear complexity can slow down cross-node message delivery and cluster management. Fortunately, even with this complexity, the RabbitMQ management UI can handle large clusters.

7.1.1 Clusters and the management UI

The RabbitMQ management UI is built to perform all of the same actions on a cluster that it performs with a single node, and it's a great tool for understanding your RabbitMQ clusters once they've been created. The Overview page of the management UI contains top-level information about a RabbitMQ cluster and its nodes (figure 7.2).

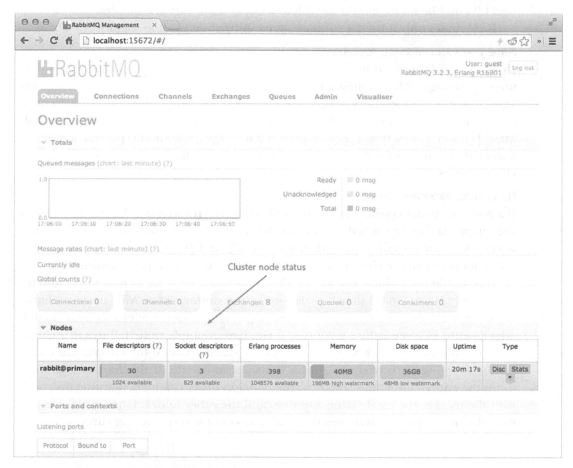

Figure 7.2 The management interface, highlighting cluster status with a single node

In the highlighted area of figure 7.2, cluster nodes are listed with columns that describe their general health and state. As you add nodes to a cluster, they'll be added to the table. In larger clusters, this table may take more time to refresh, as each time the API is called to gather the information, each node in the cluster is queried for updated information prior to returning a response.

But before we go too deep into the management UI with regard to clusters, it's important to understand the types of nodes in a RabbitMQ cluster.

7.1.2 Cluster node types

There are multiple node types with different behavior in a RabbitMQ cluster. When a node is added to a cluster, it carries with it one of two primary designations: disk node or RAM node.

Disk nodes store the runtime state of a cluster to both RAM and disk. In RabbitMQ, runtime state includes the definition of exchanges, queues, bindings, virtual hosts, users, and policies. Because of this, in clusters with large amounts of runtime state, disk I/O may be more of an issue with disk nodes than with RAM nodes.

RAM nodes only store the runtime state information in an in-memory database.

NODE TYPES AND MESSAGE PERSISTENCE

Designation of a disk node or a RAM node doesn't control the behavior of persistent message storage. When a message is marked as persistent in the `delivery-mode` message property, the message will be written to disk regardless of the node type. Because of this, it's important to consider the impact that disk I/O may have on your RabbitMQ cluster nodes. If you require persisted messages, you should provide a disk subsystem that can handle the write velocity required by the queues that live on your cluster nodes.

NODE TYPES AND CRASH BEHAVIOR

If a node or cluster crashes, disk nodes will be used to reconstruct the runtime state of the cluster as they're started and rejoin the cluster. RAM nodes, on the other hand, won't contain any runtime state data when they join a cluster. Upon rejoining a cluster, other nodes in the cluster will send it information such as queue definitions.

You should always have at least one disk node when creating a cluster, and in some cases more. Having more than one disk node in a cluster can provide more resilience in the event of hardware failures. But having multiple disk nodes can be a double-edged sword in some failure scenarios. If you have multiple node failures in a cluster with two disk nodes that don't agree about the shared state of the cluster, you'll have problems trying to recover the cluster to its previous state. If this happens, shutting down the entire cluster and restarting the nodes in order can help. Start the disk node with the most correct state data, and then add the other nodes. Later in this chapter we'll discuss additional strategies for troubleshooting and recovering clusters.

THE STATS NODE

If you use the rabbitmq-management plugin, there's an additional node type that only works in conjunction with disk nodes: the stats node. The stats node is responsible for gathering all of the statistical and state data from each node in a cluster. Only one node in a cluster can be the stats node at any given time. A good strategy for larger cluster setups is to have a dedicated management node that's your primary disk node and the stats node, and to have at least one more disk node to provide failover capabilities (figure 7.3).

Depending on the frequency and use of the management API and the quantity of resources used in RabbitMQ, there can be a high CPU cost for running the management API. Running a dedicated management node ensures that message delivery doesn't slow statistics gathering, and statistics gathering doesn't impact message delivery rates.

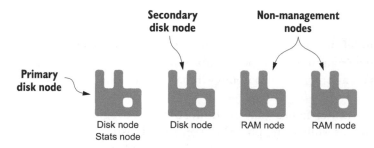

Figure 7.3   A cluster with a secondary disk node and two RAM-only nodes

In a cluster topology setup with two disk nodes, if the primary node fails, the stats node designation will be transferred to the secondary disk node. Should the primary disk node come back up, it will not regain the stats node designation unless the secondary disk node with the stats node designation stops or leaves the cluster.

The stats node plays an important part in managing your RabbitMQ clusters. Without the rabbitmq-management plugin and a stats node, it can be difficult to get cluster-wide visibility of performance, connections, queue depths, and operational issues.

7.1.3   *Clusters and queue behavior*

A message published into any cluster node will be properly routed to a queue without regard to where that queue exists in the cluster. When a queue is declared, it's created on the cluster node the `Queue.Declare` RPC request was sent to. Which node a queue is declared on can have an impact on message throughput and performance. A node with too many queues, publishers, and consumers can be slower than if the queues, publishers, and consumers were balanced across nodes in a cluster. In addition to not evenly distributing resource utilization, not considering the location of a queue in a cluster can have an impact on both publishing and consuming.

You might recognize figure 7.4, which is slightly modified from a figure in chapter 4. When publishing to a cluster, this scale becomes even more important than on a single RabbitMQ server.

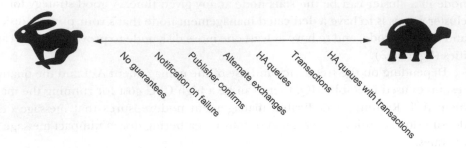

Figure 7.4   Performance of delivery guarantee options in RabbitMQ

As you move from left to right on the scale, the amount of cross-cluster communication between nodes is amplified. If you're publishing messages on one node that are routed to queues on another, the two nodes will have to coordinate on a delivery guarantee method.

For example, consider figure 7.5, which illustrates the logical steps for messages published across nodes while using publisher confirmations.

Although the steps outlined in figure 7.5 wouldn't greatly reduce message throughput, you should consider the complexity of confirmation behavior when creating your messaging architecture using clusters. Benchmark the various methods with publishers

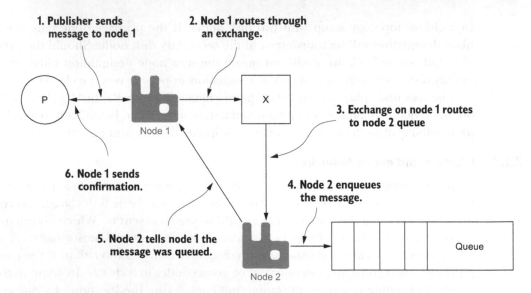

Figure 7.5   Multi-node publishing with consumer confirmations

and consumers on the various nodes, and see what works best for you. Throughput might not be the best indicator of the successful implementation of a messaging architecture; poor performance can surely have a negative impact.

As with a single node, publishing is only one side of the coin when it comes to message throughput. Clusters can have an impact on message throughput for consumers too.

NODE-SPECIFIC CONSUMERS

To improve message throughput in a cluster, RabbitMQ tries to route newly published messages to pre-existing consumers whenever possible. But in queues with a backlog of messages, new messages are published across the cluster into the nodes where the queues are defined. In this scenario, performance can suffer when you connect a consumer to a node that's different than the node where the queue is defined (figure 7.6).

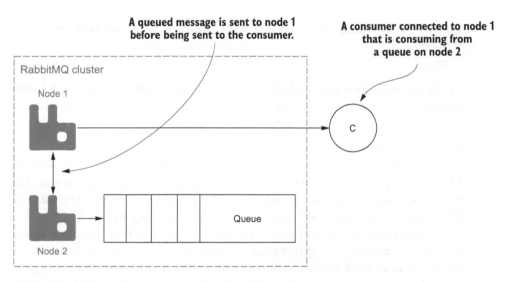

Figure 7.6 Cross-cluster node message consuming

In this scenario, messages are published into a queue located on node 2, and a consumer is connected to node 1. When messages are retrieved from the queue for the consumer connected to node 1, they must first travel through the cluster to node 1 before being delivered to the consumer. If you consider where the queue lives when connecting a consumer, you can reduce the overhead required to send the message to the consumer. Instead of having messages travel through the cluster to your consumers, the node where the queue lives can directly deliver messages to consumers connected to it (figure 7.7).

By considering queue locality and connecting to the appropriate node for consumers and publishers alike, you can reduce cross-cluster communication and improve

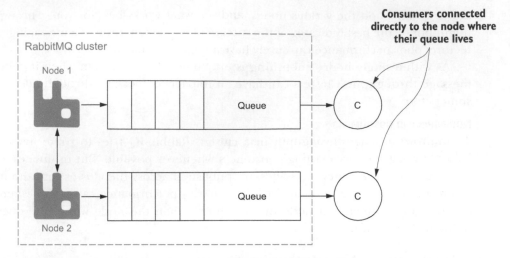

Figure 7.7   By connecting to the same node that a queue lives on, consumers can see improved throughput.

overall message throughput. High-velocity publishers and consumers will see the greatest impact on directly connecting to the appropriate nodes for their queues. That is, of course, unless you're using HA queues.

HIGHLY AVAILABLE QUEUES

It should be no surprise that using HA queues can come with a performance penalty. When placing a message in a queue or consuming a message from a queue, RabbitMQ must coordinate among all the nodes that the HA queue lives on. The more nodes an HA queue lives on, the more coordination there is among nodes.

In large clusters, you should consider just how many nodes your queue should use prior to declaring it. If you're asking for all nodes on a 24-node cluster, you're likely creating a lot of work for RabbitMQ with very little reward. Because HA queues have a copy of each message on each node, you should ask yourself if you need more than two or three nodes to ensure that you don't lose any messages.

7.2   *Cluster setup*

A RabbitMQ cluster requires two or more nodes. In this section, you'll set up a cluster using two Vagrant VMs. The Vagrant configuration you downloaded in the appendix (while doing the setup for chapter 2) has a configuration for both VMs used in the following examples. The primary VM you've used to this point will be the first server in the cluster, and you'll use the secondary VM definition in Vagrant for this chapter.

To start the process of setting up a cluster, you'll boot the secondary VM and log into it via a secure shell.

7.2.1 *Virtual machine setup*

Change to the location where you unzipped the rmqid-vagrant.zip file when setting up the environment for the book. Start the second VM by telling Vagrant to start the VM:

```
vagrant up secondary
```

This will start a second VM that you'll use to set up and experiment with RabbitMQ clustering. When it has finished setting up the VM, you should see output similar to figure 7.8.

```
○ ○ ○                    Release — vagrant@secondary: ~ — bash — 93×28
[2014-02-23T21:54:50+00:00] INFO: Enabling RabbitMQ plugin 'rabbitmq_web_stomp_examples'.
[2014-02-23T21:54:50+00:00] INFO: rabbitmq_plugin[rabbitmq_web_stomp_examples] not queuing de
layed action restart on service[rabbitmq-server] (delayed), as it's already been queued
[2014-02-23T21:54:50+00:00] INFO: execute[rabbitmq-plugins enable rabbitmq_web_stomp_examples
] ran successfully
[2014-02-23T21:55:02+00:00] INFO: execute[aptitude-update] ran successfully
[2014-02-23T21:55:03+00:00] INFO: Upgrading python_pip[pika] version from uninstalled to late
st
[2014-02-23T21:55:09+00:00] INFO: Upgrading python_pip[pamqp] version from uninstalled to lat
est
[2014-02-23T21:55:15+00:00] INFO: Upgrading python_pip[rabbitpy] version from uninstalled to
latest
[2014-02-23T21:55:21+00:00] INFO: Upgrading python_pip[mosquitto] version from uninstalled to
 latest
[2014-02-23T21:55:27+00:00] INFO: Upgrading python_pip[stomp.py] version from uninstalled to
latest
[2014-02-23T21:55:33+00:00] INFO: cookbook_file[/etc/hosts] backed up to /var/chef/backup/etc
/hosts.chef-20140223215533.386396
[2014-02-23T21:55:33+00:00] INFO: cookbook_file[/etc/hosts] updated file contents /etc/hosts
[2014-02-23T21:55:38+00:00] INFO: execute[update-cookie] ran successfully
[2014-02-23T21:55:38+00:00] INFO: file[/var/lib/rabbitmq/.erlang.cookie] sending restart acti
on to service[rabbitmq-server] (delayed)
[2014-02-23T21:55:43+00:00] INFO: service[rabbitmq-server] restarted
[2014-02-23T21:55:43+00:00] INFO: Chef Run complete in 72.684514531 seconds
[2014-02-23T21:55:43+00:00] INFO: Running report handlers
[2014-02-23T21:55:43+00:00] INFO: Report handlers complete
[2014-02-23T21:54:31+00:00] INFO: Forking chef instance to converge...
gmr-home:Release gmr$ ▊
```

Figure 7.8 Output of `vagrant up secondary`

With the VM running, you can now open a secure shell by running the following Vagrant command in the same directory:

```
vagrant ssh secondary
```

You should now be connected into the second VM as the `vagrant` user. You'll need to run your commands as the root user, however, so switch to the root user with the following command:

```
sudo su -
```

When you run this command, the prompt you see in the secure shell should change from `vagrant@secondary:~$` to `root@secondary:~#` indicating that you're now logged in as the root user in the VM. As the root user, you'll have permission to run the `rabbit-mqctl` script to communicate with the local RabbitMQ server instance on the box.

Now it's time to set up the cluster.

7.2.2   *Adding nodes to the cluster*

There are two ways to add nodes to a cluster with RabbitMQ.

The first involves editing the rabbitmq.config configuration file and defining each node in a cluster. This method is preferred if you're using an automated configuration management tool, such as Chef (www.getchef.com) or Puppet (www.puppetlabs.com) and you have a well-defined cluster from the outset. Before you create a cluster via the rabbitmq.config file, it's useful to create one manually.

Alternatively, you can add and remove nodes from a cluster in an ad hoc manner by using the `rabbitmqctl` command-line tool. This method provides a less rigid structure for learning about RabbitMQ cluster behavior and is good to know for troubleshooting degraded clusters. You'll use `rabbitmqctl` to create a cluster between the VMs in this section, but prior to doing so, you should know something about Erlang cookies and their impact on RabbitMQ clustering.

ERLANG COOKIES

To communicate between nodes, RabbitMQ uses the built-in, multi-node communication mechanisms in Erlang. To secure this multi-node communication, Erlang and the RabbitMQ process have a shared secret file called a *cookie*. The Erlang cookie file for RabbitMQ is contained in the RabbitMQ data directory. On *NIX platforms, the file is usually at /var/lib/rabbitmq/.erlang.cookie, though this can vary by distribution and package. The cookie file contains a short string and should be the same on every node in a cluster. If the cookie file isn't the same on each node in the cluster, the nodes won't be able to communicate with each other.

The cookie file will be created the first time you run RabbitMQ on any given server, or if the file is missing. When setting up a cluster, you should ensure that RabbitMQ isn't running and you overwrite the cookie file with the shared cookie file prior to starting RabbitMQ again. The Chef cookbooks that set up the Vagrant VMs for this book have already set up the Erlang cookie to match on both machines. That means you can get started creating a cluster using `rabbitmqctl`.

> **NOTE**   Using `rabbitmqctl` is an easy way to add and remove nodes in a cluster. It can also be used to change a node from a disk node to a RAM node and back. `rabbitmqctl` is a wrapper to an Erlang application that communicates with RabbitMQ. As such, it also needs access to the Erlang cookie. When you run the command as root, it knows where to look for the cookie file and will use it if it can. If you have trouble using `rabbitmqctl` in your production environment, make sure the user you're running `rabbitmqctl` as either has access to the RabbitMQ Erlang cookie, or has a copy of the file in its home directory.

CREATING AD HOC CLUSTERS

With RabbitMQ running on the node, and you logged in as the root user, you can now add the secondary VM node, creating a cluster with the primary VM node.

To do so, you must first tell RabbitMQ on the secondary node to stop using `rabbitmqctl`. You won't be stopping the RabbitMQ server process itself, but using `rabbitmq` to instruct RabbitMQ to halt internal processes in Erlang that allow it to process connections. Run the following command in the terminal:

```
rabbitmqctl stop_app
```

You should see output similar to the following:

```
Stopping node rabbit@secondary ...
...done.
```

Now that the process has stopped, you need to erase the state in this RabbitMQ node, making it forget any runtime configuration data or state that it has. To do this, you'll instruct it to reset its internal database:

```
rabbitmqctl reset
```

You should see a response similar to this:

```
Resetting node rabbit@secondary ...
...done.
```

Now you can join it to the primary node and form the cluster:

```
rabbitmqctl join_cluster rabbit@primary
```

This should return with the following output:

```
Clustering node rabbit@secondary with rabbit@primary ...
...done.
```

Finally, start the server again using the following command:

```
rabbitmqctl start_app
```

You should see the output that follows:

```
Starting node rabbit@secondary ...
...done.
```

Congratulations! You now have a running RabbitMQ cluster with two nodes. If you open the management UI in your browser at http://localhost:15672 you should see an Overview page similar to figure 7.9.

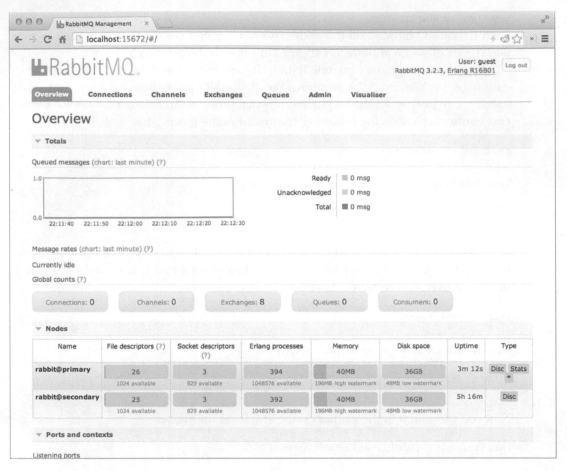

Figure 7.9   A two-node RabbitMQ cluster

CONFIGURATION-BASED CLUSTERS

Creating a cluster using the configuration file can be a little trickier. When you set up the cluster using `rabbitmqctl`, you issued the `reset` command to the server, telling it to forget all of its state and internal data. With configuration-file-based clusters, you can't do this, as RabbitMQ attempts to join a node to the cluster when the server starts. If you install RabbitMQ and the server starts before you create the configuration file that has the cluster definition in it, the node will fail to join the cluster.

If you're using a configuration management tool, one way around this is to create the /etc/rabbitmq.config file prior to installing RabbitMQ. The new installation shouldn't overwrite the pre-existing configuration file. During this same phase of configuration, it's a good idea to write the Erlang cookie file that's shared across all nodes of the cluster.

Defining a cluster in configuration is straightforward. In the /etc/rabbitmq.config file, there's a stanza named `cluster_nodes` that carries the list of nodes in the cluster and indicates whether the node is a disk node or a RAM node. The following configuration snippet would be used to define the VM cluster you previously created:

```
[{rabbit,
  [{cluster_nodes, {['rabbit@primary', 'rabbit@secondary'], disc}}]
}].
```

If you were to use this configuration on both nodes, they'd both be set up as disk nodes in the cluster. If you wanted to make the secondary node a RAM node, you could change the configuration, substituting the `disc` keyword with `ram`:

```
[{rabbit,
  [{cluster_nodes, {['rabbit@primary', 'rabbit@secondary'], ram}}]
}].
```

A downside to configuration-based clusters is that because they're defined in the configuration file, adding and removing nodes requires updating the configuration of all nodes in the cluster prior to a node being added or removed. It's also worth noting that cluster information is ultimately stored as state data in the disk nodes in a cluster. Defining the cluster in the configuration file tells RabbitMQ nodes to join a cluster the first time they start up. This means that if you change your topology or configuration, it won't impact that node's membership in a cluster.

7.3 Summary

Clustering in RabbitMQ is a powerful way to scale your messaging architecture and create redundancy in your publishing and consuming endpoints. Although RabbitMQ's cohesive cluster topology allows for publishing and consuming from any node in a cluster, publishers and consumers should consider the location of the queues they're working with to achieve the highest throughput.

For LAN environments, clusters provide a solid platform for the growth of your messaging platform, but clusters aren't meant for high-latency networks such as WANs and the internet. To connect RabbitMQ nodes across WANs or the internet, RabbitMQ comes with two plugins that we'll discuss in the next chapter.

Cross-cluster
message distribution

This chapter covers

- Federated exchanges and queues
- How to set up multiple federated RabbitMQ nodes in Amazon Web Services
- Different patterns of use for RabbitMQ federation

Whether you're looking to implement messaging across data centers, upgrade RabbitMQ, or provide transparent access to messages in different RabbitMQ clusters, you'll want to take a look at the federation plugin. Distributed with RabbitMQ as a stock plugin, the federation plugin provides two different ways to get messages from one cluster to another. By using a federated exchange, messages published to an exchange in another RabbitMQ server or cluster are automatically routed to bound exchanges and queues on the downstream host. Alternatively, if your needs are more specific, federated queues provide a way to target the messages in a single queue instead of an exchange. In either scenario, the goal is to transparently relay messages from the upstream node where they were originally published to the downstream node (figure 8.1).

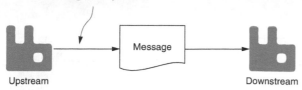

Messages are sent from the upstream node to the downstream node's exchanges or queues.

Upstream

Message

Downstream

Figure 8.1   Messages are sent to the downstream node's exchanges and queues from the upstream node.

8.1   Federating exchanges and queues

To figure out if federation has a place in your message topology, it helps to understand how federation works and what you can expect when you use the federation plugin. Provided as part of the core RabbitMQ distribution, the federation plugin provides flexible ways to transparently relay messages between nodes and clusters. The functionality of the plugin is divided into two main components: federated exchanges and federated queues.

Federated exchanges allow for messages published to an exchange on an upstream node to transparently be published to an exchange of the same name on the downstream node. Federated queues, on the other hand, allow for downstream nodes to act as consumers of shared queues on upstream nodes, providing the ability to round-robin messages across multiple downstream nodes.

Later in this chapter you'll set up a test environment where you can experiment with both types of federation, but first let's explore how each works.

8.1.1   Federated exchanges

Suppose you're tasked with adding the ability to do large-scale data processing of user behavior related to your pre-existing web application running in the cloud. The application is a large-scale, user-driven news site, like Reddit or Slashdot, and the application already uses a messaging-based topology where events are raised when the user takes actions on your site. When users log in, post articles, or leave comments, instead of directly writing the content to the database, messages are published to RabbitMQ and consumers perform the database writes (figure 8.2).

Because the web application's database write operations are decoupled using RabbitMQ as the middleware between the application and the consumer that writes to the database, you can easily tap into the message stream to write the data to a data warehouse for analysis as well. One way you could go about this is to add a consumer local to the web application that writes to the data warehouse. But what do you do when the infrastructure and storage for your data warehouse is located elsewhere?

As we discussed in the last chapter, RabbitMQ's built-in clustering capabilities require low-latency networks where network partitions are rare. The term *network partition* refers to nodes on a network being unable to communicate with each other.

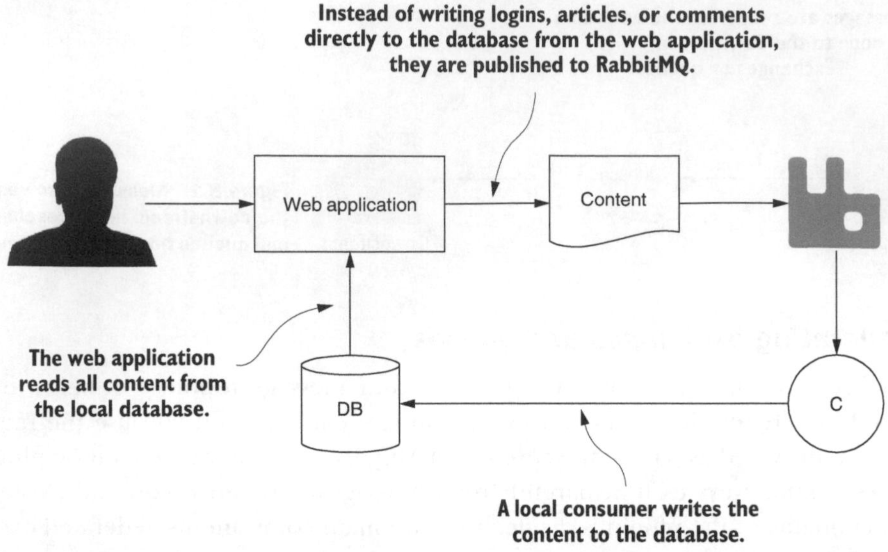
Instead of writing logins, articles, or comments directly to the database from the web application, they are published to RabbitMQ.
Web application
Content
The web application reads all content from the local database.
DB
C
A local consumer writes the content to the database.

Figure 8.2 A web application with decoupled writes, prior to adding federation

When you're connecting over high-latency network connections, such as the internet, network partitions aren't uncommon and should be accounted for. Fortunately, RabbitMQ has a bundled plugin for federating nodes that can be used in these very situations. The federation plugin allows for a downstream RabbitMQ server that federates messages from the pre-existing RabbitMQ server (figure 8.3).

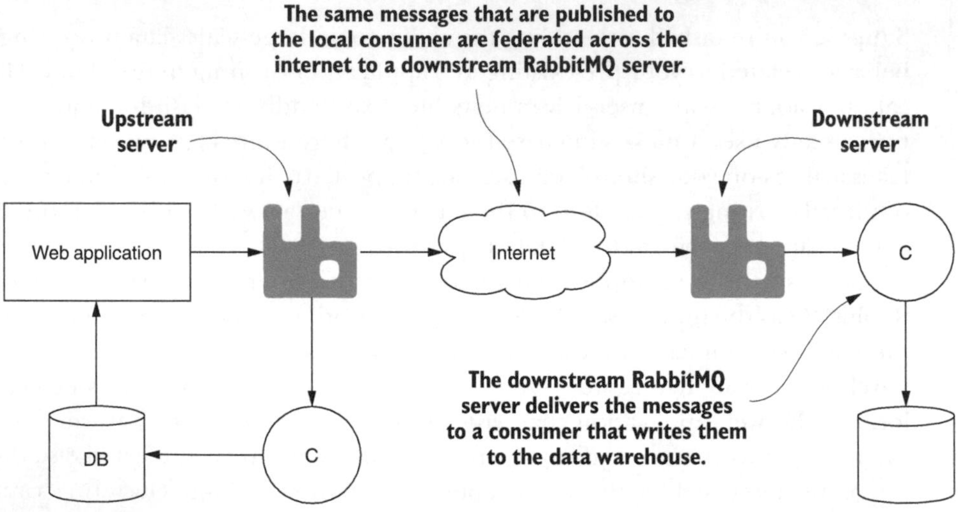
The same messages that are published to the local consumer are federated across the internet to a downstream RabbitMQ server.
Upstream server
Downstream server
Web application
Internet
C
DB
C
The downstream RabbitMQ server delivers the messages to a consumer that writes them to the data warehouse.

Figure 8.3 The same web application with a federated downstream RabbitMQ server storing messages in the data warehouse

When the federated server is set up, all you have to do is create policies that apply to the exchanges you need the messages from. If the upstream RabbitMQ server has an exchange called events that the login, article, and comment messages are published into, your downstream RabbitMQ server should create a federation policy matching that exchange name. When you create the exchange on the downstream RabbitMQ and bind a queue to it, the policy will tell RabbitMQ to connect to the upstream server and start publishing messages to the downstream queue.

Once RabbitMQ is publishing messages from the upstream server to the downstream queue, you don't have to worry about what will happen if the internet connectivity is severed between the two. When connectivity is restored, RabbitMQ will dutifully reconnect to the main RabbitMQ cluster and start locally queuing all of the messages that were published by the website while the connection was down. After a bit of time, the downstream consumer should catch up, and you won't need to lift a finger. Does this sound like magic? Perhaps, but there's nothing magical about it under the covers.

An exchange with a federation policy on the host gets its own special process in RabbitMQ. When an exchange has a policy applied, it will connect to all of the upstream nodes defined in the policy and create a work queue where it can receive messages. The process for that exchange then registers as a consumer of the work queue and waits for messages to start arriving. Bindings on exchange in the downstream node are automatically applied to the exchange and work queue in the upstream node, causing the upstream RabbitMQ node to publish messages to the downstream consumer. When that consumer receives a message, it publishes the message to the local exchange, just as any other message publisher would. The messages, with a few extra headers attached, are routed to their proper destination (figure 8.4).

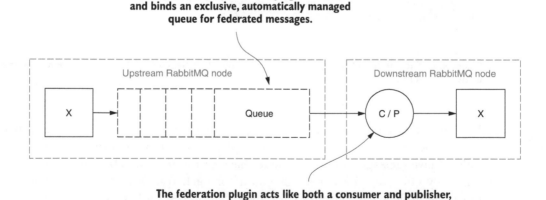

Figure 8.4   The federation plugin creates a work queue on the upstream RabbitMQ node.

As you can see, federated exchanges provide a simple, reliable, and robust way to extend your RabbitMQ infrastructure across network latencies that RabbitMQ clustering doesn't allow. Additionally, it allows you to bridge logically separated RabbitMQ clusters, such as two clusters in the same data center running different versions of RabbitMQ.

The federated exchange is a powerful tool that can cast a wide net in your messaging infrastructure, but what if your needs are more specific? Federated queues can also provide a more focused way of distributing messages across RabbitMQ clusters that even allows for round-robin behavior among multiple downstream nodes and RabbitMQ consumers.

8.1.2 Federated queues

A newer addition to the federation plugin—*queue-based federation*—provides a way to scale out queue capacity. This is especially useful for messaging workloads where a particular queue may have heavy spikes of publishing activity and much slower or throttled consuming. When using a federated queue, message publishers use the upstream node or cluster, and messages are distributed to the same-named queue across all downstream nodes (figure 8.5).

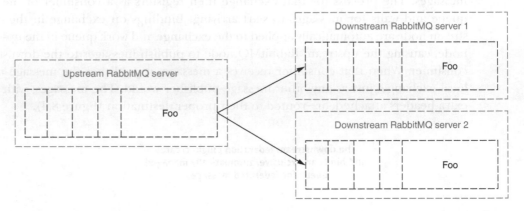

Figure 8.5   The upstream "foo" queue has its messages load-balanced between two RabbitMQ servers using the federation plugin.

Like the upstream queue, downstream queues can exist on a single node or as part of an HA queue in a cluster. The federation plugin ensures that downstream queues will only receive messages when the queues have consumers available for processing messages. By checking the consumer count for each queue and only binding to the upstream node when consumers are present, it prevents idle messages from collecting in consumerless queues.

As you go through the configuration-related examples later in this chapter, you'll see that there's very little difference between the configuration of federated queues and exchanges. In fact, the default configuration for federation targets both exchanges and queues.

8.2 Creating the RabbitMQ virtual machines

In the rest of this chapter, we'll use free Amazon EC2 instances to set up multiple RabbitMQ servers that will use federation to transparently distribute messages without clustering. If you'd rather use your own cloud provider or pre-existing network and servers, the concepts remain the same. If you choose not to use Amazon Web Services (AWS) for the examples in this chapter, just create your own servers and try to match the environment setup as closely as possible. In either scenario, you should set up two RabbitMQ servers to work with the examples.

To set up the VMs on Amazon EC2, you'll create the first instance, install and configure RabbitMQ, and then create an image of the instance, allowing you to create one or more copies of the server for experimentation. If you're not providing your own virtual servers, you'll need an AWS account. If you don't already have one, you can create one for free at http://aws.amazon.com.

8.2.1 Creating the first instance

To begin, log into the AWS console and click Create Instance. You'll be presented with a list of image templates for creating a VM. Select Ubuntu Server from the list (figure 8.6).

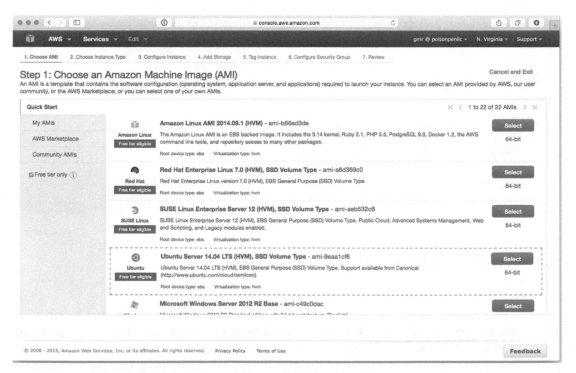

Figure 8.6   Selecting an AMI to launch an Amazon EC2 instance

Once it's selected, you'll be presented with the next step, choosing the instance type. Select the general purpose t2.micro instance, which should be labeled as Free Tier Eligible.

Once the instance type is selected, you'll be presented with a configuration screen for the instance. You can leave the defaults selected on that screen and click the Next: Add Storage button. Leave the defaults on this screen as well, clicking on the Next: Tag Instance button. You don't need to do anything on this screen either. Click Next: Configure Security Group, and you'll be presented with the Security Group configuration. You'll want to modify these settings so that you can communicate with RabbitMQ. Because this is just an example, you can open ports 5672 and 15672 to the internet without any source restrictions. Click the Add Rule button to allow for a new firewall rule to be defined, and create entries for each port with the Source set to Anywhere, as illustrated in figure 8.7.

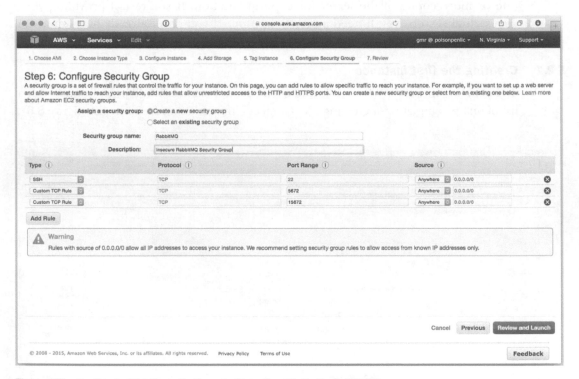

Figure 8.7   Configuring the Security Group's firewall settings for RabbitMQ

Once you've added the two rules, click the Review and Launch button. Once you're on the review screen, click Launch. You'll be presented with a dialog box allowing you to select an SSH key pair or create a new one. Select Create a New Key Pair from the first drop-down box, enter a name for it, and click Download Key Pair (figure 8.8). You'll want to save the key pair to an accessible location on your computer, as it will be used to SSH into the EC2 instance.

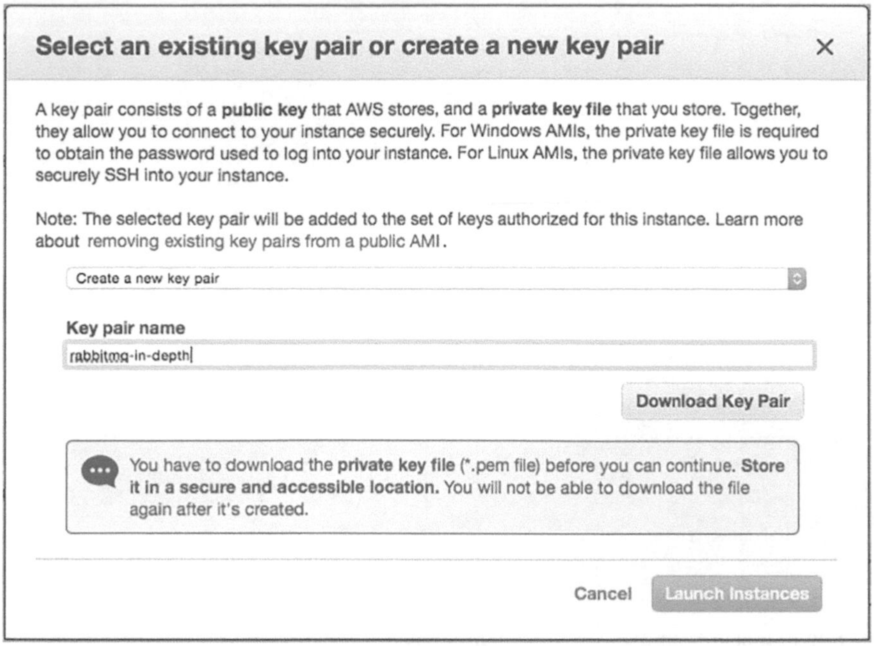

Figure 8.8   Creating a new key pair for accessing the VM

When you've downloaded the key pair, click the Launch Instance button. AWS will then begin the process of creating and starting your new VM instance. Navigate back to the EC2 dashboard, and you should see the new instance starting up or running (figure 8.9).

Once the new EC2 instance has started, it will have a public IP address and DNS. Make note of the IP address, as you'll use it to connect to the VM to configure RabbitMQ.

CONNECTING TO THE EC2 INSTANCE

With the EC2 instance IP address and path to the SSH key pair in hand, you can now SSH into the VM and begin the process of setting up RabbitMQ. Connecting as the ubuntu user, you'll need to specify the path to the SSH key pair. The following command references the file in the Downloads folder in my home directory.

```
ssh -i ~/Downloads/rabbitmq-in-depth.pem.txt ubuntu@[Public IP]
```

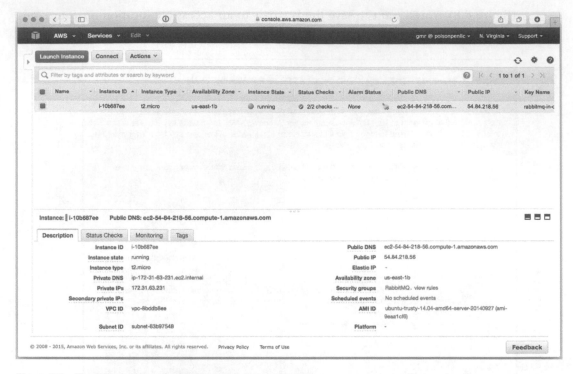

Figure 8.9   The EC2 dashboard with the newly created instance

> **NOTE**   If you're in a Windows environment, there are several good applications for connecting over SSH to remote systems, including PuTTY (free, at www.chiark.greenend.org.uk/~sgtatham/putty/) and SecureCRT (commercial, www.vandyke.com/products/securecrt/).

Once connected, you'll be logged in as the ubuntu user, and you should see the MOTD banner, similar to the following:

```
Welcome to Ubuntu 14.04.1 LTS (GNU/Linux 3.13.0-36-generic x86_64)

 * Documentation:  https://help.ubuntu.com/

  System information as of Sun Jan  4 23:36:53 UTC 2015

  System load: 0.0              Memory usage: 5%   Processes:       82

  Usage of /:  9.7% of 7.74GB   Swap usage:   0%   Users logged in: 0

Ubuntu comes with ABSOLUTELY NO WARRANTY, to the extent permitted by
applicable law.

ubuntu@ip-172-31-63-231:~$
```

Because there are a number of commands you need to issue as the `root` user, go ahead and switch users so you're not typing the `sudo` command all of the time:

```
sudo su -
```

As the root user, you can now install the Erlang runtime and RabbitMQ on the first EC2 instance.

INSTALLING ERLANG AND RABBITMQ

To install RabbitMQ and Erlang, you can use the official RabbitMQ and Erlang Solutions repositories. Although the main Ubuntu package repositories have support for both RabbitMQ and Erlang, it's advisable to get the latest versions of both, and the distribution repositories can often be significantly out of date. To use the external repositories, you'll need to add the package-signing keys and configuration for the external repositories.

First, add the RabbitMQ public key that enables Ubuntu to verify the file signatures of the packages being installed:

```
apt-key adv --keyserver hkp://keyserver.ubuntu.com:80 \
    --recv 6B73A36E6026DFCA
```

You'll see output from the `apt-key` application stating that it imported the "RabbitMQ Release Signing Key <info@rabbitmq.com>."

With the key imported to the database of trusted packaging keys, you can now add the official RabbitMQ package repository for Ubuntu. The following command will add a new file to the proper location, adding the RabbitMQ repository for use:

```
echo "deb http://www.rabbitmq.com/debian/ testing main" \
    > /etc/apt/sources.list.d/rabbitmq.list
```

Now that the RabbitMQ repository has been configured, you'll need to add the Erlang Solutions key to the trusted keys database:

```
apt-key adv --keyserver hkp://keyserver.ubuntu.com:80 --recv \
    D208507CA14F4FCA
```

When `apt-key` has completed, you'll see that it imported the "Erlang Solutions Ltd. <packages@erlang-solutions.com>" key.

Now add the Erlang Solutions Ltd. repository configuration:

```
echo "deb http://packages.erlang-solutions.com/debian precise contrib" \
    > /etc/apt/sources.list.d/erlang-solutions.list
```

With the configuration and keys in place, the following command will synchronize the local database of packages and allow you to install RabbitMQ:

```
apt-get update
```

Now you can install Erlang and RabbitMQ. The `rabbitmq-server` package will automatically resolve the Erlang dependencies and install the proper packages.

```
apt-get install -y rabbitmq-server
```

Once the command has finished, you'll have RabbitMQ up and running, but you'll need to run a few more commands to enable the proper plugins and allow you to connect to both the AMQP port and the management interface.

CONFIGURING RABBITMQ

RabbitMQ contains all of the functionality for both managing the server and using federation, but it's not enabled by default. The first step in configuring the RabbitMQ instance is to enable the plugins that ship with RabbitMQ, which will allow you to set up and use its federation capabilities. To do so, use the `rabbitmq-plugins` command:

```
rabbitmq-plugins enable rabbitmq_management rabbitmq_federation \
    rabbitmq_federation_management
```

As of RabbitMQ 3.4.0, this will automatically load the plugins without requiring a restart of the broker. But you'll want to enable the default `guest` user to allow logins from IP addresses beyond `localhost`. To do so, you'll need to create a RabbitMQ configuration file at /etc/rabbitmq/rabbitmq.config with the following content:

```
[{rabbit, [{loopback_users, []}]}].
```

You now need to restart RabbitMQ for the `loopback_users` setting to take effect:

```
service rabbitmq-server restart
```

To prevent confusion later when using both VMs, you can update the cluster name using the `rabbitmqctl` command. When you're using the management interface, the cluster name is displayed in the top-right corner. To set the name via the command line, run the following command:

```
rabbitmqctl set_cluster_name cluster-a
```

You can now test that the installation and configuration worked. Open the management interface in your web browser using the IP address of the EC2 instance on port 15672 in this URL format: `http://[Public IP]:15672`. Once you log in as the `guest` user with the password "guest", you should see the Overview screen (figure 8.10).

With the first instance created, you can leverage the Amazon EC2 dashboard to create an image from the running instance you just created, and use that image to launch a duplicate VM. The new image will make it easy to spin up new, pre-configured, standalone RabbitMQ servers for testing RabbitMQ's federation capabilities.

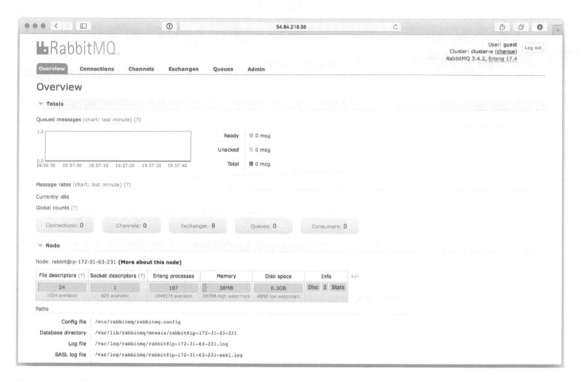

Figure 8.10   The RabbitMQ management UI Overview screen

8.2.2   Duplicating the EC2 instance

Instead of duplicating the previous steps to create a standalone instance of RabbitMQ, let's have Amazon do the work. To do so, you'll need to tell EC2 to create a new image or AMI from the running VM instance you just created.

Navigate to the EC2 Instances dashboard in your web browser, and click on the running instance. When you do, a context-sensitive menu will pop up that allows you to perform commands on that instance. From that menu, navigate to Image > Create Image (figure 8.11).

Once you select Create Image, a pop-up dialog box will appear, allowing you to set options for creating the image. Give the image a name and leave the rest of the options alone. When you click on the Create Image button, the exiting VM will be shut down, and the disk image for the VM will be used to create a new AMI (figure 8.12).

When the system has created the snapshot of the filesystem for the original VM, it will automatically be restarted, and the task of creating a new AMI will be queued in Amazon's system. It will take a few minutes for the AMI to be available for use. You can

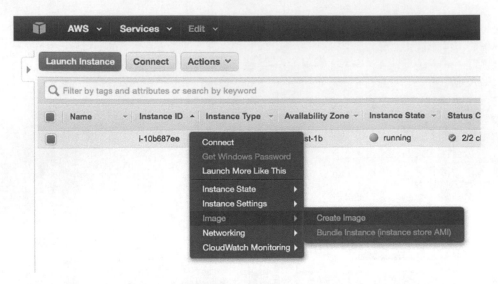

Figure 8.11   Creating a new image based on the running instance

Create Image   ✕

	Instance ID ⓘ	i-10b687ee
Image name ⓘ		
Image description ⓘ		
No reboot ⓘ	☐

Instance Volumes

Type ⓘ	Device ⓘ	Snapshot ⓘ	Size (GiB) ⓘ	Volume Type ⓘ	IOPS ⓘ	Delete on Termination ⓘ	Encrypted ⓘ
Root	/dev/sda1	snap-1f806dbb	8	General Purpose (SSD)	24 / 3000	☑	Not Encrypted

Add New Volume

Total size of EBS Volumes: 8 GiB
When you create an EBS image, an EBS snapshot will also be created for each of the above volumes.

Cancel   **Create Image**

Figure 8.12   The Create Image dialog box

check the status by clicking on the Images > AMIs option in the sidebar navigation (figure 8.13).

Figure 8.13   The AMI section of the EC2 dashboard

Once your AMI is available, select it in the AMI dashboard, and then click the Launch button on the top button bar. This will start you at step two of creating the VM. You'll go through all the steps you previously went through to create the original VM, but instead of creating a new security policy and SSH key pair, select the ones you created for the first VM.

When you've completed the steps to create the VM, navigate back to the EC2 Instances dashboard. Wait for the instance to become available, making note of its public IP address. One it's running, you should be able to connect to its management interface via your web browser on port 15672 using the URL format http://[Public IP]:15672. Log in to the management interface and change the cluster name to "cluster-b" by clicking on the Change link at the top right corner and following the instructions on the page you're sent to (figure 8.14). This name change will make it easy to distinguish which server you're logged in to when using the management interface.

Figure 8.14   The cluster name is displayed in the top right of the management interface.

With both EC2 instances up and running, you're ready to set up federation between the two nodes. Although we've used Amazon EC2 in the same availability zone for both nodes in this example, federation is designed to work well in environments where network partitions can occur, allowing RabbitMQ to share messages across data centers and large geographic distances.

To get started, let's use federation to copy messages from one node to another.

8.3   Connecting upstream

Whether you're looking to leverage federation for cross-data-center delivery of messages or you're using federation to seamlessly migrate your consumers and publishers to a new RabbitMQ cluster, you start in the same place: upstream configuration. Although the upstream node is responsible for delivering the messages to the downstream node, it's the downstream node where the configuration takes place.

Federation configuration has two parts: the upstream configuration and a federation policy. First, the downstream node is configured with the information required for the node to make an AMQP connection to the upstream node. Then policies are created that apply upstream connections and configuration options to downstream exchanges or queues. A single RabbitMQ server can have many federation upstreams and many federation policies.

To start receiving messages from the upstream node, cluster-a, to the downstream node, cluster-b, you must first define the upstream in the RabbitMQ management interface.

8.3.1   Defining federation upstreams

When installed, the federation management plugin adds two new Admin tabs to the RabbitMQ management interface: Federation Status and Federation Upstreams. Although the status screen will be blank until you create policies that configure exchanges or queues to use federation, the Federation Upstreams tab (figure 8.15) is the first place you'll go to start the configuration process.

There are multiple options for adding a new upstream connection, but only the name and AMQP URI for the connection are required. In a production environment, you'll likely want to configure the other options as well. If these options look familiar, it's because they represent a combination of options available when defining a queue and when consuming messages. For your first upstream connection, leave them blank and let RabbitMQ use the default settings.

To define the connection information for the upstream node, enter the AMQP URI for the remote server. The AMQP URI specification allows for flexible configuration of the connection, including the ability to tweak the heartbeat interval, maximum frame size, connection port, username and password, and much more. The full specification for the AMQP URI syntax, including the available query parameters, is available on the RabbitMQ website at www.rabbitmq.com/uri-spec.html. Because the test

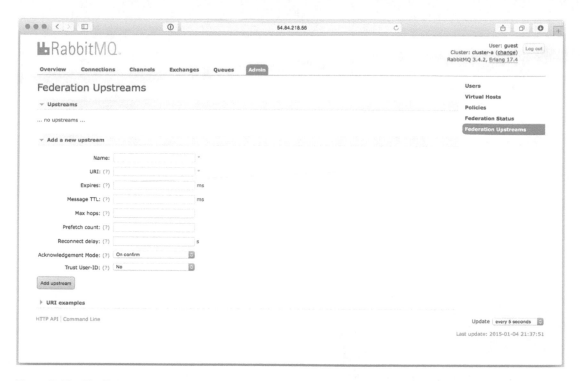

Figure 8.15   **The Federation Upstreams tab in the Admin section of the management interface**

environment we're using is as simple as possible, you can use the defaults for everything but the hostname in the URL.

In your testing environment, the node representing `cluster-b` will act as the downstream node and connect to the node representing `cluster-a`. Open the management interface in your web browser and navigate to the Federation Upstreams tab in the Admin section. Expand the Add a New Upstream section and enter `cluster-a` as the name for the upstream. For the URI, enter `amqp://[Public IP]`, replacing `[Public IP]` with the IP address of the first node you set up in this chapter (figure 8.16).

The information you enter here defines a single connection to another RabbitMQ node. The connection won't be used until a policy is created that references the upstream. When a policy is applied using the upstream, the federation plugin will connect to the upstream node. Should it be disconnected due to a routing error or some other network event, the default behavior is to try to reconnect once per second; you can change this behavior when defining the upstream in the Reconnect Delay field. If you want to change this after you've created an upstream, you must delete and recreate the upstream.

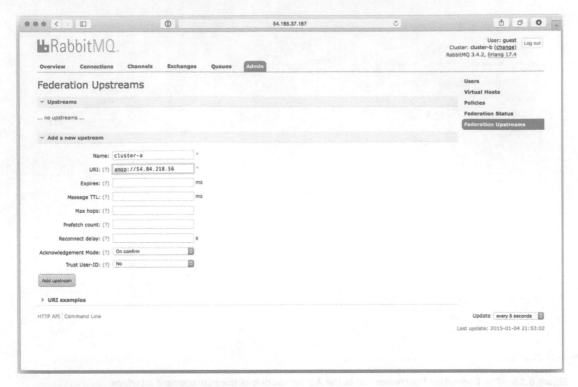

Figure 8.16   Adding a new federation upstream

Once you've entered the name and URI, click Add Upstream to save the upstream configuration with RabbitMQ. After the upstream has been added, you can define the policy and test out exchange-based federation.

> **NOTE**   Although the examples in this chapter use the management interface to create upstream nodes, you can also use the HTTP management API and the rabbitmqctl CLI application. For examples of using rabbitmqctl for adding upstreams, visit the federation plugin documentation at http://rabbitmq.com.

8.3.2   *Defining a policy*

Federation configuration is managed using RabbitMQ's policy system, which provides a flexible way to dynamically configure the rules that tell the federation plugin what to do. When you create a policy, you first specify a policy name and a pattern. The pattern can either evaluate for direct string matching or it can specify a regular expression (regex) pattern to match against RabbitMQ objects. The pattern can be compared against exchanges, queues, or both exchanges and queues. Policies can also specify a priority that's used to determine which policy should be applied to queues or exchanges that match multiple policies. When a queue or exchange is matched by multiple policies, the policy with the highest priority value wins. Finally, a policy has a definition table that allows for arbitrary key/value pairs to be specified.

For a first example, you'll create a policy named `federation-test` that will do string-equality checking against an exchange named `test` (figure 8.17). To tell the federation plugin that you want to federate the exchange from the `cluster-a` upstream, enter a key of `federation-upstream` with a value of `cluster-a` in the definition table. Once you've entered that information, click the Add Policy button to add it to the system.

Figure 8.17   Adding a new policy using the `cluster-a` federation upstream node

With the policy added, you'll need to add the `test` exchange to both nodes. You can use the Exchanges tab of each management interface to add the exchange. To prevent the `cluster-b` node from trying to federate a non-existent exchange on the `cluster-a` node, declare the exchange on the `cluster-a` node first. You can use any of the built-in exchange types, but I recommend using a topic exchange for flexibility in experimenting. Whichever type you select, you should be consistent and use the same exchange type for the `test` exchange on both `cluster-a` and `cluster-b`.

Once you've added the exchange to both nodes, you'll notice in the Exchanges tab of the management interface on the `cluster-b` node that the `test` exchange has a label matching the federation policy in the Features column (figure 8.18). The label indicates that you successfully matched the policy to the exchange.

Name	Type	Features		Message rate in	Message rate out
(AMQP default)	direct	D			
amq.direct	direct	D			
amq.fanout	fanout	D			
amq.headers	headers	D			
amq.match	headers	D			
amq.rabbitmq.log	topic	D	I		
amq.rabbitmq.trace	topic	D	I		
amq.topic	topic	D			
test	topic	D	federation-test		

Figure 8.18   The Exchanges table showing that the `test` **exchange has the** `federation-test` **policy applied to it**

After verifying that the policy was applied correctly, check the federation status to make sure that the `cluster-b` node was able to connect properly to its upstream, `cluster-a`. Click on the Admin tab and then the Federation Status menu item on the right to see if everything was configured properly. If everything worked, you should see a table with a single entry, with `cluster-a` in the Upstream column. The State column should indicate the upstream is running (figure 8.19).

Figure 8.19   The Federation Status page indicates that the `cluster-a` **upstream is running for the** `test` **exchange.**

Now that you've verified that RabbitMQ thinks everything is configured and running properly, you can test it by publishing messages on `cluster-a` and having them queued on `cluster-b`. To do so, create a test queue on `cluster-b` and bind it to the `test` exchange with a binding key of `demo`. This will set up the binding both locally on `cluster-b` and for the federation of messages to the test exchange on `cluster-a`.

Switch to the management interface for `cluster-a` and select the `test` exchange on the Exchanges tab. On the `test` exchange page, expand the Publish Message section. Enter the routing key demo and whatever content you'd like in the Payload field. When you click the Publish Message button, the message will be published to the test exchange on both cluster-a and cluster-b, and it should have been queued in your test queue on cluster-b.

Using the management interface for cluster-b, navigate to the Queues tab, and then select your test queue. Expand the Get Messages section and click the Get Message(s) button and you should see the message you published on cluster-a (figure 8.20).

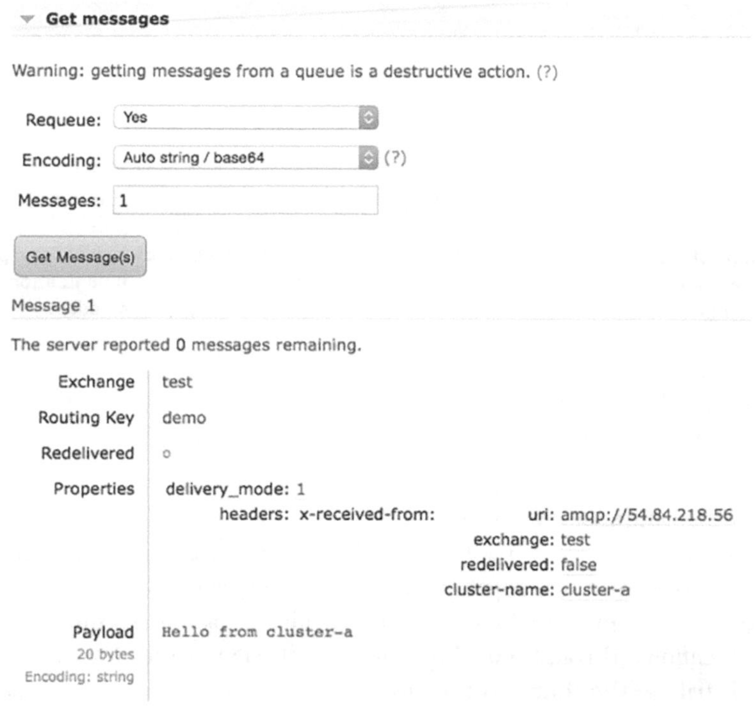

Figure 8.20 **The message published from** cluster-a

To help identify messages that were distributed via federation, the federation plugin adds an x-received-from field to the headers table in the message properties. The value of the field is a key/value table that includes the upstream uri, exchange, cluster-name, and a flag indicating if the message was redelivered.

8.3.3 *Leveraging upstream sets*

In addition to defining individual upstream nodes, the federation plugin provides the ability to group multiple nodes together for use in a policy. This grouping functionality provides quite a bit of versatility in how you define your federation topology.

PROVIDING REDUNDANCY

For example, imagine your upstream node is part of a cluster. You could create an upstream set that defines each node in the upstream cluster, allowing the downstream node to connect to every node in the cluster, ensuring that should any one node go down, messages published into the upstream cluster won't be missed downstream (figure 8.21).

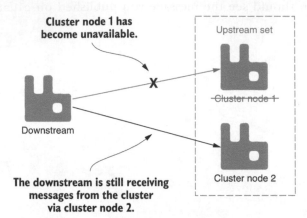

Cluster node 1 has become unavailable.

Upstream set

X

Cluster node 1

Downstream

Cluster node 2

The downstream is still receiving messages from the cluster via cluster node 2.

Figure 8.21   A cluster set can provide redundancy for communication with clustered upstream nodes.

If you're using a federated exchange in a downstream cluster, should the node connecting to the upstream fail in the cluster, another node will automatically take over the role, connecting upstream.

GEOGRAPHICALLY DISTRIBUTED APPLICATIONS

A more complex scenario could involve a geographically distributed web application. Suppose you're tasked with developing a service that records views of a banner advertisement. The goal is to serve the banner ad as quickly as possible, so the application is deployed to locations throughout the world, and DNS-based load balancing is employed to distribute the traffic to the closest data center for any given user. When the user views the advertisement, a message is published to a local RabbitMQ node that acts as a federation upstream node for a central processing system. The centralized RabbitMQ node has defined a federation upstream set that contains the RabbitMQ server in each geographically distributed location. As messages come into each location, they're relayed to the central RabbitMQ server and processed by consumer applications (figure 8.22).

Because the client-like behavior of the federation plugin allows for connection failures, should any of the geographically distributed nodes go offline, the processing of traffic from the rest of the system isn't impacted. Should it just be a regional routing issue, all of the queued messages from the disconnected upstream will be delivered once the downstream is able to reconnect.

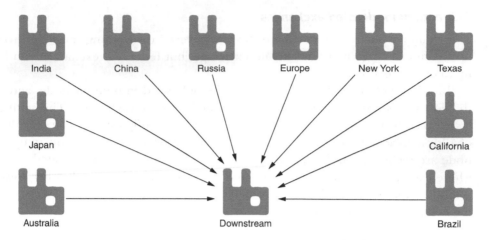

Figure 8.22 Geographically distributed upstreams in a set deliver messages to the downstream node.

CREATING AN UPSTREAM SET

To create an upstream set, first define each upstream node either in the management interface or via the rabbitmqctl CLI application. Because there's no interface for creating upstream sets in the federation management interface, you must use the rabbitmqctl command-line tool. As with any other use of rabbitmqctl, you must run it locally on the RabbitMQ node you wish to perform the configuration on and as a user that has access to RabbitMQ's Erlang cookie, which was discussed in section 7.2.2.

With your list of upstream nodes in hand, create a JSON string that contains the list of the names you used when creating the upstream definitions. For example, if you created upstreams named a-rabbit1 and a-rabbit2, you'd create the following JSON snippet:

```
[{"upstream": " a-rabbit1"}, [{"upstream": " a-rabbit2"}]
```

Then, to define an upstream set named cluster-a, run the rabbitmqctl command set_parameter, which allows you to define a federation-upstream-set named cluster-a.

```
rabbitmqctl set_parameter federation-upstream-set cluster-a \
    '[{"upstream": " a-rabbit1"}, {"upstream: " a-rabbit2"}]'
```

Once the upstream set is defined, you can reference it by name when creating a federation policy by using the federation-upstream-set key to define the policy instead of using the federation-upstream key you used to reference an individual node.

It's also worth noting that there's an implicitly defined upstream set named all that doesn't require any configuration. As you might expect, the all set will include every defined federation upstream.

8.3.4 *Bidirectional federated exchanges*

The examples in this chapter have thus far covered distributing messages from an upstream exchange to a downstream exchange, but federated exchanges can be set up to be bidirectional.

In a bidirectional setup, messages can be published into either node, and using the default configuration, they'll only be routed once on each node. This setting can be tweaked by the max-hops setting in the upstream configuration. The default value of 1 for max-hops prevents message loops where messages received from an upstream node are cyclically sent back to the same node. When you use a federated exchange where each node acts as an upstream and downstream node to each other, messages published into either node will be routed on each node, similar to how message routing behaves in a cluster (figure 8.23).

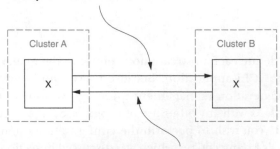

Messages published into cluster A are relayed to and routed on cluster B.

Messages published into cluster B are relayed to and routed on cluster A.

Figure 8.23   Messages published to either node of a bidirectional federated exchange will be routed on each node.

This type of federation behavior works well for creating a fault-tolerant, multi-data-center application structure. Instead of sharding data across data centers or locations, this type of federation allows for each location to receive the same messages for processing data.

Although this is a very powerful way to provide a highly available service, it also creates additional complexity. All of the complexities and concerns around multi-master databases become concerns when trying to keep a consistent view of data across locations using federation. Consensus management becomes very important to ensure that when data is acted upon it's done so consistently across locations. Fortunately, federated exchanges can provide an easy way to achieve consensus messaging across locations. It's also worth considering that this behavior isn't limited to two nodes, but can be set up in a graph where all nodes connect to all other nodes (figure 8.24). As in a two-node setup, setting max-hops to 1 for an upstream will prevent messages from cyclically republishing around the graph.

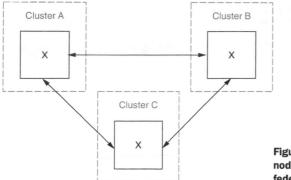

Figure 8.24 More than two nodes in a graph-like setup for federated exchanges

It's important to recognize that like any graph structure, the more nodes you add, the more complex things become. As with all aspects of implementing a message-oriented architecture, you should benchmark the performance of your architecture prior to production use. Fortunately, cloud service providers like Amazon have different availability zones, so it's easy to build-out and test complex federation environments with RabbitMQ.

8.3.5 *Federation for cluster upgrades*

One of the more difficult operational concerns with managing a RabbitMQ cluster is handling upgrades in a production environment where downtime is undesirable. There are multiple strategies for dealing with such a scenario.

If the cluster is large enough, you can move all traffic off a node, remove it from the cluster, and upgrade it. Then you could take another node offline, remove it from the cluster, upgrade it, and add it to a new cluster consisting of the node that was removed first. You continue to shuffle through your cluster like this, taking nodes offline one by one, until they're all removed, upgraded, and re-added in reverse order. If your publishers and consumers handle reconnection gracefully, this approach can work, but it's laborious. Alternatively, provided that you have the resources to set up a mirror of the cluster setup on a new version of the cluster, federation can provide a seamless way to migrate your messaging traffic from one cluster to another.

When using federation as a means to upgrade RabbitMQ, you start by rolling out the new cluster, creating the same runtime configuration on the new cluster, including virtual hosts, users, exchanges, and queues. Once you've set up and configured the new cluster, add the federation configuration, including the upstreams and policies to wildcard-match on all exchanges. Then you can start migrating your consumer applications, changing their connections from the old cluster to the new cluster (figure 8.25).

**Publishers continue to
publish to the old cluster.**

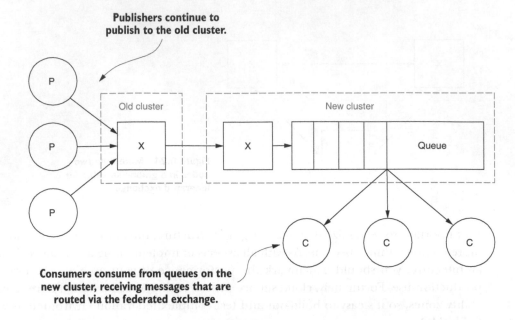

**Consumers consume from queues on the
new cluster, receiving messages that are
routed via the federated exchange.**

Figure 8.25   The second stage of using federation to upgrade a RabbitMQ cluster

As you migrate the consumers off a queue, you should unbind the queue on the old cluster, but don't delete it. Instead, you can create a temporary policy on the new cluster to federate that queue, moving the messages from the old cluster to the new one. It's advisable to automate this process as much as possible, because you want to minimize the chance of duplicate messages being added to the new cluster's queues due to using both the federated exchange and the federated queue.

Once you've finished moving all of the consumers off, and you've unbound the queues on the old cluster, you can migrate the publishers. When all of your publishers have been moved, you should be fully migrated to the upgraded RabbitMQ cluster. Of course, you may want to keep the federation going for a while to ensure that no rogue publishers are connecting to the old cluster when they're not expected to do so. This will allow you to keep your application operating properly, and you can use the RabbitMQ logs on the old cluster nodes to monitor for connections and disconnections. Although the federation plugin may not have originally been intended for such a task, it proves to be the perfect tool for zero-downtime RabbitMQ upgrades.

8.4 Summary

The flexibility and power provided by the federation plugin is limited only by your imagination. Whether you're looking to transparently migrate traffic from one RabbitMQ cluster to another, or you'd like to create a multi-data-center application that shares all messages across all nodes, the federation plugin is a reliable and efficient solution. As a scale-out tool, federated queues provide a way to greatly increase the capacity of a single queue by defining it on an upstream node and any number of downstream nodes. Combined with clustering and HA queues, federation not only allows for network partition tolerance between clusters, but also provides a fault-tolerance should nodes in either the upstream set or downstream clusters fail.

And failures do occasionally happen. In the next chapter you'll learn multiple strategies for monitoring and alerting when things go wrong.

Part 3

Integrations and customization

RabbitMQ doesn't stop at AMQP and exchanges. There are more options allowing some interesting integration opportunities. In this part of the book, we'll look at the MQTT and STOMP protocols, stateless publishing using HTTP, and integrating RabbitMQ with PostgreSQL and InfluxDB.

Using alternative protocols

This chapter covers

- The advantages of and how to use the MQTT protocol
- How to use STOMP-based applications with RabbitMQ
- How to communicate directly from a web browser using Web STOMP
- How to publish messages to RabbitMQ over HTTP using statelessd

While AMQP 0-9-1 is designed to be a robust protocol that supports the needs of most applications that communicate with RabbitMQ, there are specific use cases where there are better choices. For example, the high-latency, unreliable networking of mobile devices can be problematic for AMQP. In contrast, AMQP's state-based protocol may be too complicated for some application environments where client applications aren't able to maintain long-running connections but need to publish at a high velocity. Additionally, some applications may already contain support for messaging, but not using the AMQP protocol. In each of these scenarios, RabbitMQ's ecosystem of applications and plugins enables it to continue to be the centerpiece in your messaging architecture.

In this chapter, we'll look at a few alternatives to the standard AMQP 0-9-1 protocol: the MQTT protocol, which is ideal for mobile applications; STOMP, a simpler alternative to AMQP; Web STOMP, designed for use in web browsers; and statelessd for high-velocity message publishing.

9.1   MQTT and RabbitMQ

The MQ Telemetry Transport (MQTT) protocol is a lightweight messaging protocol that's growing in popularity for mobile applications, and support for it is distributed with RabbitMQ as a plugin. Created as a publish-subscribe pattern-based protocol, MQTT was originally invented in 1999 by Andy Stanford-Clark of IBM and Arien Nipper of Eurotech. MQTT was designed for messaging on resource-constrained devices and in low-bandwidth environments, without sacrificing reliable messaging constraints. Although it's not as feature-rich as AMQP, the explosive growth of mobile applications has resulted in MQTT's growing popularity in recent years.

From mobile applications to smart cars and home automation, MQTT's mainstream use has grabbed technology news headlines in recent years. Facebook uses MQTT for real-time messaging and notifications in their mobile applications. In 2013, the Ford Motor Company teamed up with IBM to implement smart car technology using IBM's MessageSight product line based on MQTT for the Ford Evo concept cars. Commercial home-automation products may be somewhat down the road, but there are numerous open source and open-standard-based home-automation systems using MQTT, such as the FunTechHouse project at www.fun-tech.se/FunTechHouse/. Also in 2013, MQTT, like AMQP 1.0 the year before, was accepted as an open standard through OASIS, a non-profit organization that works to encourage the development and adoption of open standards. This has provided MQTT with an open, vendor-neutral home for its further development and stewardship.

Should you consider MQTT as a protocol for your messaging architecture? Quite possibly, but you should look at the benefits and drawbacks first: Will your architecture benefit from MQTT's Last Will and Testament (LWT) feature? (LWT enables clients to specify a message that should be published if the client is unintentionally disconnected.) Or you may run into limitations with MQTT's maximum message size of 256 MB. Even with RabbitMQ's MQTT plugin transparently translating between MQTT and AMQP for your applications, to properly evaluate MQTT, as with AMQP, a good understanding of the protocol's communication process is quite helpful.

9.1.1   The MQTT protocol

There are some commonalities between the AMQ and MQTT protocols. After all, most messaging protocols share many of the same concerns, such as supporting connection negotiation, including authentication and message publishing. Under the covers, however, the protocols are structured differently. Instead of having protocol level constructs like AMQP's exchanges and queues, MQTT is limited to publishers and subscribers. Of course, this limitation has less impact if you're using RabbitMQ, because MQTT messages published into RabbitMQ are treated like messages published via AMQP, and subscribers are treated like AMQP consumers.

Although RabbitMQ supports MQTT out of the box, there are differences in messages published via MQTT and AMQP that underscore the value proposition of each protocol. As a lightweight protocol, MQTT is better for constrained hardware without reliable network connections, whereas AMQP is designed to be more flexible but requires more robust and reliable network environments. If you don't account for these differences, your applications may encounter interoperability problems when using both protocols in the same messaging architecture. In this section, we'll consider the anatomy of an MQTT message and what impact it can have on your message architecture and applications.

MESSAGE STRUCTURE

At the base of MQTT is a message structure referred to as command message, much like AMQP's low-level frames. Command messages are the low-level data structure that encapsulates the data in MQTT messages (figure 9.1).

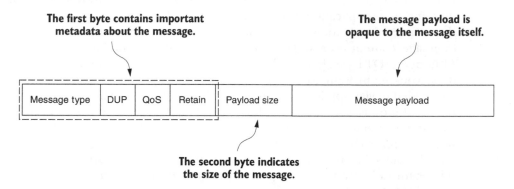

Figure 9.1   Anatomy of an MQTT command message

An MQTT command message has a fixed two-byte header that describes the message. Marshaled in the first header byte are four values:

1   The message type—A four-bit value that indicates the action for a message, similar to an AMQP method frame. Examples of message types include CONNECT, PUBLISH, and SUBSCRIBE.

2   The DUP flag—A single bit indicating whether the message is a redelivery, without regard to whether a client or server is redelivering the message.

3   The QoS flag—A two-bit value used to indicate the quality of service for a message. In MQTT, the QoS specifies whether a message must be delivered once at most, at least once, or exactly once.

4   The Retain flag—A single-bit flag indicating to the server whether a message should be retained when it has been published to all current subscribers. An

MQTT broker will only retain the last message with the Retain flag set, providing a mechanism for new subscribers to always receive the last good message. Suppose you're using MQTT for a mobile application. Should the application lose its connection to the RabbitMQ server, getting the last good message via the Retain feature allows your app to know the last good message, which will help it resynchronize state when it reconnects.

The second byte of the MQTT message header carries the size of the message payload. MQTT messages have a maximum payload size of 256 MB. In contrast, the maximum message size in AMQP is 16 exabytes, and RabbitMQ limits message size to 2 GB. MQTT's maximum message size is something to consider when creating your messaging architecture, as you'll need to create your own protocol on top of MQTT for splitting up payloads larger than 256 MB into individual messages, and then reconstruct them on the subscriber end.

> **NOTE** According to Maslow's Law, if all you have is a hammer, everything looks like a nail. It's very easy to use a protocol like MQTT or AMQP as a hammer for inter-application communication. But for different types of data, there can be better tools. For example, sending large messages such as video or image content over MQTT can be problematic for mobile applications. Although MQTT excels at sending smaller messages such as application-state data, you might want to consider HTTP 1.1 when you want a mobile or embedded device application to upload videos or photos. When using MQTT for small messages, it can outperform HTTP, but when it comes to transferring things like files, HTTP will be faster. It may be easy to overlook HTTP, but it supports chunked file uploads, which is perfect for large media transferred on less than reliable networks. Most mature client libraries will support this feature without your having to create an extra layer to manage such features, as you would with MQTT.

VARIABLE HEADERS

In the message payload of some MQTT command messages is binary packed data containing message details in a data structure referred to as *variable headers*. The format of variables can vary from command message to command message. For example, the variable headers of a CONNECT message contain data allowing for connection negotiation, whereas the variables of a PUBLISH message contain the topic to publish the message to and a unique identifier. In the case of a PUBLISH command message, the payload contains the variable headers and the opaque application-level message (figure 9.2).

For values in variable headers that aren't fixed in size, such as the topic name, the values are prefixed with two bytes that indicate the size of the value (figure 9.3). This structure allows servers and clients alike to read and decode messages as they're being streamed across the socket instead of having to wait for all of a message to be read prior to decoding.

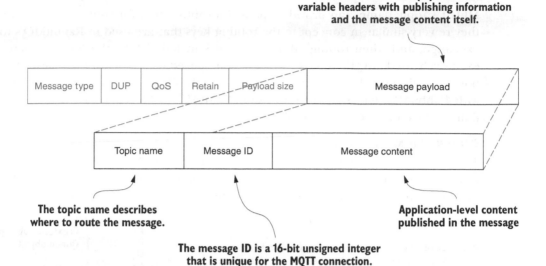

A PUBLISH command payload contains variable headers with publishing information and the message content itself.

The topic name describes where to route the message.

The message ID is a 16-bit unsigned integer that is unique for the MQTT connection.

Application-level content published in the message

Figure 9.2   Message payload of a PUBLISH command message

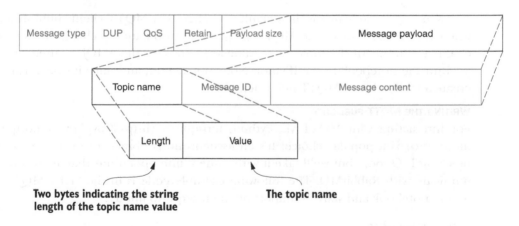

Two bytes indicating the string length of the topic name value

The topic name

Figure 9.3   Structure of the topic-name field of a PUBLISH command message's variable headers

All values in the variable fields are specified to be UTF-8 encoded strings, and they allow for a 32 KB length. It's important to remember that any values in the variable headers of a PUBLISH message subtract from the maximum message size for the message itself. For example, if you use the topic name my/very/long/topic to publish to, you've used up 23 available bytes from the message payload, so your message content can only be 268,435,433 bytes in length.

9.1.2 *Publishing via MQTT*

MQTT's topic names can provide a powerful routing tool for your messages. In fact, they're very similar in concept to the routing keys that are used in RabbitMQ's topic exchange, and when routing MQTT messages in RabbitMQ, the topic exchange is exclusively used. MQTT topic strings are namespaced using the forward slash (/) symbol as a delimiter when a message is published. To illustrate how MQTT can be used with RabbitMQ, let's start with an example MQTT publisher publishing a message that will be consumed over AMQP.

CREATING THE MESSAGE DESTINATION

To create a queue for the MQTT published message to be routed to, the following example from the "7.1.2 Setup" IPython notebook creates a queue named `mqtt-messages` and binds it to the `amq.topic` exchange using the routing key #.

```
import rabbitpy

with rabbitpy.Connection() as connection:
    with connection.channel() as channel:
        queue = rabbitpy.Queue(channel, 'mqtt-messages')
        queue.declare()
        queue.bind('amq.topic', '#')
```

Creates a rabbitpy Queue object

Declares the mqtt-messages queue

Binds the queue to the amq.topic exchange

The `amq.topic` exchange is the default exchange that MQTT clients publish to, and when they're published, the MQTT plugin will automatically change forward-slash characters in the MQTT topic name value to periods for the AMQP routing key.

Run the notebook in the IPython Notebook Server, and once it's been run, we'll create a Python-based MQTT publisher.

WRITING THE MQTT PUBLISHER

For interacting with MQTT via Python, mosquitto (https://pypi.python.org/pypi/mosquitto) is a popular choice. It's an asynchronous library meant to be run via a blocking I/O loop, but we'll fake it with some inline operations that allow it to communicate with RabbitMQ. The following example code is in the "7.1.2 MQTT Publisher" notebook and starts by importing the mosquitto library:

```
import mosquitto
```

With the library imported, a mosquitto client class should be created with a unique name for the client connection. In this case we'll just use the value `rmqid-test`, but for production using the string representation of the operating system's process ID is a good idea:

```
client = mosquitto.Mosquitto('rmqid-test')
```

The client class has a `connect` method where you can pass in the connection information for the MQTT server. The `connect` method accepts multiple arguments, including the `hostname`, `port`, and `keepalive` values. In this example, only the hostname is specified, using the default values for `port` and `keepalive`.

```
client.connect('localhost')
```

The library will return a `0` if it connects successfully. A return value that's greater than `0` indicates there was a problem connecting to the server.

With a connected client, you can now publish a message, passing in the topic name, message content, and a QoS value of `1`, indicating that the message should be published at least once, expecting an acknowledgment from RabbitMQ.

```
client.publish('mqtt/example', 'hello world from MQTT via Python', 1)
```

Because you're not running a blocking I/O loop, you need to instruct the client to process I/O events. Invoke the `client.loop()` method to process I/O events that should return a `0`, indicating success:

```
client.loop()
```

Now you can disconnect from RabbitMQ and run the `client.loop` method to process any other I/O events.

```
client.disconnect()
client.loop()
```

When you run this notebook, you should successfully publish a message that has been placed in the mqtt-messages queue you previously declared. Let's validate that it's there with rabbitpy.

GETTING AN MQTT-PUBLISHED MESSAGE VIA AMQP

The "7.1.2 Confirm MQTT Publish" notebook contains the following code for fetching a message from the `mqtt-messages` queue using `Basic.Get`, and it uses the `Message.pprint()` method to print the content of the message.

```
import rabbitpy                                          Fetches a message from
                                                         RabbitMQ using Basic.Get
message = rabbitpy.get(queue_name='mqtt-messages')   ◁
if message:                                                    ◁   Evaluates if a message
                    message.pprint(True)        ◁┐             was retrieved
Acknowledges        message.ack()                │  Prints the message,
the message    └▷ else:                          including properties
                    print('No message in queue')     ◁┐
                                                      │ If no message,
                                                        lets user know
```

When you run the code, you should see the AMQP message from RabbitMQ that was transparently mapped from MQTT semantics to AMQP semantics.

```
Exchange: amq.topic
```

```
Routing Key: mqtt.example
```

```
Properties:

{'app_id': '',
 'cluster_id': '',
 'content_encoding': '',
 'content_type': '',
 'correlation_id': '',
 'delivery_mode': None,
 'expiration': '',
 'headers': {'x-mqtt-dup': False, 'x-mqtt-publish-qos': 1},
 'message_id': '',
 'message_type': '',
 'priority': None,
 'reply_to': '',
 'timestamp': None,
 'user_id': ''}

Body:

'hello world from MQTT via Python'
```

The routing key is no longer `mqtt/example` like the topic name that was published, but this is the message that was published. RabbitMQ replaced the forward slash with a period to match the topic exchange semantics. Also note that the AMQP message properties headers table contains two values—`x-mqtt-dup` and `x-mqtt-publish-qos`— containing the values of the MQTT PUBLISH message header values.

Now that you've validated the publisher, let's explore what the MQTT subscriber experience is like with RabbitMQ.

9.1.3 *MQTT subscribers*

When connecting to RabbitMQ via MQTT to subscribe for messages, RabbitMQ will create a new queue. The queue will be named using the format `mqtt-subscriber-`[NAME]`qos`[N], where [NAME] is the unique client name and [N] is the QoS level set on the client connection. For example, a queue named `mqtt-subscriber-facebookqos0` would be created for a subscriber named `facebook` with a QoS setting of 0. Once a queue is created for a subscription request, it will be bound to the topic exchange using the AMQP period-delimited routing-key semantics.

Subscribers can bind to topics with string matching or pattern matching using semantics similar to AMQP topic-exchange routing-key bindings. The pound symbol (#) is for multilevel matching in both AMQP and MQTT. But when publishing with MQTT clients, the plus symbol (+) is used for single-level matching in a routing key, instead of using an asterisk (*). For example, if you were to publish new image messages over MQTT using the topic names of `image/new/profile` and `image/new/gallery`, MQTT subscribers could receive all image messages by subscribing to `image/#`, all new image messages by subscribing to `image/new/+`, and only new profile images by subscribing to `image/new/profile`.

The following example, from the "7.1.3 MQTT Subscriber" notebook, will connect to RabbitMQ via the MQTT protocol, set itself up as a subscriber, and loop until a single message is received. Once the message is received, it will unsubscribe and disconnect from RabbitMQ. To start, the mosquitto and os libraries are included:

```
import mosquitto
import os
```

You can use Python's standard library os module to get the process ID of the subscriber, which allows you to create a unique MQTT client name when creating the new mosquitto client. You may want a more random or robust method of naming your subscriber to prevent duplicate client names in production code, but using the process ID should work for this example.

```
client = mosquitto.Mosquitto('Subscriber-%s' % os.getpid())
```

Now you can define a few callback methods that will be invoked by the mosquitto library during each phase of execution. To start off, you can create a callback that's invoked when the client connects:

```
def on_connect(mosq, obj, rc):
    if rc == 0:
        print('Connected')
    else:
        print('Connection Error')
client.on_connect = on_connect
```

When an MQTT message is delivered, the mosquitto client invokes the on_message callback. This callback prints information about the message, and then the client will unsubscribe.

```
def on_message(mosq, obj, msg):
    print('Topic: %s' % msg.topic)
    print('QoS: %s' % msg.qos)
    print('Retain: %s' % msg.retain)
    print('Payload: %s' % msg.payload)
    client.unsubscribe('mqtt/example')
client.on_message = on_message
```

The final callback is invoked when the client is unsubscribed, and it will disconnect the client from RabbitMQ.

```
def on_unsubscribe(mosq, obj, mid):
    print("Unsubscribe with mid %s received." % mid)
    client.disconnect()
client.on_unsubscribe = on_unsubscribe
```

With all of the callbacks defined, you can connect to RabbitMQ and subscribe to the topic:

```
client.connect("127.0.0.1")
client.subscribe("mqtt/example", 0)
```

Finally, you can invoke the I/O event loop by calling `client.loop()` and specifying a timeout of 1 second. The following code will do this, looping until `client.loop()` no longer returns 1 because it has been disconnected from RabbitMQ.

```
while client.loop(timeout=1) == 0:
    pass
```

Once you open the notebook, you can run all of the cells at once by clicking on the Cell dropdown and choosing Run All. Click over to the "7.1.2 MQTT Publisher" tab and choose Cell > Run All, publishing a new message. In the subscriber tab you should now see output like what's shown in figure 9.4.

As you can see, the period-delimited routing key has been transformed back into the forward-slash delimited topic name `mqtt/example`. With the bidirectional transformation from MQTT topic name to AMQP routing key, RabbitMQ successfully bridges the protocols in a transparent and native way for either type of client connecting. In

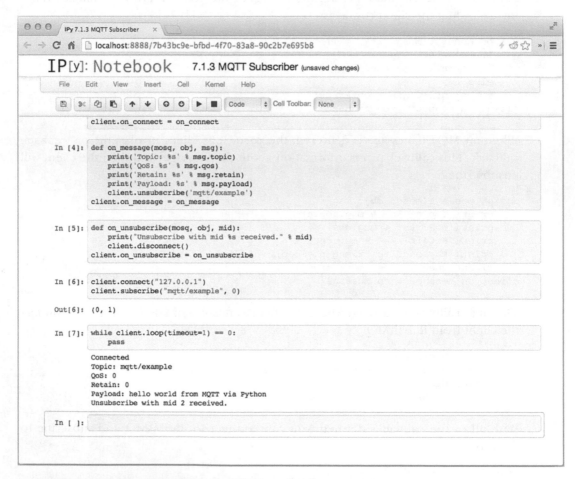

Figure 9.4   Output of the "MQTT Subscriber" IPython notebook

doing so, not only does RabbitMQ create a compelling platform for MQTT applications but it makes for a much more robust messaging platform than brokers that are protocol-specific.

9.1.4 *MQTT plugin configuration*

With the basics of MQTT out of the way, you may find that you want to customize the MQTT behaviors to match various aspects of your RabbitMQ cluster, such as providing MQTT-specific authentication credentials or queue-specific configuration for subscribers. To change these and other configuration values, you'll need to edit the main RabbitMQ configuration file, rabbitmq.config.

RabbitMQ's configuration file is typically located at /etc/rabbitmq/rabbit.config in UNIX-based systems. Where most configuration files use a data serialization format, the rabbitmq.config file uses the code format of native Erlang data structures. Almost like a JSON array of objects, the RabbitMQ configuration contains a top-level stanza for RabbitMQ itself and then a stanza for each plugin that you wish to configure. In the following snippet, RabbitMQ's AMQP listening port is set to 5672 and the MQTT plugin listening port is set to 1883.

```
[{rabbit,        [{tcp_listeners,    [5672]}]},
 {rabbitmq_mqtt, [{tcp_listeners,    [1883]}]}].
```

Many of the default settings, such as the virtual host and default username and password for the MQTT plugin, mirror the defaults for RabbitMQ. Unlike with AMQP, MQTT clients aren't able to select which virtual host to use. Although this behavior may change in future versions, currently the only way to change the virtual host used by MQTT clients is by changing the default value of the forward slash using the vhost directive in the MQTT configuration stanza from / to the desired value:

```
[{rabbitmq_mqtt, [{vhost, <<"/">>}]}]
```

Although MQTT does provide a facility for authentication, there may be use cases where this isn't desired. For those cases, the MQTT plugin has a default username and password combination of guest and guest. These defaults are changed with the default_user and default_pass configuration directives. If you'd like to require authentication for MQTT clients, you can disable the default user behavior by setting the allow_anonymous configuration directive to false.

> **TIP** Your MQTT application architecture may require different settings for different types of MQTT clients. Using a RabbitMQ cluster is one way around the limitation imposed by a single virtual host and the default username and password settings. By having different per-node configurations, you can share MQTT messages in a RabbitMQ cluster, with each node accepting MQTT connections configured with different default settings. There's no requirement for uniform configuration across RabbitMQ cluster nodes.

Table 9.1 describes each of the MQTT plugin configuration directives and their default values. These values directly impact the behavior of the MQTT plugin with regard to MQTT clients and message routing.

Table 9.1   MQTT plugin configuration options

Directive	Type	Description	Default value
allow_anonymous	Boolean	Enable MQTT clients to connect without authentication.	true
default_user	String	The username to use when an MQTT client doesn't present authentication credentials.	guest
default_password	String	The password to use when an MQTT client doesn't present authentication credentials.	guest
exchange	String	The topic exchange to use when publishing MQTT messages.	amq.topic
prefetch	Integer	The AMQP QoS prefetch count setting for MQTT listener queues.	10
ssl_listeners	Array	TCP ports to listen on for MQTT over SSL connections. If specified, the top-level rabbit stanza of the configuration file must contain the ssl_options configuration stanza.	[]
subscription_ttl	Integer	The duration to keep a subscriber queue, in milliseconds, after a subscriber unexpectedly disconnects.	1800000
tcp_listeners	Array	TCP ports to listen on for MQTT connections.	1833
tcp_listen_options	Array	An array of configuration directives for altering the TCP behavior of the MQTT plugin.	See table 9.2

Some directives, such as exchange, prefetch, and vhost, are more likely to be candidates for change in your environment, whereas others like the tcp_listen_options should be tweaked carefully.

Table 9.2 describes the tcp_listen_options directives specified by the RabbitMQ documentation and their effect on the TCP connection behavior for MQTT clients and the MQTT plugin. These values are a subset of those the Erlang TCP API provides for TCP socket tweaking. For more detailed information on what other directives are available, consult the Erlang gen_tcp documentation at http://erlang.org/doc/man/gen_tcp.html. Due to the way RabbitMQ configuration works, the values specified in the configuration file are transparently passed to the Erlang gen_tcp:start_link in the listen_option parameter. In a majority of use cases, the default values specified by the MQTT plugin shouldn't be changed; they are the tested and optimized values recommended by the RabbitMQ team.

Table 9.2 `tcp_listen_options` **for the MQTT plugin**

Directive	Type	Description	Default value
binary	Atom	Indicates that the socket is a binary TCP socket. Do not remove.	N/A
packet	Atom	Tweaks how the Erlang kernel handles TCP data prior to handing off to RabbitMQ. For more information see the Erlang `gen_tcp` documentation.	`raw`
reuseaddr	Boolean	Instructs the operating system to allow RabbitMQ to reuse the listening socket if it wants to, even if the socket is busy.	`true`
backlog	Integer	Specifies how many pending client connections can exist before refusing new connections. Pending client connections are new TCP socket connections that RabbitMQ hasn't processed yet.	`10`
nodelay	Boolean	Indicates whether a TCP socket should use the Nagle algorithm, waiting to aggregate low-level TCP data for more efficient data transmission. By default this is `false`, allowing for faster MQTT messaging in most cases by sending TCP data when RabbitMQ wants to, instead of buffering smaller message packets and sending them grouped together.	`true`

To review, MQTT is a powerful tool for lightweight messaging in the ever-evolving world of mobile computing and embedded devices. If you're considering RabbitMQ as the centerpiece of a messaging architecture that includes mobile devices, you should strongly consider the use of MQTT and the RabbitMQ MQTT plugin. Not only does it provide transparent translation of MQTT semantics into RabbitMQ's AMQP worldview, it transparently translates AMQP semantics for MQTT clients, simplifying the development required for a unified message bus. Although the configuration shortcomings prevent complex MQTT ecosystems on an individual node, there's an effort underway to expand the MQTT plugin to provide dynamic virtual host and exchange use. In the meantime, multiple RabbitMQ nodes in a cluster may be leveraged to create more complex MQTT topologies.

If your messaging architecture won't benefit from MQTT but you'd still like a more lightweight solution than AMQP for communicating with RabbitMQ, perhaps STOMP is for you.

9.2 STOMP and RabbitMQ

Originally named TMPP, the Streaming Text Oriented Message Protocol (STOMP) was first specified in 2005 by Brian McCallister. Loosely modeled after HTTP, STOMP leverages an easy-to-read, text-based protocol. Initially implemented in Apache ActiveMQ and designed with simplicity in mind, STOMP now enjoys support in numerous message broker implementations and has client libraries in most popular programming languages.

The specification of STOMP 1.2 was released in 2012 and it's supported by RabbitMQ, along with both of the previous versions. STOMP support is provided by a plugin that's distributed as part of the core RabbitMQ package. Like with AMQP and MQTT, understanding the STOMP protocol can help shape your opinion on its use in your application or environment.

9.2.1 *The STOMP protocol*

Designed to allow for stream-based processing, STOMP frames are UTF-8 text that consist of a command and the payload for the command, terminated with a null (0x00) byte. Unlike the binary AMQP and MQTT protocols, STOMP is human-readable and doesn't require binary bit-packed information to define STOMP message frames and their content.

For example, the following snippet is a STOMP frame for connecting to a message broker. It uses ^@, control-@ in ASCII, to represent the null byte at the end of a frame.

```
CONNECT
accept-version:1.2
host:rabbitmq-node

^@
```

In this example, the CONNECT command tells the receiving broker that the client would like to connect. It's followed by two header fields, accept-version and host, that instruct the broker about the connection the client would like to negotiate. Finally, a blank line is followed by the null byte, indicating the end of the CONNECT frame.

If the request is successful, the broker will return a CONNECTED frame to the client. This frame is very similar to the CONNECT frame:

```
CONNECTED
version:1.2

^@
```

Much like AMQP, STOMP commands are RPC-style requests of the message broker, and some will have replies for the client. The standard set of STOMP commands covers similar concepts as AMQP and MQTT, including connection negotiation, publishing messages, and subscribing to receive messages from a message broker. If you'd like more information on the protocol itself, the specifications are available on the STOMP protocol page at https://stomp.github.io/.

To illustrate how you can leverage STOMP with RabbitMQ, let's start with a simple message publisher.

9.2.2　*Publishing messages*

When publishing messages with STOMP, the generic concept of a destination is used to describe where a message should be sent. When using RabbitMQ, a STOMP destination is one of the following:

- A queue automatically created by the STOMP plugin when a message is published or when a client sends a subscription request
- A queue created by normal means, such as an AMQP client or via the management API
- The combination of an exchange and routing key
- The automatically mapped `amq.topic` exchange using the STOMP `topic` destination
- A temporary queue when using `reply-to` headers in a STOMP `SEND` command

Each of these destinations is delimited by a forward slash separating out the destination type, in most cases, and additional information specifying the exchange, routing key, or queue.

To illustrate the use of message destinations and publishing, let's start by sending a message to a STOMP queue using the stomp.py Python library.

NOTE The STOMP plugin acts as a translation or proxy layer in RabbitMQ itself. As such, it acts as an AMQP client, creating an AMQP channel and issuing AMQP RPC requests to RabbitMQ itself. STOMP publishers are subject to the same rate limiting and connection blocking that AMQP publishers are limited to, except there are no semantics in the STOMP protocol to let your publisher know that it's being blocked or throttled.

SENDING TO A STOMP-DEFINED QUEUE

Sending a message via STOMP is very similar to sending a message via MQTT or AMQP. To send a message directly to a queue, use a destination string with a format of `/queue/<queue-name>`.

In the following example, we'll use the destination `/queue/stomp-messages`. Sending the message to this destination will publish messages into the `stomp-messages` queue using RabbitMQ's default exchange behavior. If the queue doesn't exist, the queue will automatically be created. The example code is in the "7.2.2 STOMP Publisher" notebook.

```
import stomp

conn = stomp.Connection()
conn.start()
conn.connect()
conn.send(body='Example Message', destination='/queue/stomp-messages')
conn.disconnect()
```

When the queue is created by the STOMP plugin, it will be created using default argument values by issuing the `Queue.Declare` RPC request internally. This means that if you have an existing queue in the RabbitMQ server that was created using default values, you can still publish to it using the STOMP queue destination. If you have a queue that was created with a message TTL or other custom arguments, you'll need to use an AMQP-defined queue destination instead.

SENDING TO AN **AMQP**-DEFINED QUEUE

The STOMP plugin has an extended destination syntax that's specific to RabbitMQ's implementation of STOMP, allowing for AMQP-defined queues with custom settings to be published to. To achieve this, you first need to create a queue with a maximum length, using the rabbitpy library in the "7.2.2 Queue Declare" notebook.

```
import rabbitpy

with rabbitpy.Connection() as connection:
    with connection.channel() as channel:
        queue = rabbitpy.Queue(channel, 'custom-queue',
                               arguments={'x-max-length': 10})
        queue.declare()
```

Now that the queue is declared, you'll need to use the AMQP-defined queue destination syntax. By creating a destination string using the /amq/queue/<queue-name> format, the STOMP plugin will be able to route the message to the custom-queue queue. This example is in the "7.2.2 Custom Queue" notebook.

```
import stomp

conn = stomp.Connection()
conn.start()
conn.connect()
conn.send(body='Example Message', destination='/amq/queue/custom-queue')
conn.disconnect()
```

The problem with sending to queues directly is that you don't enjoy the benefit that AMQP messages receive by using the various exchange types and routing keys. Fortunately, the STOMP plugin allows for specially formatted destination strings, which achieve that purpose.

SENDING TO AN EXCHANGE

To send a message to an exchange using a routing key with the RabbitMQ STOMP plugin, you use the /exchange/<exchange-name>/<routing-key> format. This allows you to publish via STOMP as flexibly as you would be able to using AMQP.

The following example from the "7.2.2 Exchange and Queue Declare" notebook will set things up so you can publish a STOMP message through a custom exchange.

```
import rabbitpy

with rabbitpy.Connection() as connection:
    with connection.channel() as channel:
        exchange = rabbitpy.Exchange(channel, 'stomp-routing')
        exchange.declare()
        queue = rabbitpy.Queue(channel, 'bound-queue',
                               arguments={'x-max-length': 10})
        queue.declare()
        queue.bind(exchange, 'example')
```

With an exchange and queue declared, and the queue bound to the exchange, it's time to publish a message to the new queue. The following example is from the "7.2.2 Exchange Publishing" notebook.

```
import stomp

conn = stomp.Connection()
conn.start()
conn.connect()
conn.send(body='Example Message',
          destination='/exchange/stomp-routing/example')
conn.disconnect()
```

With this example under your belt, the flexibility of exchange routing should be apparent. But you can benefit from the flexibility of topic exchange routing without having to declare an exchange or use the longer exchange destination string. Instead, you can send your messages using a STOMP topic destination string.

SENDING TO A STOMP TOPIC

Topic destination strings, like queue destination strings, use a common format recognized by all message brokers that support the STOMP protocol. By formatting a destination string using a format of /topic/<routing-key>, messages sent to RabbitMQ via STOMP will be routed through the amq.topic exchange to all queues bound to the routing key.

Instead of creating a new queue, you can bind the previously created bound-queue queue to the amq.topic exchange using a routing key of # to receive all messages sent to that exchange. The following example code to bind the queue is in the "7.2.2 Bind Topic" notebook.

```
import rabbitpy

with rabbitpy.Connection() as connection:
    with connection.channel() as channel:
        queue = rabbitpy.Queue(channel, 'bound-queue')
        queue.bind('amq.topic', '#')
```

With the queue bound, you can now publish via STOMP by sending a message to the /topic/routing.key routing key using the example from the "7.2.2 Topic Publishing" notebook.

```
import stomp

conn = stomp.Connection()
conn.start()
conn.connect()
conn.send(body='Example Message',
          destination='/exchange/stomp-routing/example')
conn.disconnect()
```

Between the queue, amq queue, exchange, and topic destination strings, a large portion of message-publishing use cases are covered. But STOMP adds one nice feature that replicates some of the work we did in chapter 6. If you publish a message via

STOMP and set a `reply-to` header value, the STOMP plugin will automatically create an RPC reply queue for your publisher to consume messages from.

USING TEMPORARY REPLY QUEUES

When your messaging architecture calls for RPC behavior between your publishers and consumers, if you use STOMP there is convenient behavior built into the RabbitMQ STOMP plugin. By setting the `reply-to` header when you send a message via STOMP, the reply queue will automatically be created, setting both the exclusive and auto-delete flags on the queue so that the publishing STOMP connection is the only connection that can consume messages from the reply queue. In addition, the reply queue will automatically be deleted from RabbitMQ should your publishing application be disconnected.

The following example from the "7.2.2 Reply-To" notebook demonstrates how to set the `reply-to` header. We'll be covering how to consume messages via STOMP in the next section of this chapter, so for now we'll let the reply queue be automatically removed once the message is published.

```
import stomp

conn = stomp.Connection()
conn.start()
conn.connect()
conn.send(body='Example Message',
          destination='/exchange/stomp-routing/example',
          headers={'reply-to': 'my-reply-queue'})
conn.disconnect()
```

A major take-away from setting the `reply-to` header is that STOMP messages can have arbitrary message headers. These header values are most analogous to AMQP message properties.

AMQP MESSAGE PROPERTIES VIA STOMP

STOMP message headers allow you to pass arbitrary message header values to a message broker. This functionality is what enables the reply-to functionality of auto-creation of reply queues for publishers. Although arbitrary message header values can be useful for your applications, if you're considering a mixed protocol environment that leverages both STOMP and AMQP, you'll want to consider a more limited set of message headers that will be available in both protocols. If you use message headers that map to the AMQP message property names, the STOMP plugin will automatically map the header values to AMQP message properties.

The following example, from the "7.2.2 Send with Message Headers" notebook, sets message headers that will be converted to AMQP message properties.

```
import stomp
import time

conn = stomp.Connection()
conn.start()
conn.connect()
```

```
conn.send(body='Example message with Headers',
          destination='/queue/stomp-messages',
          headers={'app-id': '7.2.2 Example',
                   'priority': 5,
                   'reply-to': 'reply-to-example',
                   'timestamp': int(time.time())})
conn.disconnect()
```

If you set STOMP message headers that don't map to AMQP message properties, the AMQP `headers` message property will be populated with those values. As you might expect, when you consume messages with AMQP message properties populated, those values will come through as STOMP message header values.

There's one exception to this behavior—the `message-id` AMQP message property. This value is automatically set as part of the STOMP protocol and shouldn't be manually set when sending a message to RabbitMQ using the STOMP protocol.

Publishing messages to RabbitMQ using STOMP has a little more overhead than doing so via AMQP, but there are some nice features of doing so, such as automatic queue creation and auto-creation of reply-to queues. By leveraging the different destination string formats, your messages can be sent directly to a queue or published to an exchange just like with AMQP message publishing. The STOMP plugin automatically maps AMQP semantics into STOMP messages, and STOMP semantics into AMQP messages.

To see this automatic mapping in action, you can consume the messages published in the previous examples. In the next section, we'll consume messages via STOMP subscribers, including messages with header values.

9.2.3 Consuming messages

Similar to MQTT, STOMP clients are considered subscribers instead of consumers. But because RabbitMQ is first and foremost an AMQP broker, the STOMP plugin treats STOMP subscribers as AMQP consumers that get their messages from RabbitMQ queues. What happens in most cases when you subscribe via STOMP is that a queue will be created for messages to be consumed from.

One of the neater features of the STOMP plugin is that all of the destination string types for sending messages via STOMP exist for subscribing to messages in STOMP. In this section you'll leverage destination strings in a STOMP subscriber to do the following:

- Consume messages from an automatically created queue
- Consume messages from a predefined AMQP queue
- Consume messages by subscribing to an exchange
- Consume messages by subscribing to a STOMP topic

When sending a message via STOMP, you can set a reply-to header that will automatically create an exclusive auto-delete queue for the STOMP connection. In contrast, consuming the reply-to messages is handled the same way as consuming messages when subscribing to a STOMP-defined queue.

Let's start by subscribing to the same queue we sent messages to in the last section, the stomp-messages queue.

SUBSCRIBING TO A STOMP-DEFINED QUEUE

STOMP-defined queues are queues that are created by RabbitMQ when messages are published using the /queue/<queue-name> formatted destination string. In the previous section, we published messages into RabbitMQ using the STOMP send command in the "7.2.2 Stomp Publisher" notebook. In the following example from the "7.2.3 Queue Subscriber" notebook, you'll consume those messages, printing out the message body for each message sent. Because the subscriber code is a bit more complex, let's step through it in sections.

First, you'll import all of the Python libraries required to run the subscriber:

```
import stomp
import pprint
import time
```

The Python stomp.py library requires a ConnectionListener object to process messages received from a message broker. This object should contain an on_message method that will be invoked whenever the subscriber receives a message. In this example, you'll print out headers if there are any, and the message. In addition, you only want to receive one message and then quit. In the demo listener, you'll add a flag named can_stop that will let the example know when to stop.

```
class Listener(stomp.ConnectionListener):
    can_stop = False
    def on_message(self, headers, message):
        if headers:
            print('\nHeaders:\n')
            pprint.pprint(headers)
        print('\nMessage Body:\n')
        print(message)
        self.can_stop = True
```

With the Listener class defined, you can create an instance of the object, a STOMP connection, set the connections listener object, start the connection, and then connect to RabbitMQ:

```
listener = Listener()

conn = stomp.Connection()
conn.set_listener('', listener)
conn.start()
conn.connect()
```

Once a connection is established, the Connection.subscribe method sends a STOMP subscription request to RabbitMQ that will automatically acknowledge any received messages.

```
conn.subscribe('/queue/stomp-messages', id=1, ack='auto')
```

To ensure that the code waits until a message is received, you'll loop, sleeping one second at a time until `Listener.can_stop` is set to `True`:

```
while not listener.can_stop:
    time.sleep(1)
```

Finally, once a message is received, you disconnect from the connection:

```
conn.disconnect()
```

Run the code until you receive the message with defined message headers, from the "7.2.2 Send with Message Headers" notebook. Once it's received, you should see output similar to figure 9.5.

What you'll notice is that the AMQP message properties are merged with the STOMP message headers, including `content-length` and `destination`. If there are

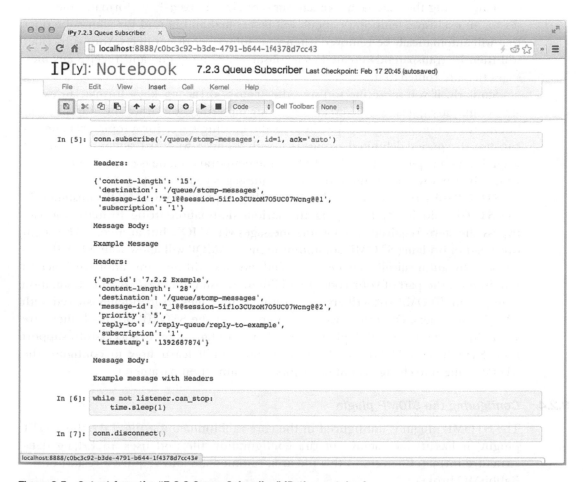

Figure 9.5   Output from the "7.2.3 Queue Subscriber" IPython notebook

any values in the AMQP message properties of a message that's received, they too will be flattened down into the headers that are received as part of a STOMP message.

Like when sending a STOMP message, if you send to a queue destination for a queue that was declared via AMQP using custom arguments, the subscription will fail and you won't receive any messages. Fortunately, the RabbitMQ team added the AMQ queue destination string format for such scenarios.

SUBSCRIBING TO AN AMQP-DEFINED QUEUE

If you need to intermix STOMP subscribers and AMQP consumers that consume from the same queue with custom arguments, or if you need a single STOMP subscriber that receives messages from a queue with custom arguments, you can use the /amq/queue/<queue-name> destination format when using your STOMP subscriber.

SUBSCRIBING TO AN EXCHANGE OR TOPIC

Another neat feature of the STOMP plugin is that it allows you to subscribe to an exchange using the /exchange/<exchange-name>/<binding-key> format. When you do so, an exclusive, temporary queue will be created and bound for your subscriber that will automatically be removed when your subscriber disconnects. Your subscriber will then be transparently created as a consumer of the queue and receive any messages that are routed to it.

Similarly, if you subscribe to using the /topic/<binding-key> format, an exclusive, temporary queue will be created for your subscriber, and it will be automatically bound using the binding key specified. As the binding key is for a topic exchange, it can use the period-delimited namespace with # and * wildcard semantics, just like when binding a queue using AMQP. Once the temporary queue is created and bound, your subscriber will be set up to receive any messages routed to it.

STOMP subscribers connected to RabbitMQ are proxied into AMQP consumers in the STOMP plugin. By leveraging the various destination string formats, you can bypass the steps required to consume messages via AMQP, but at a cost. The slight overhead of bridging STOMP communications to AMQP will allow your STOMP subscribers to automatically create and bind queues without any additional action required on the part of your code. In addition, by using the AMQ queue destination string, your STOMP subscribers can consume messages from queues shared with AMQP consumers. Of course, with the simplicity of the STOMP protocol, there are some things that the STOMP plugin must do via configuration to successfully support both STOMP and AMQP. In the next section you'll learn how to configure the STOMP plugin to change client behaviors and connection parameters.

9.2.4 *Configuring the STOMP plugin*

The STOMP plugin is configured in the core rabbitmq.config file. Like the MQTT plugin, it has its own stanza in the configuration file and uses an Erlang data-structure format. Changes to this file aren't immediate and require a restart of the RabbitMQ broker.

As the following snippet shows, the top-level configuration of the STOMP plugin is placed in the `rabbitmq_stomp` configuration section.

```
[{rabbit,         [{tcp_listeners,    [5672]}]},
 {rabbitmq_stomp, [{tcp_listeners,    [61613]}]}].
```

Table 9.3 details the configuration options for the STOMP plugin.

Table 9.3 STOMP plugin configuration options

Directive	Type	Description	Default value
default_user	String	The username to use when a STOMP client doesn't present authentication credentials.	[{login, "guest", passcode, "guest"}]
implicit_connect	Integer	Allows for STOMP connections to not send the CONNECT frames upon connection. If enabled, a CONNECTED frame won't be sent upon connection.	False
ssl_listeners	Array	TCP ports to listen on for STOMP over SSL connections. If specified, the top-level `rabbit` stanza of the configuration file must contain the `ssl_options` configuration stanza.	[]
ssl_cert_login	Boolean	Allows for SSL certificate-based authentication.	False
tcp_listeners	Array	TCP ports to listen on for STOMP connections.	[61613]

9.2.5 Using STOMP in the web browser

Bundled with RabbitMQ is the Web STOMP plugin. Leveraging the SockJS library, Web STOMP is a RabbitMQ-specific extension that adds a websocket-compatible HTTP server that allows web browsers to communicate directly with RabbitMQ. The Web STOMP plugin listens, by default, to port 15670 and supports the entire STOMP protocol, with one small exception—the STOMP heartbeat feature. Due to the nature of SockJS, the library used by Web STOMP to communicate with RabbitMQ, heartbeats can't be used.

Web STOMP is enabled in the Vagrant virtual machine and includes examples that show you how it can be used. To see multiple examples demonstrating the Web STOMP library and service, visit http://localhost:15670/web-stomp-examples/.

Before you run out and implement Web STOMP as a solution for your application, consider the security implications of opening up your RabbitMQ server to the internet, just as you would with any other application or service. It may make sense to isolate

RabbitMQ Web STOMP servers as standalone clusters or servers that bridge to your main servers using tools like the Shovel and Federation plugins to mitigate the impact of malicious or abusive clients. For more information on Web STOMP, visit the plugin page at www.rabbitmq.com/web-stomp.html.

The STOMP protocol is a human-readable, text-based streaming protocol designed to be simple and easy to implement. Although binary protocols such as AMQP and MQTT may be more efficient on the wire, using less data to transfer the same message, the STOMP protocol has some advantages, especially when using the STOMP plugin with RabbitMQ. The queue creation and binding behaviors require less code on your end, but they also come at a cost. The proxied AMQP connections created by the STOMP plugin that are used to communicate the translated STOMP data with RabbitMQ have overhead that direct AMQP connections do not have.

As with the various options that are available to you in publishing and consuming AMQP messages, I highly recommend that you benchmark the use of STOMP with RabbitMQ prior to using it in production. Each protocol has its advantages and disadvantages, and in some cases, neither is ideal.

In the next section, we'll cover statelessd, a web application used for high-performance, stateless publishing into RabbitMQ. It was created for scenarios where both the AMQP and STOMP protocols carry too much protocol overhead for single-transaction, fire-and-forget publishing.

9.3   Stateless publishing via HTTP

In some scenarios, AMQP, MQTT, STOMP, and other stateful protocols are expensive for environments with high message velocities that can't maintain long-running connections to RabbitMQ. Because these protocols have a bit of overhead related to connecting prior to being able to take message-related actions, they can be less than ideal, from a performance perspective, for short-lived connections. It was this realization that led to the development of statelessd, an HTTP-to-AMQP publishing proxy that enables high-performance, fire-and-forget message publishing for client applications without requiring the overhead of connection state management.

9.3.1   How statelessd came to be

Sometime in mid-2008 we started to build out our asynchronous messaging architecture at MeetMe.com (then myYearbook.com) as a way to decouple database writes from our PHP-based web application. Initially we built this architecture using Apache ActiveMQ, a Java-based message broker service with support for the STOMP protocol. As foundationally important as memcached was to the success of our database-read scaling, messaging, STOMP, and ActiveMQ allowed us to create consumer applications that fundamentally changed how we thought about database writes, constraining workloads, and scaling out computationally expensive workloads.

As our traffic grew, we encountered scaling issues with ActiveMQ and started to evaluate other brokers. At the time, RabbitMQ showed a lot of promise and supported the same STOMP protocol we used with ActiveMQ. As we migrated to RabbitMQ, we found it to be a good choice for our environment, but it introduced new issues.

One of the things we immediately discovered when we started using RabbitMQ was that the stateful AMQ protocol was very expensive for our PHP application stack. We found that PHP couldn't maintain the state of open connections and channels across client requests. Every request that a PHP application processed required a new connection to RabbitMQ in order to publish any messages that needed to be sent.

Don't get me wrong, the amount of time required to create an AMQP connection with RabbitMQ isn't terribly substantial and can be measured in milliseconds. But when you're publishing tens of thousands of messages per second, usually once or twice per web request, you're turning over tens of thousands of connections to RabbitMQ per second. To address this we eventually created statelessd, an HTTP-to-AMQP publishing gateway. This application needed to accept a high velocity of HTTP requests while managing the connection stack required for our message publishing. In addition, it couldn't be a bottleneck for performance and needed to reliably get messages into RabbitMQ.

After releasing statelessd as open source, we found that we weren't unique in facing this issue. In 2013, the folks over at Weebly created a statelessd clone named Hare (https://github.com/Weebly/Hare) that's written in Go.

9.3.2 Using statelessd

Designed to require as little overhead as possible, statelessd expects that clients publishing messages through it via HTTP will use native HTTP conventions to convey all the information required to publish native AMQP messages. The first part of the path in the HTTP URI contains the virtual host in RabbitMQ that a message should be published to. Additionally, the exchange and routing key to be used are path components in the request:

```
http://host[:port]/<virtual-host>/<exchange>/<routing-key>
```

For the username and password, HTTP Basic Authentication headers are used. When a request comes in, the statelessd daemon will look to see if the combination of the RabbitMQ username, password, and virtual host exists in its stack of open connections. If it does, the daemon will use that open connection to publish the message posted down to it, returning a "request processed, no content returned" (204) status to the client.

Because statelessd is generally run in a controlled environment where authentication issues are very rare, a design tradeoff for optimum request efficiency was made. If the connection isn't established, statelessd will internally buffer the message, start an asynchronous process to connect to RabbitMQ, and return a 204 status to the client. Once the connection is established, any buffered messages for the specific combination of credentials will be sent. Should there be a problem connecting, the combination of credentials will be marked as bad, and any subsequent requests will receive a 424 or "request failed due to the nature of a previous request" error.

Statelessd requests use HTTP POST to send standard form-encoded key/value pairs that carry the body and properties of the message to be published. Valid keys for statelessd requests include body, the value of the actual message body itself, and the standard AMQP message property names, with the dash character replaced with an underscore. For example, to set the message-id property, the payload of the request should include a value assigned to the message_id key. For a full list of the valid keys in a statelessd request payload, refer to the documentation at https://github.com/gmr/statelessd.

9.3.3   *Operational architecture*

Statelessd is designed to be run on the same server as the RabbitMQ servers that messages should be published to. It's a Python-based daemon that's usually configured to have a backend process running for each CPU core on the server. Each backend process has its own HTTP port that it listens on. These processes are aggregated and can be proxied by a single port using a reverse proxy server like Nginx (figure 9.6), providing a scale-out solution that has benchmarked up to hundreds of thousands of messages per second per server.

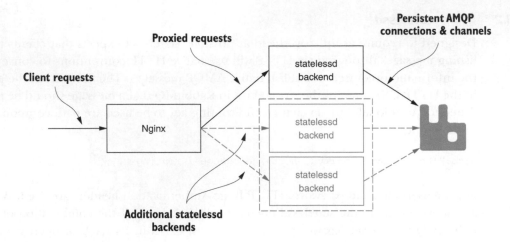

Figure 9.6   Statelessd operational architecture

If you need to run statelessd on multiple servers, each server's Nginx instance can be added to a load balancer, distributing the publishing requests across multiple servers in a cluster. Statelessd includes a URL endpoint for gathering statistical data that can be used to compare message-throughput rates between a cluster of statelessd nodes and RabbitMQ servers. Refer to the statelessd documentation at https://github.com/gmr/statelessd for information on installing and configuring statelessd.

9.3.4 *Publishing messages via statelessd*

To publish a message to RabbitMQ, any standard HTTP library should do. For this example, we'll use the Python library named `requests`. Prior to publishing a message, you should create and bind a queue to publish messages to. The following code from the "7.4.4 Queue Setup" notebook does just that.

```
import rabbitpy

with rabbitpy.Connection() as connection:
    with connection.channel() as channel:
        queue = rabbitpy.Queue(channel, 'statelessd-messages')
        queue.declare()
        queue.bind('amq.topic', '#')
```

With the queue declared, all that's left is to publish a message. Statelessd should already be running in the Vagrant virtual machine, so running the following code from "7.4.4 Publish Message" will publish a message to the "statelessd-messages" queue.

```
import requests

payload = {'body': 'from statelessd', 'app_id': 'example'}
response = requests.post('http://localhost:8900/%2f/amq.topic/example',
                         auth=('guest', 'guest'),
                         data=payload)
```

To verify that the message is published, navigate to the RabbitMQ management interface at http://localhost:15672/#/queues/%2F/statelessd-messages.

Now that you've published a message through statelessd, it's worth reiterating that statelessd solves a specific use case for publishing messages to RabbitMQ. As you think about where it may fit into your messaging architecture, consider the goals and performance of statelessd. It was designed to enable high-velocity publishing from many different publishing applications. It doesn't support the full AMQP protocol and doesn't support many of the more advanced publishing features in RabbitMQ, like Publisher Confirms or transactional publishing. It isn't for every project, but it's worth keeping in the back of your mind for projects were it does add tremendous value.

9.4 *Summary*

RabbitMQ goes beyond the AMQP goal of vendor and platform neutrality by supporting additional protocols such as STOMP and MQTT. In addition, there's a vibrant ecosystem of plugins and applications that allow applications to speak to RabbitMQ in different ways. For example, instead of using a protocol like AMQP for mobile applications that may be prone to network interruptions and slow transfer speeds, use MQTT, a protocol designed for such a task. Applications like Hare and statelessd exist to allow for more efficient message publishing.

Additionally, here's a list of plugins that add additional protocol support to RabbitMQ:

- rabbithub—Adds PubSubHubBub support to RabbitMQ (https://github.com/tonyg/rabbithub)
- udp_exchange—Uses UDP to publish messages to RabbitMQ (https://github.com/tonyg/udp-exchange)
- rabbitmq-smtp—An SMTP-to-AMQP gateway for RabbitMQ (https://github.com/rabbitmq/rabbitmq-smtp)
- rabbitmq-xmpp—An XMPP-to-AMQP gateway for RabbitMQ (https://github.com/tonyg/rabbitmq-xmpp)

These examples demonstrate the variety of messaging protocols that can be used with RabbitMQ. Although the rabbitmq-smtp plugin may have limited use cases compared to the Web STOMP plugin, your application may have unique requirements, and I encourage you to make sure you're using the right tool for the job when it comes to communicating with RabbitMQ.

Database integrations 10

This chapter covers

- Publishing AMQP messages from PostgreSQL
- Making RabbitMQ listen to PostgreSQL notifications
- Using the InfluxDB storage exchange to store messages

Using RabbitMQ to decouple write operations against OLTP databases is a common way to achieve great data warehousing and event-stream processing techniques. When you publish messages with serialized data that will be written to the database, a simple consumer application can act as the bridge between events and your database. But it's possible to skip the consumer step altogether and use a RabbitMQ plugin, such as the InfluxDB storage exchange, and automatically store messages in your database, directly from RabbitMQ.

The integration of RabbitMQ with an external database doesn't stop there. Another powerful pattern is for your database to directly publish messages to RabbitMQ. This can be achieved by using extensions or plugins in the database, or by having a RabbitMQ plugin that acts as a database client, publishing messages whenever database events occur.

205

NOTE   Both of these patterns of database integration can simplify operational complexity, reducing the need for external consumer applications to perform the same type of work. But this simplification comes at a price. With your database and RabbitMQ more tightly coupled, failure scenarios can become more complex. For example, what happens if your database server becomes slow or unresponsive when RabbitMQ is trying to insert records into it? It's important to answer questions like this by testing your integrations for failure scenarios and determining proper troubleshooting and recovery steps prior to production use.

This chapter explores both these patterns of database integration with RabbitMQ. First you'll learn how the PostgreSQL pg_amqp extension can be employed to publish messages using stored procedures. Then you'll learn how you can achieve the same type of behavior using PostgreSQL's LISTEN/NOTIFY functionality with the PostgreSQL LISTEN exchange. We'll then move from the relational world to the NoSQL world, and you'll see how the InfluxDB storage exchange can be leveraged to store messages as time-series data as they're published into RabbitMQ.

10.1   The pg_amqp PostgreSQL extension

The idea of publishing messages directly from PostgreSQL when triggers are executed is neither new nor novel. It was as early as 2003 that the Slony replication system (http://slony.info) used PostgreSQL's trigger functions to send event messages, implementing master-slave replication. In 2008, to create a loosely coupled replication system offering more flexibility than the existing replication systems, I created Golconde. Golconde (https://code.google.com/p/golconde) leveraged POST COMMIT triggers and PL/Python to send transactional data to other PostgreSQL servers via the STOMP messaging protocol. The latest versions of PostgreSQL use event messaging to stream transactional data to hot-standby PostgreSQL instances that act as read-only slaves with the ability to failover if a master becomes unresponsive.

Given this solid history of event-based replication for PostgreSQL, it seems only natural that someone would add flexible messaging capabilities to its ecosystem. In 2009, Theo Schlossnagle of OmniTI released pg_amqp, a PostgreSQL extension that exposes AMQP publishing via PostgreSQL functions. Although pg_amqp only exposes a subset of the AMQP 0-8 specification, it performs solidly when publishing messages from PostgreSQL's trigger functions. The functionality exposed by pg_amqp is accessible just like any other PostgreSQL function and can be invoked in SQL statements and stored procedures alike. Pg_amqp exposes a simple AMQP with two methods for interacting with RabbitMQ: `amqp.publish` and `amqp.disconnect`. The `amqp.publish` method creates an AMQP message and delivers it using the `Basic.Publish` RPC method, just like any other AMQP publisher (figure 10.1). Connections are automatically established and destroyed, but if you want to directly terminate a connection after publishing a message, you can invoke the `amqp.disconnect` function.

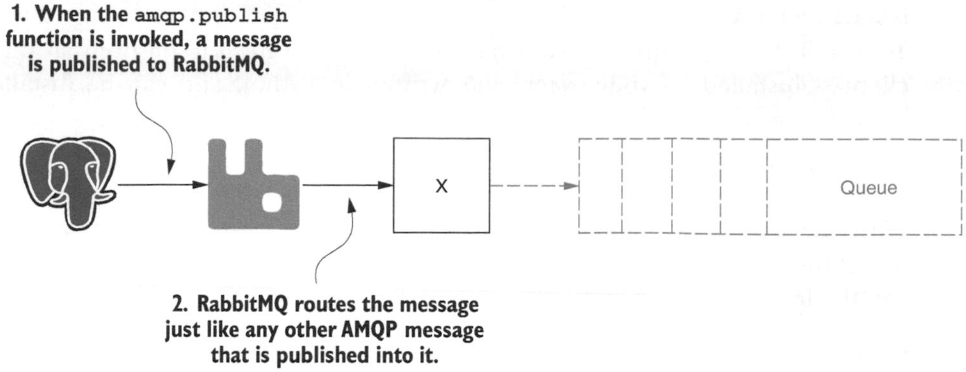

1. When the `amqp.publish`
function is invoked, a message
is published to RabbitMQ.

2. RabbitMQ routes the message
just like any other AMQP message
that is published into it.

Figure 10.1 `pg_amqp.publish` uses `Basic.Publish` to send a message to RabbitMQ.

When you use pg_amqp, you're invoking synchronous communication with RabbitMQ, and care should be taken to ensure that your use doesn't impact your overall query velocity. As with any tightly coupled integration, benchmarking should be performed and failure scenarios should be tested prior to putting a system into production. For example, if you wrap your use of `amqp.publish` in a transaction, what happens if pg_amqp can't connect to the RabbitMQ broker? Will your database transactions complete if there's a publishing failure?

To find out, you must first install the pg_amqp extension.

10.1.1 Installing the pg_amqp extension

There are two ways to install the pg_amqp extension: You can install it by downloading and compiling the source manually or by using the PostgreSQL Extension Network (PGXN) client. PGXN (http://pgxn.org) is a package repository for PostgreSQL extensions. PGXN-based installation is dramatically easier, but it doesn't work with PostgreSQL 9.3 installations. Unless you're using PostgreSQL 9.3 or later, I recommend that you start with the PGXN install and fall back to manual installation if that fails.

> **NOTE** Before you attempt to install pg_amqp, you should first ensure that you have fully installed PostgreSQL version 9.1 or greater, including the development files, because the extension is compiled as part of the installation process. In addition, you'll need the tool chain for compiling PostgreSQL from source. If you need help installing PostgreSQL or the developer tool chain required for compiling PostgreSQL, you can find installation guides on the official Wiki at https://wiki.postgresql.org/wiki/Detailed_installation _guides.

INSTALLATION VIA PGXN

To install the pg_amqp extension via PGXN, you first need to ensure that the PGXN client is installed on your system. It's written in Python and can be installed with `easy_install`:

```
easy_install pgxnclient
```

With the `pgxnclient` application installed, you can now attempt to automatically install the extension. As a user with permission to write to PostgreSQL's `lib` directory, run the following command:

```
pgxnclient install pg_amqp
```

If everything worked as expected, the command won't have returned an error. But don't worry if you encountered an error. Although the manual installation has more steps, it's nearly as easy.

MANUAL INSTALLATION

The source code for pg_amqp is available on GitHub at https://github.com/omniti-labs/pg_amqp. If you're not familiar with Git, you can download the source code from https://github.com/omniti-labs/pg_amqp/archive/v0.3.0.zip and extract it to a directory for compilation. The following code listing, written in BASH script, fixes the installation for PostgreSQL 9.3 or later systems and should be run in the top-level directory of the extracted source.

> **Listing 10.1   Compiling and installing pg_amqp**

```bash
#!/bin/bash
LIBDIR=`pg_config --libdir`
INSTALLSH="$LIBDIR/pgxs/config/install-sh"
make && make INSTALL=$INSTALLSH install
```

Once you've successfully installed the pg_amqp extension, you'll need to load it into a PostgreSQL database. For ease of illustration, the following example uses the default `postgres` superuser and `postgres` database; this is not required for use, though the user must be a superuser.

To load the extension, connect to the PostgreSQL database using `psql`:

```
$ psql -U postgres postgres
```

When you've connected, you should see output similar to the following:

```
psql (9.3.5)
Type "help" for help.

postgres=>
```

Now you can load the extension using the CREATE EXTENSION syntax:

```
postgres=> CREATE EXTENSION amqp;
```

If the extension was loaded successfully, you'll receive a confirmation similar to the following:

```
CREATE EXTENSION
```

With the extension loaded, you can move on to configuring the extension and then publishing messages.

10.1.2 Configuring the pg_amqp extension

The extension is configured by populating the amqp.broker table that was automatically created when you ran the CREATE EXTENSION query in the previous section. As shown in table 10.1, amqp.broker contains the normal AMQP connection settings along with a broker_id field that's used when invoking both the amqp.publish and amqp.disconnect functions.

Table 10.1   The amqp.broker table definition

Column	Type	Modifiers
broker_id	Integer	not null default nextval('broker_broker_id_seq')
host	Text	not null
port	Integer	not null default 5672
vhost	Text	
username	Text	
password	Text	

If you're running PostgreSQL locally and RabbitMQ in the Vagrant VM used in earlier chapters, you should be able to connect on localhost. The following SQL statement will configure pg_amqp by inserting a row into the table that connects to RabbitMQ on localhost, port 5672, using the / virtual host and the guest/guest username and password combination. If the connection settings won't work due to differences in your testing environment, adjust the SQL accordingly.

```
INSERT INTO amqp.broker (host, port, vhost, username, password)
  VALUES ('localhost', 5672, '/', 'guest', 'guest')
  RETURNING broker_id;
```

When you execute the command, you'll get the broker_id value back, confirming successful insertion into the table:

```
broker_id
-----------
          1
(1 row)

INSERT 0 1
```

Remember the `broker_id` value because you'll be using that to publish messages into RabbitMQ.

10.1.3   *Publishing a message via pg_amqp*

With pg_amqp installed and configured, it's nearly time to publish your first message. Before you do, you should set up a queue in the RabbitMQ management UI to receive the message. Open your web browser to http://localhost:15672/#/queues and create a queue named `pg_amqp-test`, as in figure 10.2.

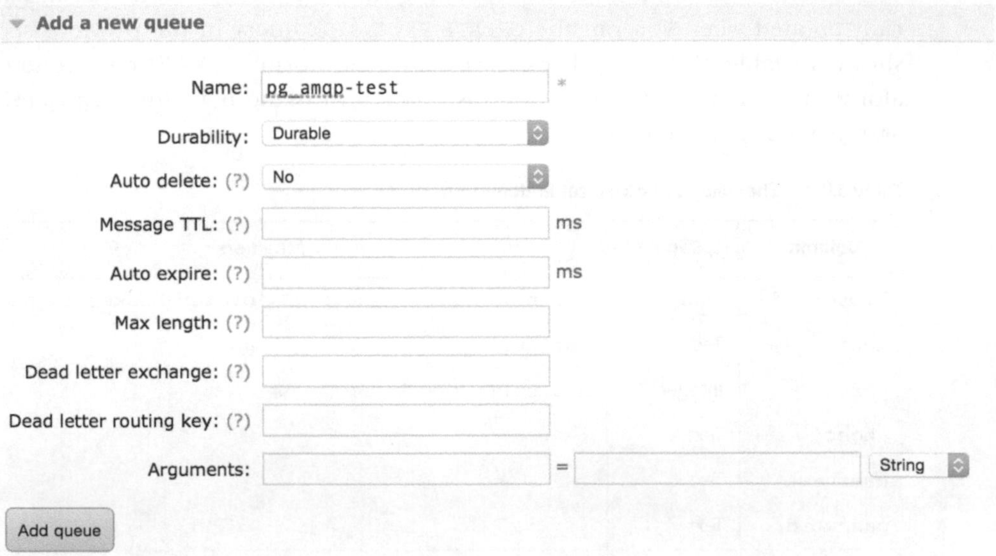

Figure 10.2   Creating the `pg_amqp-test` queue

Once you've created the queue, you can test publishing to the queue from Postgre-SQL via the default direct exchange using the queue name (`pg_amqp-test`) as the routing key. Using `psql` connected to the `postgres` database, issue the following query that passes the broker ID, exchange, routing key, and message:

```
SELECT amqp.publish(1, '', 'pg_amqp-test',
                'Test message from PostgreSQL');
```

Once it's submitted, you should receive confirmation that the query executed successfully:

```
publish
---------
 t
(1 row)
```

Although PostgreSQL has said the message was published, a better validation would be to use the management UI to retrieve the published message. On the queue detail page at http://localhost:15672/#/queues/%2F/pg_amqp-test you can use the Get Messages section to retrieve and inspect the message. As shown in figure 10.3, once you click the Get Message(s) button, you should see the message that was published via the PostgreSQL amqp.publish function.

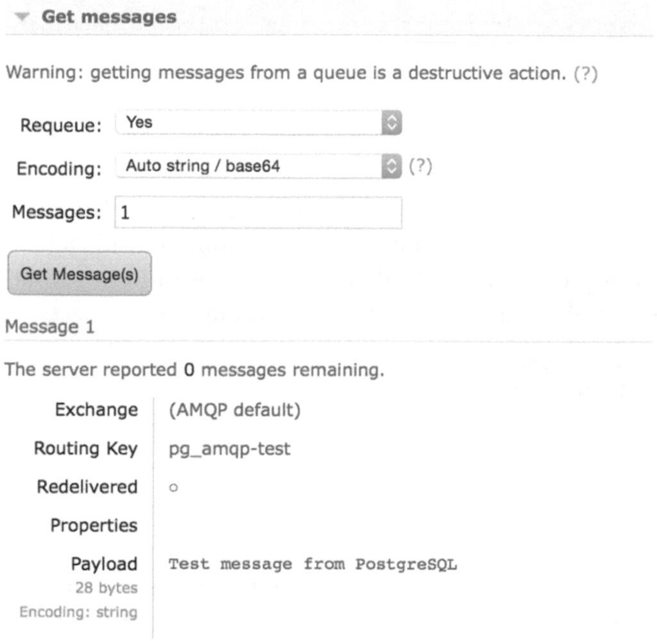

▼ **Get messages**

Warning: getting messages from a queue is a destructive action. (?)

Requeue: `Yes`

Encoding: `Auto string / base64` (?)

Messages: `1`

Get Message(s)

Message 1

The server reported **0** messages remaining.

Exchange	(AMQP default)
Routing Key	pg_amqp-test
Redelivered	○
Properties	
Payload 28 bytes Encoding: string	Test message from PostgreSQL

Figure 10.3 Using the management UI to confirm the message was published

As you can see, publishing messages via pg_amqp is a fairly trivial exercise once you have it set up and configured. It's worth noting that you can't set the AMQP message properties as of version 0.3. Additionally, message publishing is wrapped in an AMQP transaction. Should you invoke the amqp.publish function in a PostgreSQL transaction and then roll back the transaction, the RabbitMQ transaction will be rolled back as well. In most cases, publish will be wrapped within a stored procedure, either along with other actions inside the stored procedure, or as a trigger function that's executed on the INSERT, UPDATE, or DELETE of rows in a table.

NOTE   The management UI warns you that the Get Messages(s) operation is a destructive action. What it means by this is that the message is actually removed from the queue to display it, and if the Requeue option is set to Yes, it will republish the message back into the queue, so it will now be at the end of the queue instead of at the front.

DEALING WITH FAILURE

You may have noticed that when you called the `amqp.publish` function, it returned a Boolean value. In the case of success, it returned a `t` or true, but what happens if it can't connect to RabbitMQ? Issuing the same statement in a new transaction with a new connection attempt will return `f` or false and log a warning:

```
postgres=# SELECT amqp.publish(1, '', 'pg_amqp-test',
                   'Test message from PostgreSQL');

WARNING: amqp[localhost:5672] login socket/connect failed: Connection refused

 publish
---------
 f
(1 row)
```

In this scenario it's pretty easy to test for the result of the `amqp.publish` call, and if it's false, you weren't able to publish. But what if something happens inside a long-running transaction and RabbitMQ disconnects? In this scenario, the call will invoke true but log a warning that the AMQP transaction couldn't be committed:

```
postgres=# SELECT amqp.publish(1, '', 'pg_amqp-test',
                   'Test message from PostgreSQL');
WARNING:  amqp could not commit tx mode on broker 1
 publish
---------
 t
(1 row)
```

Unfortunately, as of version 0.3.0 of pg_amqp, you can't catch this error, and if you're not watching your PostgreSQL logs, you could be losing messages without knowing it. Although this is problematic behavior, it's better than losing your database transaction. Like with all operational systems, monitoring is key. If you use a system like Splunk, you can create a job that periodically searches for AMQP errors in PostgreSQL's logs. Alternatively, you could write your own app or plugin for systems like Nagios that scans the logs looking for such warnings.

10.2 *Listening to PostgreSQL notifications*

Although pg_amqp provides a convenient and fast way of publishing messages directly from PostgreSQL, it creates a tightly coupled integration between the server instances. Should your RabbitMQ cluster become unavailable for any reason, it could have an adverse impact on your PostgreSQL server. To avoid such tight coupling while retaining the direct integration, I created the PostgreSQL LISTEN exchange.

The PostgreSQL LISTEN exchange acts as a PostgreSQL client, listening for notifications issued in PostgreSQL by the NOTIFY SQL statement. PostgreSQL notifications are sent to a channel, a text value that clients subscribe to. This value is used in the PostgreSQL LISTEN exchange as the routing key for the published message. When notifications are sent on a channel that the LISTEN exchange has registered on, the notification will be turned into a message that's then published using direct-exchange-like behavior (figure 10.4).

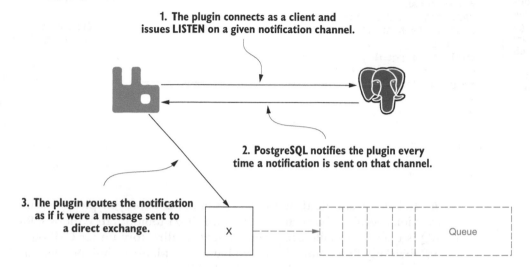

1. The plugin connects as a client and issues LISTEN on a given notification channel.

2. PostgreSQL notifies the plugin every time a notification is sent on that channel.

3. The plugin routes the notification as if it were a message sent to a direct exchange.

X

Queue

Figure 10.4   The LISTEN exchange acts as a PostgreSQL client, publishing notifications as messages.

Of course, with any technology decision there are trade-offs. With pg_amqp, should PostgreSQL be unable to connect to RabbitMQ, the calls to amqp.publish will fail. With the LISTEN exchange, should the PostgreSQL connection fail, it can't register for notifications and, in turn, it won't publish any messages. You can watch for such a scenario by monitoring the throughput rate of the exchange using the RabbitMQ management API.

10.2.1   Installing the PostgreSQL LISTEN exchange

The PostgreSQL LISTEN exchange can be downloaded from its GitHub project page at https://github.com/AWeber/pgsql-listen-exchange. In the README displayed on the project page are downloads of precompiled binary plugins for specific RabbitMQ versions. When you download and install the plugin, make sure you're getting the latest version for your version of RabbitMQ.

The download is a zip file with two RabbitMQ plugins: the exchange and a PostgreSQL driver. The following code listing will download and install the plugin on an OS X system running RabbitMQ 3.3.5 installed via Homebrew. For other systems, you'll need to alter the RABBITMQ_DIR assignment, specifying the correct path to the RabbitMQ base directory.

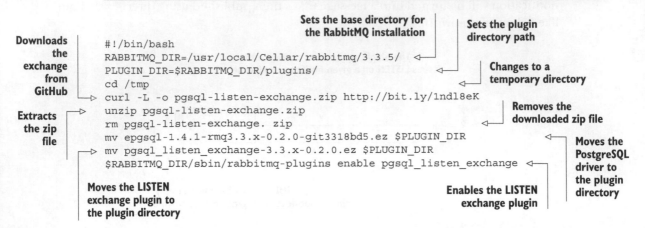

Listing 10.2   OS X installation script for the LISTEN exchange

Downloads the exchange from GitHub

Extracts the zip file

Sets the base directory for the RabbitMQ installation

Sets the plugin directory path

Changes to a temporary directory

Removes the downloaded zip file

Moves the PostgreSQL driver to the plugin directory

Moves the LISTEN exchange plugin to the plugin directory

Enables the LISTEN exchange plugin

```bash
#!/bin/bash
RABBITMQ_DIR=/usr/local/Cellar/rabbitmq/3.3.5/
PLUGIN_DIR=$RABBITMQ_DIR/plugins/
cd /tmp
curl -L -o pgsql-listen-exchange.zip http://bit.ly/1ndl8eK
unzip pgsql-listen-exchange.zip
rm pgsql-listen-exchange. zip
mv epgsql-1.4.1-rmq3.3.x-0.2.0-git3318bd5.ez $PLUGIN_DIR
mv pgsql_listen_exchange-3.3.x-0.2.0.ez $PLUGIN_DIR
$RABBITMQ_DIR/sbin/rabbitmq-plugins enable pgsql_listen_exchange
```

NOTE   In Ubuntu and RedHat/CentOS systems, RabbitMQ is typically installed to a version-specific subdirectory under /usr/lib/rabbitmq. In Windows, RabbitMQ is typically installed to a version-specific directory under C:\Program Files\RabbitMQ. Precompiled binary plugins are platform independent and can be run on any platform that runs RabbitMQ.

To verify that the plugin has been installed correctly, navigate to the management UI's Exchanges tab at http://localhost:15672/#/exchanges. In the Add a New Exchange section, you should see the x-pgsql-listen value in the Type drop-down list (figure 10.5).

After validating that the plugin was installed correctly, you can now move on to configuring the exchange. If you don't see the option in the drop-down list, it's possible

Figure 10.5   Validating that the x-pgsql-listen option exists in the Type drop-down list

that either the plugins weren't copied to the appropriate directory or that you're running an older version of Erlang than the plugins were compiled with. It's recommended that you use Erlang R16 or later.

There are multiple ways to configure the plugin: by directly configuring the exchange with connection arguments passed in during exchange declaration, by configuring the exchange in the rabbitmq.config file, or via a policy that's applied to the exchange. Policies provide the most flexible way of configuring the exchange and should be used until you have experience with the plugin and are confident about how it behaves.

10.2.2 Policy-based configuration

To get started, navigate to the Admin tab of the management UI. From there, click Policies on the right side of the page (figure 10.6).

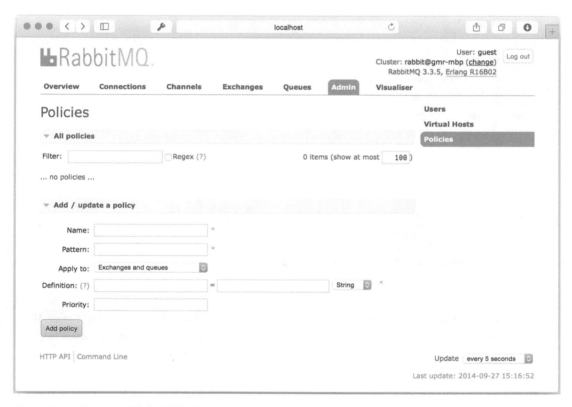

Figure 10.6   The management UI Policies page

To create the policy required for connecting to PostgreSQL, specify a name for the policy, a regular expression pattern for matching the exchange name, and the PostgreSQL host, port, database name, user name, and optionally password. Additionally, you can narrow down the policy by specifying that it only applies to exchanges. Figure 10.7 shows a policy that will connect to PostgreSQL on `localhost`, port `5432`, using the `postgres` database and username.

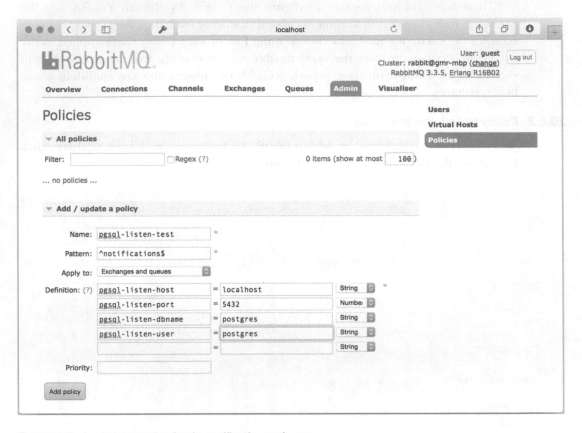

Figure 10.7   Declaring a policy for the notification exchange

Once you click Add Policy, you'll see the policy listed on the same page, as in figure 10.8.

When you add the policy, the connection information that you provide will be checked for type correctness but not validity. You won't know if the connection information is valid until the exchange is created.

Name	Pattern	Apply to	Definition	Priority
pgsql-listen-test	^notifications$	exchanges	pgsql-listen-host: localhost pgsql-listen-port: 5432 pgsql-listen-dbname: postgres pgsql-listen-user: postgres	0

Figure 10.8   The policy added to the All Policies section

10.2.3 Creating the exchange

With the policy created, navigate to the Exchanges tab of the management UI at http://localhost:15672/#/exchanges. Add a new exchange using the Add a New Exchange form at the bottom of the page. Name the exchange notification so that the policy will match, and set the exchange type to x-pgsql-listen (figure 10.9).

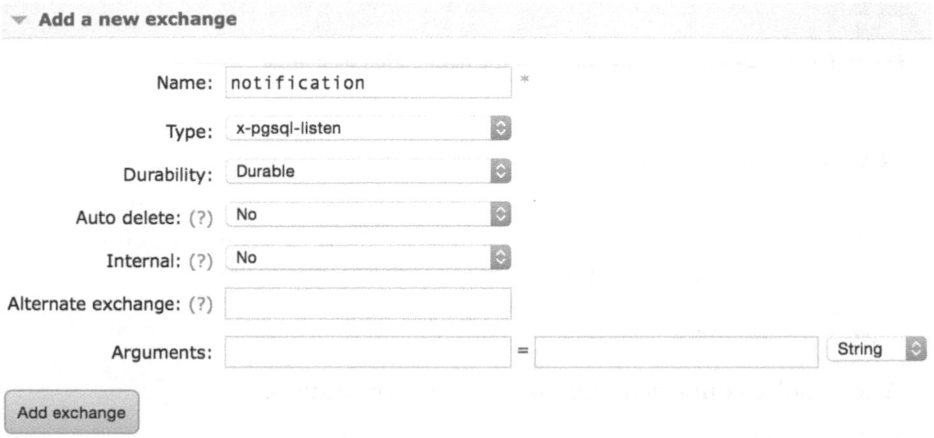

Figure 10.9 Adding the notification PostgreSQL LISTEN exchange

Once you add the exchange, it will connect to PostgreSQL, but it won't start listening for notifications. To have it start listening to exchanges, you must bind to the exchange with a routing key that matches the PostgreSQL notification channel string.

10.2.4 Creating and binding a test queue

The last setup step for testing the LISTEN exchange is creating a test queue that your notifications will be sent to. If you navigate to the Queues tab of the management UI (http://localhost:15672/#/queues), you can create a queue with the Add a New Queue section. For the purposes of this test, call the queue notification-test. You don't need to specify any custom attributes or change any of the default properties in the form when adding the queue.

Once you've added the queue, navigate to the queue's page in the management UI at http://localhost:15672/#/queues/%2F/notification-test. In the Bindings section of the page, you can create a new binding to the notification exchange with a routing key of example (figure 10.10).

Once added, the exchange will connect to PostgreSQL and execute a LISTEN statement, registering for all notifications sent on the example channel. You're now ready to send a test notification.

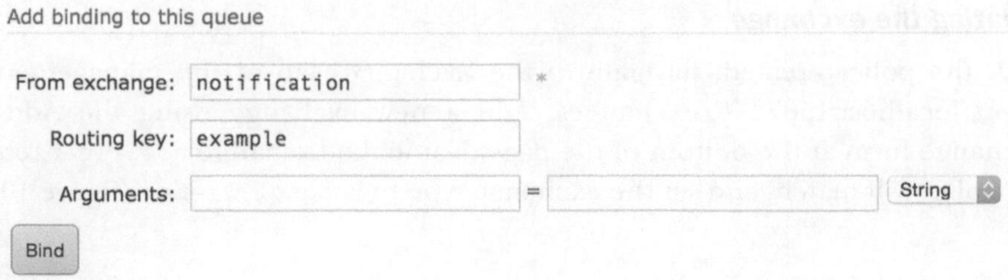

Add binding to this queue

From exchange: `notification`   *

Routing key: `example`

Arguments: ⬚ = ⬚   String ⬍

Bind

Figure 10.10   Binding the test queue to the notification exchange

10.2.5 *Publishing via NOTIFY*

To validate that the exchange setup is correct, you can now send a notification in PostgreSQL using the NOTIFY SQL statement. To do so, use psql, connecting as post-gres to the postgres database:

```
$ psql -U postgres postgres
```

When you've connected, you can send the notification:

```
psql (9.3.5)
Type "help" for help.
postgres=# NOTIFY example, 'This is a test from PostgreSQL';
NOTIFY
```

With the notification sent, switch back to the RabbitMQ management UI to get the message from the notification-test queue in the Get Messages section (figure 10.11).

As you can see, the LISTEN exchange adds metadata about the message that's not populated when using pg_amqp. The message properties specify the app_id, noting that the message originated from the pgsql-listen-exchange plugin. The timestamp is also shown, taken from the current local time of the RabbitMQ server. Additionally, headers are set that specify the PostgreSQL notification channel, database, server, and name of the source exchange.

Although this example was a plain text string, functions sending notifications can serialize data in a variety of formats, making notifications a versatile part of your application. Perhaps you want to use them for debugging complex stored procedures, making it easy to trace the state of data as it travels through your database. Or maybe you want to use them to update disparate systems in the cloud, using the exchange in combination with the RabbitMQ federation plugin. In either circumstance, the LISTEN exchange adds loosely coupled integration with PostgreSQL with very little overhead for either system.

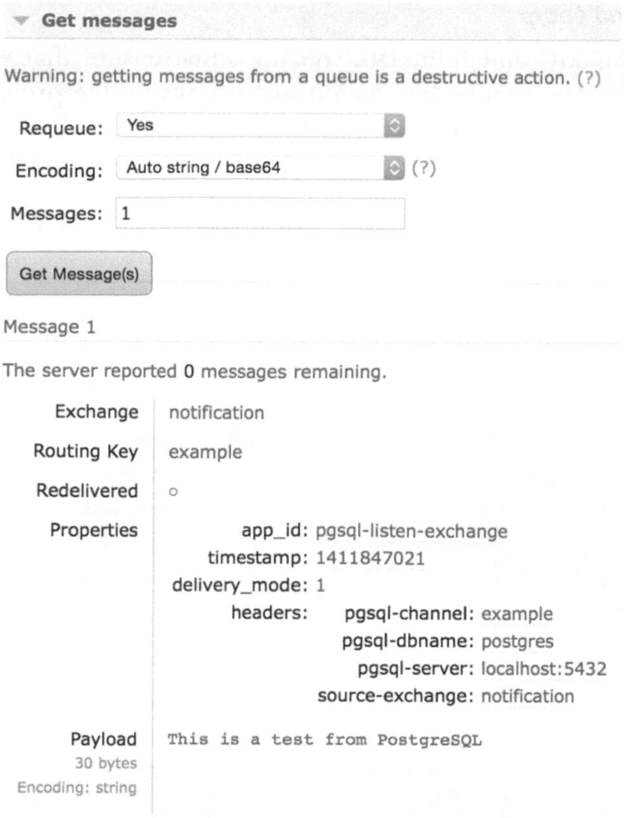

▼ **Get messages**

Warning: getting messages from a queue is a destructive action. (?)

Requeue: `Yes`

Encoding: `Auto string / base64` (?)

Messages: `1`

[Get Message(s)]

Message 1

The server reported **0** messages remaining.

Exchange	notification
Routing Key	example
Redelivered	○
Properties	app_id: pgsql-listen-exchange
	timestamp: 1411847021
	delivery_mode: 1
	headers: pgsql-channel: example
	pgsql-dbname: postgres
	pgsql-server: localhost:5432
	source-exchange: notification
Payload	`This is a test from PostgreSQL`
30 bytes	
Encoding: string	

Figure 10.11 Getting the message from the `notification-test` queue

10.3 *Storing messages in InfluxDB*

InfluxDB (http://influxdb.com) is an open source, distributed, time-series database written in Go. It's very easy to set up for both Linux and OS X systems. It's a compelling system for storing time-series data for analytical purposes, as it provides multiple easy-to-use protocols for populating data and a built-in web-based query interface for querying the data it stores. It's quickly becoming an alternative to systems like Graphite because it provides more scalable storage that's accessible via a cohesive, scale-out cluster.

Messages that are routed through the InfluxDB storage exchange are examined to determine whether they should be stored in InfluxDB. If the content type of a message is specified and it's set to application/json, the message will be transformed into the proper format and stored in InfluxDB using the routing key as the InfluxDB event name. Additionally, if the timestamp is specified, it will automatically be mapped to the InfluxDB event time column.

10.3.1 *InfluxDB installation and setup*

To get started with RabbitMQ and InfluxDB, you must first ensure that you have InfluxDB installed. There are detailed installation instructions on the project documentation page at http://influxdb.com/docs/. Pick the latest version from the documentation index, and then follow the installation instructions and the getting started instructions to check that the system is installed and set up correctly.

Alternatively, for learning about InfluxDB, the project provides a public playground server at http://play.influxdb.org. If you're using Windows or you don't want to install a server locally on your computer, you can use the public playground with the InfluxDB storage exchange to test the integration. The examples in this section of the chapter will assume a local installation, but you should only need to change the connection and authentication information to use the public playground server.

If you're setting up a local instance of InfluxDB, you'll need to create both a database and a user for RabbitMQ. To do so, open your web browser to http://localhost:8083 and log in to the administration interface using the username root and the password root (figure 10.12).

Once you log in for the first time, you'll be prompted to create a database. For validating the InfluxDB storage exchange, create an exchange called rabbitmq-test (figure 10.13).

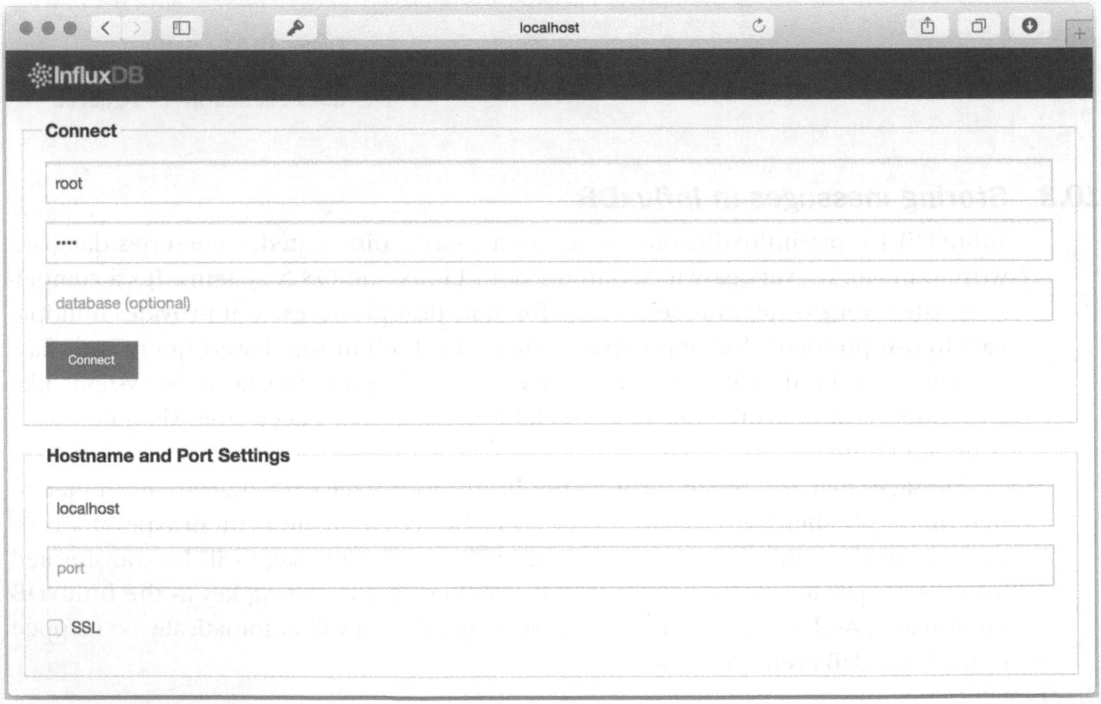

Figure 10.12   Logging into the InfluxDB administration interface

Figure 10.13 Creating the `rabbitmq-test` database

Once you've created the database, it will appear in a list at the top of the web page. Click on `rabbitmq-test` in that list and you'll be taken to a page where you can add a user for RabbitMQ that the plugin will use to authenticate to RabbitMQ (figure 10.14). On that form, enter the username `rabbitmq` and the password `test`, and then click the Create button.

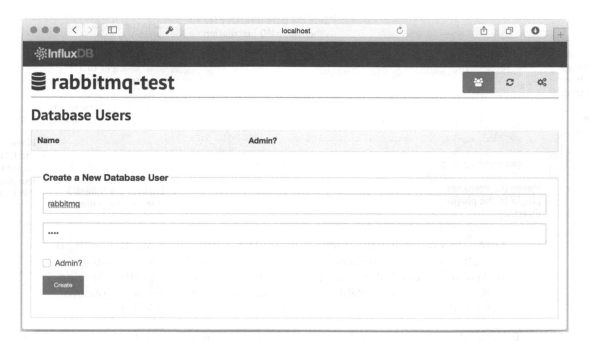

Figure 10.14 Creating the `rabbitmq` user for the `rabbitmq-test` database

Once you've created the user, it will show up in the Database Users table at the top of the page. Then you're ready to install and configure the InfluxDB storage exchange.

10.3.2 *Installing the InfluxDB storage exchange*

Installing and configuring the InfluxDB storage exchange is very similar to the process for the PostgreSQL LISTEN Exchange. The plugin can be downloaded from its GitHub project page at https://github.com/aweber/influxdb-storage-exchange. The README displayed on the project page lists download links for precompiled binary plugins for specific RabbitMQ versions. When you download and install the plugin, make sure you're getting the latest version for your version of RabbitMQ.

The download is a zip file with two RabbitMQ plugins: the exchange and an HTTP client library. The following code listing will download and install the plugin on an OS X system running RabbitMQ 3.3.5 installed via Homebrew. For other systems, you'll need to alter the RABBITMQ_DIR assignment, specifying the correct path to the RabbitMQ base directory.

> **Listing 10.3   OS X installation script for the LISTEN exchange**

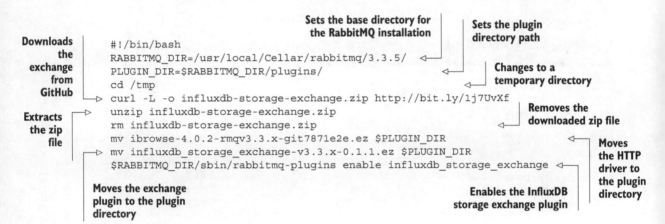

Sets the base directory for the RabbitMQ installation
Sets the plugin directory path
Downloads the exchange from GitHub
Changes to a temporary directory

```
#!/bin/bash
RABBITMQ_DIR=/usr/local/Cellar/rabbitmq/3.3.5/
PLUGIN_DIR=$RABBITMQ_DIR/plugins/
cd /tmp
curl -L -o influxdb-storage-exchange.zip http://bit.ly/1j7UvXf
unzip influxdb-storage-exchange.zip
rm influxdb-storage-exchange.zip
mv ibrowse-4.0.2-rmqv3.3.x-git7871e2e.ez $PLUGIN_DIR
mv influxdb_storage_exchange-v3.3.x-0.1.1.ez $PLUGIN_DIR
$RABBITMQ_DIR/sbin/rabbitmq-plugins enable influxdb_storage_exchange
```

Extracts the zip file
Removes the downloaded zip file
Moves the HTTP driver to the plugin directory
Moves the exchange plugin to the plugin directory
Enables the InfluxDB storage exchange plugin

> **NOTE**   As a reminder, in Ubuntu and RedHat/CentOS systems, RabbitMQ is typically installed to a version-specific subdirectory under /usr/lib/rabbitmq. In Windows, RabbitMQ is typically installed to a version-specific directory under C:\Program Files\RabbitMQ. Precompiled binary plugins are platform independent and can be run on any platform that runs RabbitMQ.

To verify that the plugin has been installed correctly, navigate to the management UI Exchanges tab at http://localhost:15672/#/exchanges. In the Add a New Exchange section, you should see the x-influxdb-storage value in the Type drop-down list (figure 10.15).

With the installation properly verified, you can now create an instance of the InfluxDB storage exchange.

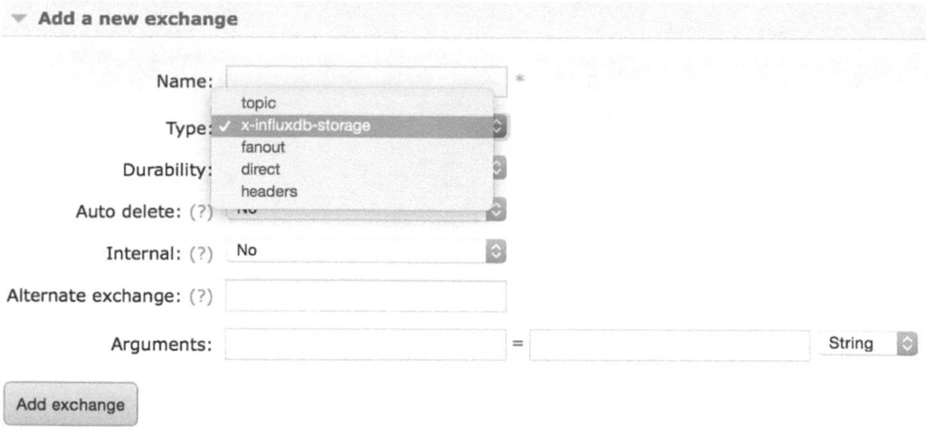

▼ **Add a new exchange**

Name: [   ] *

Type: [topic
       ✓ x-influxdb-storage
         fanout
         direct
         headers]

Durability: [◇]

Auto delete: (?) [◇]

Internal: (?) [No   ◇]

Alternate exchange: (?) [   ]

Arguments: [   ] = [   ] [String ◇]

[Add exchange]

Figure 10.15 Validating that the InfluxDB storage exchange is installed properly

10.3.3 *Creating a test exchange*

Like the PostgreSQL LISTEN Exchange, the InfluxDB storage exchange can be configured by policy, by rabbitmq.config, or by passing custom arguments when declaring the exchange. For the various configuration options and variables used for each configuration method, check the README on GitHub at https://github.com/aweber/influxdb-storage-exchange. To illustrate the difference between the policy-based configuration used with the PostgreSQL LISTEN exchange and argument-based configuration, the following example will use an argument-based configuration when creating the exchange.

First, navigate to the Exchanges tab of the RabbitMQ management UI at http://localhost:15672/#/exchanges and go to the Add a New Exchange section. Configuring the exchange with custom arguments is done with variables that have a prefix of x-, indicating that each of these arguments aren't standard AMQP or RabbitMQ variables. You'll need to configure the host, port, database name, user, and password for the InfluxDB connection. Each of these values is prefixed with x-, as illustrated in figure 10.16. Failure to prefix the variables with x- will cause the exchange to use the default values for each of the settings you provide.

When you add the exchange, the parameters will be checked for type validity, but the connection information won't be tested. Due to the immutable nature of AMQP exchanges, if you misconfigure the exchange, it will need to be deleted and re-added.

Messages published into the exchange will first be stored in InfluxDB and then routed to any queues or exchanges bound to the exchange using the topic exchange routing key behavior. Misconfigured exchanges won't prevent messages from being routed through them, but they won't be able to store the messages in InfluxDB.

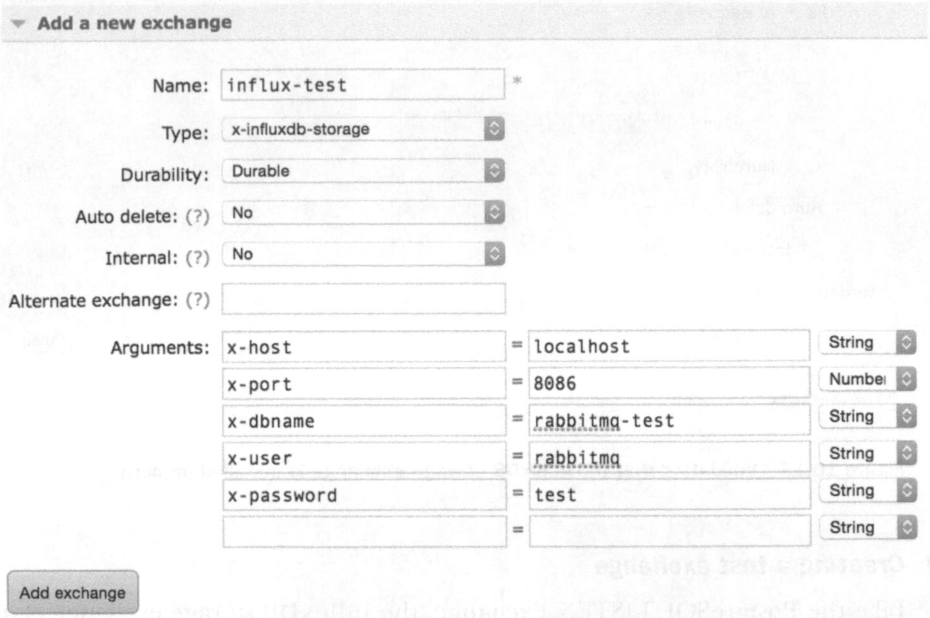

▽ Add a new exchange

Name:	`influx-test`	*
Type:	x-influxdb-storage ⬍	
Durability:	Durable ⬍	
Auto delete: (?)	No ⬍	
Internal: (?)	No ⬍	
Alternate exchange: (?)		

Arguments:				
	`x-host`	=	`localhost`	String ⬍
	`x-port`	=	`8086`	Number ⬍
	`x-dbname`	=	`rabbitmq-test`	String ⬍
	`x-user`	=	`rabbitmq`	String ⬍
	`x-password`	=	`test`	String ⬍
		=		String ⬍

Add exchange

Figure 10.16 Adding a new InfluxDB exchange with argument-based configuration

With the exchange created, you can now test the exchange by publishing messages into it. If you're using rabbitmq.config or policy-based configuration, you could leave the arguments empty and the values of either method would be applied to the exchange's configuration.

10.3.4 *Testing the exchange*

To test the proper integration of the exchange, navigate to the new exchange's page in the RabbitMQ management UI at http://localhost:15672/#/exchanges/%2F/influx-test. In the Publish a Message section, specify a message that has a content_ type of application/json, a valid timestamp value, and a well-formed JSON body (figure 10.17).

Because you didn't bind a queue to the exchange, you'll receive a warning that the message was published but not routed when you publish the message. That's OK for this test because you only want to verify that the data point made it into InfluxDB.

To validate that the event was stored properly, open the administration interface in your web browser by navigating to http://localhost:8083 and logging in as root using the password root. As illustrated in figure 10.18, you'll be presented with a list of databases. Click on the Explore Data link for the rabbitmq-test database.

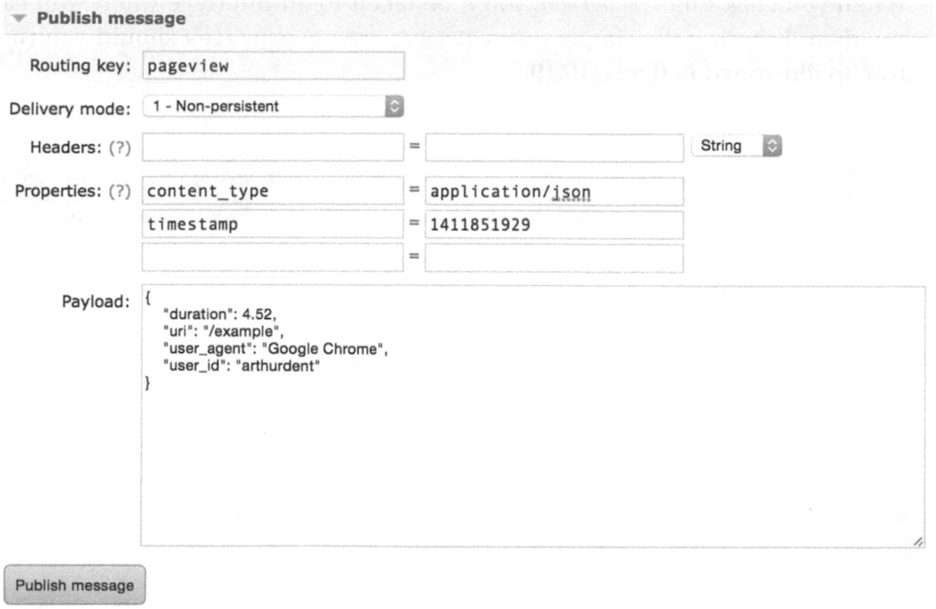

Figure 10.17 Publishing a JSON message to the InfluxDB storage exchange

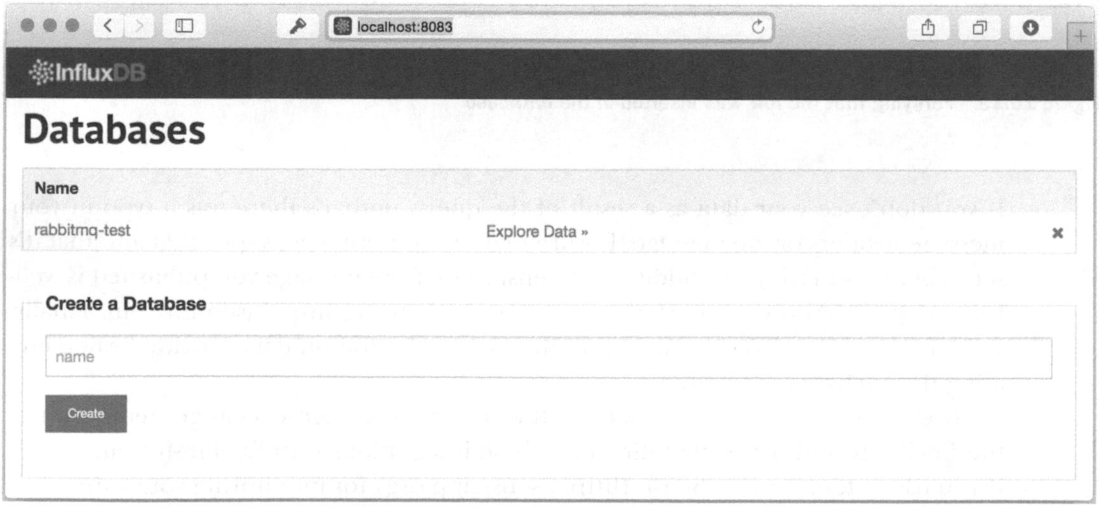

Figure 10.18 The InfluxDB administration interface showing a list of databases

When you click on *Explore Data*, you'll be taken to an interface where you can query the data. Entering the simple query SELECT * FROM pageview should return a single row, as illustrated in figure 10.19.

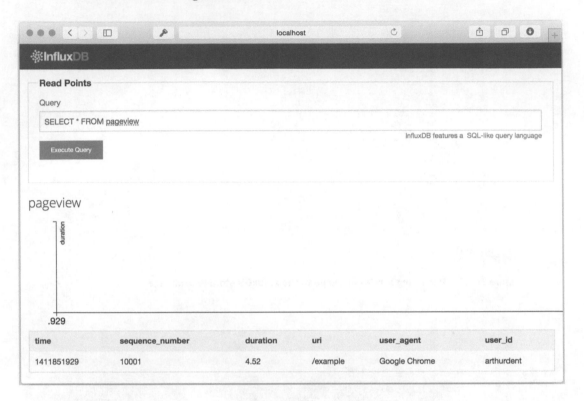

Figure 10.19   Verifying that the row was inserted in the database

If you don't see your data as a result of the query, perhaps there was a typo in your message headers or the message. Ensure that the content type is specified and that it's set to application/json. Additionally, ensure that the message you published is well-formed JSON. You can check your message body using http://jsonlint.com. Finally, validate that InfluxDB is running and that the configuration data provided when creating the exchange is accurate.

If everything worked as expected, the InfluxDB storage exchange demonstrates the flexibility and power that direct database integrations with RabbitMQ can create. If you use systems such as Sensu (http://sensuapp.org) for monitoring your infrastructure, you now have a powerful way to transparently tap into your event stream and store it in a database for further analysis, or for providing the information in a dashboard using Grafana (http://grafana.org).

10.4 *Summary*

Integrating databases with RabbitMQ reduces the operational overhead of running consumer or publisher applications outside of your database or RabbitMQ stack. Such simplification comes with a cost, however. Because RabbitMQ and your database are more tightly coupled, failure scenarios can become more complex.

In this chapter you learned how PostgreSQL can be used as a source of messages that are routed through RabbitMQ either by using the pg_amqp PostgreSQL extension or by using the PostgreSQL LISTEN exchange. Installing and using the InfluxDB storage exchange was detailed, demonstrating how messages published into RabbitMQ can be stored in a database by RabbitMQ itself.

The database integrations in this chapter are just the tip of the iceberg. There are other projects that directly integrate RabbitMQ with a database, such as the Riak exchange (https://github.com/jbrisbin/riak-exchange) and its counterpart, a project that implements Riak RabbitMQ commit hooks (https://github.com/jbrisbin/riak-rabbitmq-commit-hooks), publishing messages into RabbitMQ when write transactions occur in Riak. To see if there's a plugin for your database of choice, check out the RabbitMQ Community Plugins page at https://www.rabbitmq.com/community-plugins.html and the RabbitMQ Clients & Developer Tools page at https://www.rabbitmq.com/devtools.html.

Can't find what you're looking for? Perhaps you can contribute the next plugin providing database integration with RabbitMQ.

appendix
Getting set up

This appendix covers setting up VirtualBox, Vagrant, and the RabbitMQ in Depth Vagrant virtual machine (VM) that contains everything needed to test code samples, experiment, and follow along with the book.

VirtualBox is the virtualization software we'll use to run all of the examples, and Vagrant is an automation tool for setting up the VM. You'll need to install these two applications, and then you'll be able to set up the RabbitMQ in Depth VM by downloading a zip file containing the Vagrant configuration and Chef cookbooks. Once they're downloaded and extracted, you can start the VM by running a single command, and you'll be able to interactively test the code listings and examples in the book.

It's a fairly straightforward process in Windows, OS X, and Linux designed to keep the steps for following along with the book to a minimum. To get started, you'll need to download and install VirtualBox.

A.1   Installing VirtualBox

VirtualBox is a free virtualization product originally developed by Sun Microsystems and now made available by Oracle. It runs on Windows, Linux, Macintosh, and Solaris systems and provides the underlying VM that will be used for this book.

Setting up VirtualBox is very straightforward. You can download it from http://virtualbox.org. Just navigate to the Downloads page, chose the VirtualBox platform package for your operating system type, and download the installation package for your computer (figure A.1).

228

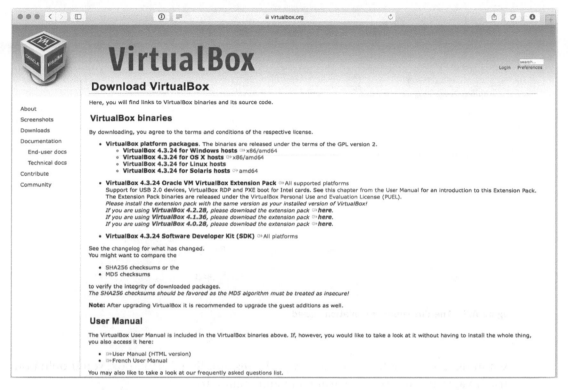

Figure A.1   The VirtualBox download page includes downloads for Windows, OS X, Linux, and Solaris.

NOTE   At the time of this writing, Vagrant supports VirtualBox versions 4.0.x, 4.1.x, 4.2.x, 4.3.x, 5.0.x, and 5.1.x. It's a safe assumption that with the popularity of both VirtualBox and Vagrant that Vagrant will continue to support new releases from the VirtualBox project shortly after they're released. In other words, you should be able to download the most current version of VirtualBox without concern for Vagrant incompatibility.

With the package downloaded, run the installer. Although each operating system will look slightly different, the installation process should be the same. It's safe in most circumstances to follow the default installation options when running the wizard (figure A.2).

If you'd like a more in-depth walkthrough of the options available for installing VirtualBox, chapter 2 of the VirtualBox user manual covers installation in a very detailed manner and is available at www.virtualbox.org/manual/ch02.html.

Should you run into problems installing VirtualBox, the best place for support is the VirtualBox community. The mailing lists, forums, and #vbox IRC channel on www.Freenode.net are all excellent resources to get you up and running if you run into any issues.

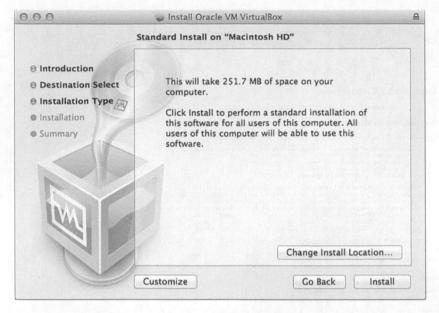

Figure A.2   The VirtualBox installation wizard

Assuming that you didn't run into any problems installing VirtualBox, you should now install Vagrant, the virtual environment automation tool.

A.2   *Installing Vagrant*

Vagrant is an automation tool for managing virtual environments. It allows for VMs to be provisioned from scratch, providing a structure for downloading and installing a base VM image, and it integrates with configuration management tools like Chef and Puppet. The result is a consistently deployed VM that makes for a solid development environment. In addition, because it's run on your local machine, it maps network access to the services running in the VM to your local computer's localhost network interface. This functionally makes it appear as if RabbitMQ and the other network-based tools you'll be using in this book are running natively on your computer instead of in a VM.

To get started, visit www.vagrantup.com (figure A.3) in your web browser and download the version of Vagrant appropriate for your computer.

When you click on the Download button, you'll be presented with a list of versions to download. Click on the latest version at the top of the list, and then you'll be presented with a list of installers and packages for specific operating systems (figure A.4). Select the version that's appropriate for your computer and download it.

> **NOTE**   Although VirtualBox supports Solaris as a host operating system, Vagrant only supports Windows, OS X, and a handful of Linux distributions.

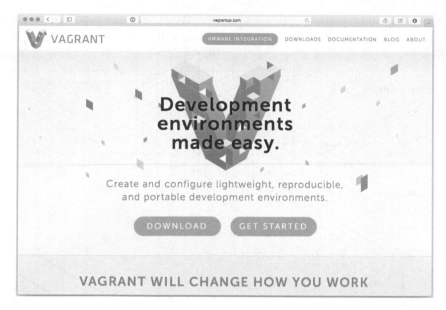

Figure A.3   VagrantUp.com, home of the Vagrant project

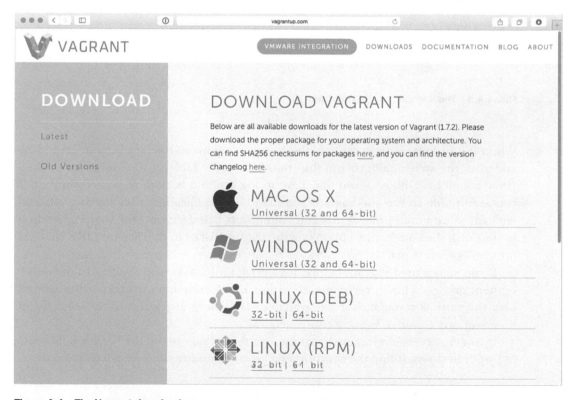

Figure A.4   The Vagrant download page

Setting up Vagrant is a straightforward process. Windows and OS X users will run the installation tool (figure A.5), whereas Linux users will install the package appropriate for their distribution using a package tool like dpkg or rpm. If you have any installation issues, the Vagrant website has support documentation available at http://docs .vagrantup.com/.

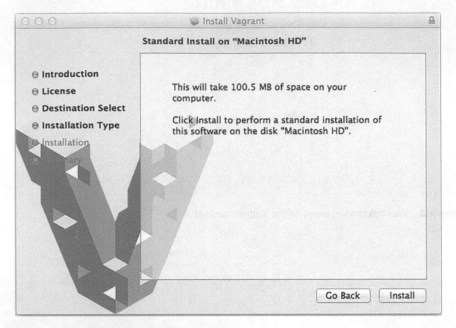

Figure A.5   The Vagrant installation wizard

When the installation is complete, the Vagrant command-line application should be added to the system path. If you find that it's not available in your terminal or shell (PowerShell in Windows), you may have to log out and back in to your computer. If you aren't able to run the Vagrant command-line application after logging out and back in, there's both professional and community-based support for Vagrant. It's best to start with the community options via the mailing list or in the #vagrant IRC channel on www.Freenode.net.

If you've not used Vagrant before, it's a great tool and is really helpful in the development process. I highly recommend reading the documentation and playing around with the various commands it has available. Try typing `vagrant help` to see a list of what you can do with a Vagrant-controlled VM.

If you've successfully installed Vagrant, you should now set up the VM for RabbitMQ in Depth by downloading the appropriate files and running a few simple commands.

A.3   *Setting up the Vagrant virtual machine*

For this next step, you'll need to download a small zip file containing the Vagrant configuration and support files required for the virtual environments used in the book. There are multiple VMs defined in the Vagrant file for the clustering tutorials in part 2 of the book. You'll be using the primary VM unless instructed otherwise in a chapter.

To get started, you'll need to download the Vagrant configuration file, rmqid-vagrant.zip, from the code files in order to configure the environment.

Once you have the zip file downloaded, extract the contents of the file to a directory that will be easy for you to remember and access via your terminal, or PowerShell if you're a Windows user. When you extract the zip file, the files will be located in a directory named rmqid-vagrant. Open your terminal and navigate to this directory, and start the Vagrant setup of the primary VM by typing the following:

```
vagrant up primary
```

This process will take 10 to 15 minutes on average but can vary depending on the speed of your computer and internet connection. When you first start the process, you should see output on your console indicating the progress of the VM, looking something similar to the following:

```
Bringing machine 'primary' up with 'virtualbox' provider...
==> primary: Box 'gmr/rmqid-primary' could not be found. Attempting to find
    and install...
    primary: Box Provider: virtualbox
    primary: Box Version: >= 0
==> primary: Loading metadata for box 'gmr/rmqid-primary'
    primary: URL: https://atlas.hashicorp.com/gmr/rmqid-primary
==> primary: Forwarding ports...
    primary: 1883 => 1883 (adapter 1)
    primary: 22 => 2222 (adapter 1)
==> primary: Booting VM...
==> primary: Waiting for machine to boot. This may take a few minutes...
    primary: SSH address: 127.0.0.1:2222
    primary: SSH username: vagrant
    primary: SSH auth method: private key
==> primary: Running provisioner: shell...
    primary: Running: inline script
==> primary: stdin: is not a tty
==> primary: From https://github.com/gmr/RabbitMQ-in-Depth
==> primary:  * branch            master      -> FETCH_HEAD
==> primary:    80e7615..469fc8c  master      -> origin/master
==> primary: Updating 80e7615..469fc8c
==> primary: Fast-forward
```

If you didn't see output similar to this, you may have an application on your computer that's already bound to and listening on one of the ports the VM is trying to use. If you're running RabbitMQ already on your local machine, shut it down before trying to run vagrant up again. The VM will attempt to use ports 1883, 2222, 5671, 5672,

8883, 8888, 9001, 15670, 15671, 15672, and 61613. That's a lot of ports, but in this machine you're running a virtual server with several services for the examples in this book. You'll need to stop any applications that are listening on these ports in order to get the VM working properly.

Additionally, if you're setting up on a Windows machine, you may be prompted by your firewall to allow connections to and from the VM. Make sure you allow this, or you'll be unable to connect to the VM, and Vagrant won't even be able to configure it.

If everything started OK and the machine has booted, there may be points while it is configuring the VM when it appears stalled or not doing anything. Once the setup of the VM is complete, you should be back at the prompt in your console.

Finally, if you need to stop the VM, use the command vagrant halt.

Now you can test a few URLs in your browser to confirm that everything was set up properly.

A.4   *Confirming your installation*

There are two applications you need to ensure are properly set up. If they're set up properly, it's an indication that everything worked as expected and you can go ahead and start with the examples in the book.

The first is RabbitMQ. To test that RabbitMQ is set up properly, open your browser to http://localhost:15672. You should see a screen similar to figure A.6.

Figure A.6   The RabbitMQ management interface login

The username and password for logging into the management UI are the default "guest" and "guest". If you log in, you'll get the main screen of the management UI, which gives an overview of the server configuration and status.

With RabbitMQ confirmed, the other application to test is the IPython Notebook server. This application allows you to run the Python-based code samples interactively in your web browser. With this VM, all of the code listings and samples are organized in the IPython Notebook server, allowing you to open each and run them independently of each other. The IPython Notebook server should be listening on port 8888, so open a new tab in your web browser and visit http://localhost:8888. You should see a page similar to the one in figure A.7.

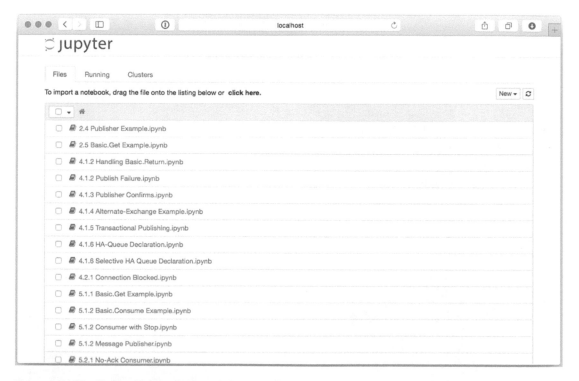

Figure A.7   The IPython Notebook server index page with the RabbitMQ in Depth notebooks

If you're interested in the capabilities of or in documentation for the IPython Notebook server, the project's website contains a wealth of information (http://ipython.org). It's a tremendously useful application and is gaining popularity in scientific and data-processing communities as an interface for crunching datasets and performing data visualization.

A.5   *Summary*

At this point you should have the RabbitMQ in Depth VM up and running. You installed VirtualBox, the virtual environment automation tool. By downloading the RabbitMQ in Depth Vagrant configuration and Chef cookbooks, you should have been able to start up a new VM using the vagrant up command. With these steps done, you can now proceed to using the tools in the VM to follow along with the examples in the book.

index